A HISTORY OF THE EARLY CHURCH

I: The Beginnings of the Christian Church
II: The Founding of the Church Universal

W9-BHG-664

Volume III, *From Constantine to Julian,* and Volume IV, *The Era of the Church Fathers,* of this work are available in a companion paperbound volume (Meridian Books, MG26B).

A HISTORY OF
THE EARLY CHURCH

I: The Beginnings of the Christian Church
II: The Founding of the Church Universal

HANS LIETZMANN

translated by Bertram Lee Woolf

Meridian Books
THE WORLD PUBLISHING COMPANY
Cleveland and New York

The Beginnings of the Christian Church: first published in 1937, translation revised 1949, 1953.

The Founding of the Church Universal: first published in 1938, translation revised 1950, 1953.

A MERIDIAN BOOK

Published by The World Publishing Company
2231 West 110 Street, Cleveland 2, Ohio
First Meridian printing August 1961

All rights reserved
Reprinted by arrangement with Lutterworth Press
Library of Congress Catalog Card Number: 61-15601
Printed in the United States of America

The Beginnings of the Christian Church

Volume I of

A HISTORY OF THE EARLY CHURCH

BIOGRAPHICAL NOTE

Hans Lietzmann was born in Düsseldorf in 1875, but spent the formative years of his youth at Luther's town of Wittenberg. The father having died before the boy was ten years old, the family was very poor. Only the heroic self-sacrificing ambition of his mother made it possible for the boy to remain at school, even when helped by a scholarship. Here his interests were mainly concentrated on the classics, in which he showed great ability, but his eager mind was almost equally attracted to the physical sciences. Indeed, practical astronomy was one of his most cherished relaxations.

After studying a short time at the University of Jena, he transferred to Bonn and made classical philology and ancient history his main interests. In 1896 he published a prize essay on the term "Son of Man", in which the young scholar tried to show that its technical sense was due not to Jesus Himself, but to its strangeness when translated into Greek. Needless to say, discussion of the matter still proceeds.

After some experience as an assistant schoolmaster, in 1900 he became Lecturer in Church History in the University of Bonn. During this period, he conceived the plan of the *Kleine Texte* now known throughout the world as reliable critical editions of important, and often otherwise inaccessible, source-material. In 1905, he became Assistant Professor of Church History in Jena, and about the same time issued the first volumes of the *Handbuch zum Neuen Testament*, a commentary which, in continually renewed editions, represents the finest scholarship of our day. Here Professor Lietzmann is himself responsible for the major Pauline Epistles, which he has dealt with in masterly fashion.

In 1908, he was raised to the rank of full professor, and, in lecturing on Church History, made it his ideal to show with what good reason history has followed its course, and to maintain that we should use the present as a preparation for the future, and that a Christian should view everything *sub specie æternitatis*. Meanwhile, his interests in paleography deepened, and resulted in many volumes of the greatest value to both young students and ripe scholars. His publications in this field are based on numerous first-hand researches in the Mediterranean lands, and these researches have brought forth some of their ripest fruit in his writings on the liturgies, the history of the sacraments, textual criticism and many other studies. Particularly important are his monographs on Peter and Paul in Rome, and on the Mass as related to the Lord's Supper.

In 1924, Professor Lietzmann succeeded to Harnack's famous chair in Berlin, an honour which was indeed his due. His labours became more diverse and important than ever. He was the editor-in-chief of numerous, learned journals and book-series, a member of the Prussian Academy of Sciences, and chairman of the section dealing with the Church Fathers. He was a corresponding member of the Bavarian Academy and of the Göttingen Science Association.

His death took place in 1943, but no particulars are known in England, up to the time of going to press. He was then, at sixty-seven, in the full tide of his vigorous mind, and the world has lost a scholar without rival to-day in the important spheres he made his own.

The present work on the Beginnings of the Christian Church is the first volume of a *History of the Early Church*. It represents the result of over forty years' first-hand study of the source-material by an unrivalled master. No scholar since Harnack has written more largely or more acutely on the historical problems surrounding the first centuries of the Christian era, and it would be hard to mention one who possessed a profounder religious insight, or who wrote in a clearer or more brilliant style.

From the beginning of the present century, there has been a growing need for a first-hand re-examination and a re-interpretation of the evidence available for the earliest and most formative period of the Christian Church. This period has hitherto been very obscure. Floods of light have been thrown on it during the last thirty years by epigraphical and other data, and Dr. Lietzmann made full use of his unique knowledge of this material in writing the present work. He tells a fascinating story in a fascinating way and, for all his restraint of judgment, presents a challenge to students on almost every page.

B. L. W.

¹ See, however, the Translator's Note on page 13 of *From Constantine to Julian*, Vol. III of this work.

TRANSLATOR'S NOTE TO THE FIRST EDITION

I SHOULD LIKE TO THANK PROFESSOR LIETZMANN FOR THE material he has willingly placed at my disposal in preparing this volume. He very kindly read and corrected the typescript in detail until it now accurately represents what he wished to write. At the same time, he took the opportunity of making minor corrections in, and additions to, his own text and supplied a Chronological Table. I am also under a deep obligation to Rev. Sydney Myers, B.A., of Bath, and to my wife, for their kind help in reading the proofs and preparing the Index. I hope readers will please bear with me in finding it impossible to devise any fully consistent system in the use of capitals when referring to intermediate deities, or in the Anglicized forms of ancient names.

B. L. W.

TRANSLATOR'S NOTE TO THE SECOND EDITION

THE decision to reset the present volume for the Second Edition afforded me a most welcome opportunity to make a thorough revision of the text, which now amounts, indeed, virtually to a new translation. Numerous critics, reviewers, and other readers, have drawn my attention to desirable amendments, for all of which suggestions I wish hereby to express my gratitude.

I am under very special obligations to certain persons in particular: Mr. Harry Cowlishaw, of Beaconsfield, has placed his rare sense of English style freely at my disposal; the Rev. H. Chadwick, M.A., Fellow of Queens' College, Cambridge, has used his extensive knowledge of the original authorities, cited in the footnotes and discussed in the text, to confirm numberless references, correct many errors, and draw attention to editions accessible to English scholars; and the Rev. Gordon Hewitt, Editor of the Lutterworth Press, has revised the English readers' Bibliography, and has been unfailing in interest and courtesy. I wish to express to all of them my profound thanks. My wife has read the revision in all its stages and every detail; the thanks due to her cannot be told.

So much skilful, painstaking, and kindly labour having been given, I hope my friend Hans Lietzmann's greatest work will be found in its English form, not only invaluable to theological students, but also a delight to non-technical readers seeking to know the facts of the early history of the Christian Church.

B. L. W.

BEACONSFIELD.
Easter, 1949.

CONTENTS

Redemption through Christ, 117. Faith, 118. Flesh
and spirit; Union with Christ, 119. Baptism and
salvation, 120. Life in the spirit as obligation, 122.
Lord's Supper, 124. Enthusiasm, 125. The second
Adam, 126. Law and Judaism, 127.

CHRONOLOGICAL TABLE

40–4 B.C.	Herod the Great.
31 B.C.–A.D. 14.	Augustus.
A.D. 6/7	Census of Quirinus.
A.D. 14–37.	Tiberius.
About A.D. 30.	Crucifixion of Jesus.
A.D. 37–41.	Caligula.
41–44.	Agrippa I.
	Philo of Alexandria.
41–54.	Claudius.
	Paul's Missionary Journeys.
About 48.	The Apostolic Council.
54–68.	Nero.
64.	Persecution of Christians in Rome.
	Death of Paul and Peter.
68.	Galba, Otho, and Vitellius.
	THE FLAVIANS.
69–79.	Vespasian.
70.	Destruction of Jerusalem.
79–81.	Titus.
	Josephus (died before A.D. 100).
81–96.	Domitian.
	THE HOUSE OF NERVA.
96–98.	Nerva.
98–117.	Trajan.
101–106.	Dacian War.
114–116.	Parthian War.
115.	Jewish Rebellion in Egypt.
	Tacitus, Dio Chrysostom, Epictetus.
117–138.	Hadrian.
132.	Rebellion of Barkochba.
	THE ANTONINES.
138–161.	Antoninus Pius.
	Marcion.
	The Gnosticism of Basilides and Valentine.
About 150.	Justin Martyr.
156.	Death of Polycarp.
161–180.	Marcus Aurelius.
177.	Persecution in Lyons.
	Irenæus.
180.	Scillitan Martyrs.

Chapter One

PALESTINE AND THE ROMAN EMPIRE

IT WAS NOT BY THE PLAN OF SOME TRANSCENDENT GENIUS, but by the compulsion of the political and military situation, that the Roman government was now preparing, inthe east, to close the circle of empire round the Mediterranean. Greece and the west of Asia Minor had been conquered by the middle and the end of the second century B.C. respectively. But the daring and the persistence of King Mithradates of Pontus endangered the whole of the eastern conquests again, and compelled the Romans for twenty-five years (88–63 B.C.) to wage a war which finally took on the character of an Asiatic struggle for liberation from the western conquerors who, in their turn, actually found themselves in the position of having to put forth their full strength and use their best men. At the same time Tigranes of Armenia, the son-in-law of Mithradates, not only invaded Media and north-west Mesopotamia but also took possession of Cappadocia and Cilicia, and even made attacks upon the northern half of the Seleucid kingdom in Syria which had long lain in ruins. He made Antioch one of the towns of his official residence, a fact which gave a definite objective to the Roman enemy, whose troops entered Syrian territory. Like an irresistible magnet the victorious general Pompey attracted embassies from all the regions of Syria, where hitherto the different parties had been quarrelling among themselves. Then the intention of Rome began to grow plain. At first it was only tentative and with slight pressure, but towards the end of 64 B.C. Pompey himself came to Syria and acted with decision. A few months later the Roman province of Syria was to be found in place of the remains of the Seleucid heritage. Its means of unifying the administration were of two kinds. Where the Hellenistic cities of the Seleucid period were of the required importance, they were given an aristocratic constitution and declared autonomous, and their city territories were constituted as small administrative districts. On the other hand where there was a region with a predominantly oriental character, a native dynasty was entrusted with control and made responsible for peace, order, and the prompt payment of taxes.

Judea proved to be one of the states of the second kind, and to require handling with special prudence on account of both the spirit and also the political history of its inhabitants. Even in the early centuries, Israel had had painful experience of its unfortunate geographical situation. On the one hand, Palestine was the bridge between the world-empires of the orient and the empire of the Pharaohs, and on the other, it was destined to be continually an apple of discord between the great rivals. Decisive battles were fought upon its soil, and armies marched through its borders. This has remained its lot to the present day, as is shown by the aftermath of two world-wars. As a consequence, it was condemned to continual political dependence upon one of the great neighbouring powers—a feature which all but the latest events have preserved.

The destruction of Jerusalem in 586 B.C. marked the absorption into Babylonia of the southern Kingdom which until then had remained independent of Assyria. When the exiles were sent back by Cyrus, they set up a state under the Persian suzerainty. The country passed from the Persians to Alexander, and was ruled by Macedonian governors. After his death, the Ptolemids and the Seleucids fought for its possession, the former being superior for a century when, in 198 B.C., Antiochus III added it to his great Syrian-Mesopotamian empire. The Egyptian period had been a time of relatively peaceful development and quiet accommodation to the Greek spirit, but the new master quickly brought tempestuous times upon Israel. The political decay of the Seleucid power led to a very large increase in the weight of taxation, and to robbing the temple treasure, while the intrigues and trickery of the city leaders at length occasioned Antiochus IV Epiphanes to pillage Jerusalem with fire and sword (168 B.C.), to raze its walls, and to station a Syrian garrison in its castle. At the same time, efforts were made to suppress the Jewish cult, to hasten the Hellenization of the city population after it had already reached a fairly high level without compulsion, to spread Hellenism throughout the land, and to extend it to the sphere of religion. The response was the insurrection of the religious peasantry under the leadership of the Hasmonæan, Judas Maccabæus, and his brothers who, in the course of a war which endured with varied fortunes for twenty-six years (167–141), not only won religious freedom for their country but, strange to say, also its political freedom. For the first time in more centuries than could be conceived, the people of Israel were free and subject to none. Its High-Priest was a prince and was soon called king by the people: the throne of David was established again. Israel's armies protected and even extended its borders, while the overwhelming empires of the Seleucids and the Ptolemids withdrew into themselves and were powerless. Under Jannæus Alexander (105–78 B.C.), who stamped the title of king in Hebrew and Greek upon his coins, the Jewish kingdom attained its greatest extent and commanded even Greek towns far into Transjordania.

This unusual condition of political freedom had lasted about a century, a period long enough to impress itself upon the memory of the nation for two more centuries as an object of yearning desire. The sons of Jannæus, the indolent Hyrcanus II, and the impassioned Aristobulus II, quarrelled for the crown, and both asked the Romans for help. The Romans came, first Scaurus the legate, who aided Aristobulus, and then Pompey himself. But Aristobulus lost the Roman confidence, and entrenched himself in the temple, when Jerusalem once more became the scene of war. After a three months' siege, the temple hill was stormed by the Romans (63 B.C.), and Pompey outraged the people by entering the Holy of Holies. The dream of Jewish freedom was ended. The conquests of Jannæus were transferred as free cities into the administrative system of the Syrian province, while the Jews received Hyrcanus II as high priest and "ethnarch", and—the Romans as masters.

The following decades saw Julius Cæsar's struggle with Pompey and the senate, and aroused even in the Jewish people and the Hasmonæan princes all sorts of hopes. But Hyrcanus' minister, the crafty Idumæan Antipater, was able to gain Cæsar's favour by certain acts, with the result that Judea was granted freedom from taxes and the obligation of military service. After Cæsar's assassination, Antipater was able to make the rulership of his rivals in Syria favourable to himself—when he was suddenly assassinated. He left behind two sons to whom he had already long entrusted governorships: Phasael in Jerusalem and Herod in Galilee. The first ended his life by a courageous suicide when a Hasmonæan pretender, Antigonus, captured Jerusalem with Parthian help. The second followed the victorious Antony through Egypt to Rome and, on the recommendation of Octavian and Antony, the senate gave him the rank of the Jewish king (40 B.C.).

Meanwhile Antigonus had deposed Hyrcanus and for greater certainty lopped off his ears so that, as a mutilated person, he could never again become High-Priest. At this moment Herod arrived in Palestine supported by Rome. Granted, this meant that Antigonus gained the supporters of Jewish freedom and so strengthened his power of resistance for three years; but in the spring of 37 B.C. Herod besieged Jerusalem, and at the same time gave a sort of dynastic legitimization to his royal title by marrying the Hasmonæan princess, Mariamne, to whom he had long been engaged. After being encircled for five months, the temple hill and the city were stormed, with dreadful bloodshed. From his own pocket, Herod bribed the soldiers to forgo their right to plunder the city. Antigonus was condemned to death by the Roman legate Sosius, and beheaded. The Hasmonæan dynasty disappeared from the stage, and the son of the house-steward assumed the crown.

But being an Idumæan and therefore not native-born, he could not wear the frontlets of the High-Priest; no matter how he might procrastinate or how reluctant he might be, he had to give that honour to the last Hasmonæan, the seventeen-year-old Aristobulus. But at the feast of booths when the jubilation of the people surged up in honour of the young representative of the Maccabæan tradition, the fatal day dawned. Herod caused him to be drowned, and in his place appointed an insignificant puppet of his own choice.

Herod required all his craft and all his good fortune once more when his neighbouring lord and master, Antony, entered into contest with Octavian for a final decision. Antony lost the game. Actium (31 B.C.) was decisive also for his companion, Cleopatra, and for Egypt. The Roman ring was now closed round the Mediterranean, and the Emperor Augustus brought lasting peace to the world. Again Herod found his way into the favour of the victor, and was rewarded with the extension of his rule westward and eastward. Herod owed what he had gained to his own power and skill, and it was attached to him personally, the Jewish people having no part in it. They shared in the outer benefits, and took it in good part when Herod favoured Jewish concerns,[1] but they hated him as a foreign usurper, and as a protégé of the Romans. The extension of his kingdom had nothing at all to do with Israel as a nation. This man ruled nearly forty years, and gave his great military and organizing abilities with relentless energy to building up a state which became a valuable part of the Roman empire. It was a bulwark against the Arab tribes of the wilderness, and it ensured the connection between Syria and Egypt. Moreover, the power and the craftiness of the king could exorcise the dangers which lay in the character of his people. In a chapter which echoes a reluctant but honourable admiration, Josephus[2] tells of his extraordinary activity as a builder: the rebuilding of the temple at Jerusalem, the founding of the city Sebaste on the site of the old Samaria, and the imposing port of Cæsarea— later the capital of the country—numberless castles, palaces, theatres, baths, aqueducts, pillared halls, temples. But the temples were dedicated to pagan gods and to emperor worship, and in their construction was reflected a love for Greek culture which led him even to institute the Olympian games. The heart of the Jewish people responded to all this, not with love, but with furious hatred, not only towards Herod himself, but also his wife, the beautiful Mariamne, whom he killed in a passion of jealousy, but whom he nevertheless could not cease to love.

With the death of Herod "the Great" (4 B.C.), his kingdom was divided to an even greater extent than he had provided in his will. The sons of the first of his ten legal marriages had originally been intended for the succession, but had succumbed to palace intrigues. Alexander and Aristobulus, the sons of Mariamne, who were beloved by the people on account of their Hasmonæan blood, had been strangled by their father's orders, and from his very death-bed he had ordered the

---

[1] Jos., *Ant.*, 16, 27–65   [2] *Bellum*, 1, 401–30

execution of his eldest son, Antipater, on account of his intrigues. Thus there remained three younger sons as heirs mentioned in the will. Philip received the outlying region of Batanea and the neighbouring districts, which lay north and east of Lake Genezareth, and which were mostly populated by pagans. Here he reigned for thirty years and was beloved by his people. Herod Antipas received Galilee and Perea. He built himself a residence, on Lake Genezareth, of a good Hellenistic kind, which he loyally named Tiberias in honour of the emperor. He laid out a fortified town in Perea, which was named after the empress Livia, and later Julia. As far as the people were concerned, he conducted himself as a professing Jew. His evil genius was Herodias whom he alienated from his half-brother, Herod. In order that he could marry her, he set aside his first wife, who was the daughter of his neighbour King Aretas of Nabatea, and whom he had married on good political grounds. This action led to strained relationships, to frontier incidents, and finally to a war in which Antipas suffered defeat, and was compelled to ask Tiberius for help. The emperor died, however, before his help became effective, and Caligula his successor banished Antipas to Lyons instead of giving him the title of king as Herodias desired. He died in exile (A.D. 39) and his rival and accuser, the Jewish king Agrippa, received his tetrarchy.

The principal portion of Herod's territory fell to Archelaos, viz. Samaria, Judea, and Idumea. According to Herod's will, he ought also to have had the royal title, but Augustus withheld it and only named him ethnarch. Almost the whole Herodian family, as well as a deputation from the people, had appeared in Rome, and attempted, in the presence of Augustus, to secure the inheritance for themselves. Meanwhile affairs in Palestine were going from bad to worse. Sabinus, the temporary procurator in Jerusalem, was taken by surprise along with his legion, and the insurrection spread over the countryside, when at least three leaders of insurgent bands had themselves proclaimed as kings of Israel.[1] In the end, Quintilius Varus the Syrian legate intervened; he scattered the rebels, seizing and crucifying 2,000 of them as an example to the rest.[2] Archelaus

[1] Jos., *Ant.*, 17, 272, 274, 278   [2] *Ibid.*, 17, 295

arrived, and even began to reign, but he soon showed himself
quite incompetent. After he had been tolerated for a few years,
a deputation of the leading Jews and Samaritans went to
Rome, and appealed for his dethronement. Augustus deposed
him (A.D. 6) and banished him to Vienne,[1] placing his lands
directly under Roman procurators. These were of equestrian
rank, and were loosely subordinated to the Syrian legate upon
whom they depended if occasion demanded. They resided in
Cæsarea, and had a modest military force of about 3,000 men
at their disposal, raised in Palestine itself from the non-Jewish
section of the population. The Jews proper, for good reasons,
were allowed to remain free from the obligation to military
service.[2] One of the Roman cohorts was continually stationed in
Jerusalem, their barracks being in the castle of Antonia. The
tribune was the chief military authority in the capital. The
procurator was responsible for the rates and taxes, but otherwise the internal government and the legal administration
were largely left to the Jews. The Jewish central magistracy,
the sanhedrin meeting under the presidency of the High Priest,
ruled in Judea, and its decisions were of moral authority far
beyond these narrow borders, and were voluntarily accepted by
the rest of Judaism. In this way, had there been goodwill,
harmonious co-operation should have been possible—if mis-
fortune, brutality, and passion had not frequently disturbed the
peace. Even such an obviously useful matter as the drawing up
of a taxation list, the "census" by Quirinus, the Syrian legate
(A.D. 6–7), was bitterly opposed by the population, and almost
occasioned open rebellion.[3] Joazar the High-Priest managed to
appease the people, but from that time Judas the "Galilean"
and Zaddok the priest conceived and preached relentless
hostility to Rome, with dreadful consequences.[4] On their side,
the procurators in authority only too frequently showed themselves deficient in tact, and they goaded the people sharply.
Pontius Pilate was outstanding in this respect, and he frequently
showed a ruthlessness which eventually brought him down.[5]
This was at the moment when Tiberius died (A.D. 37). Under
his successor Caligula, matters grew worse.

[1] *Ibid.*, 17, 342–44   [2] Schürer, i, 458   [3] Schürer, i, 510 ff.
[4] Jos., *Ant.*, 17, 1–10, 23–25   [5] Schürer, i, 488–92

Chapter Two

JUDAISM IN PALESTINE

CONDEMNED TO EXILE BY SARGON IN 722 B.C., THE TEN northern tribes of the Israelitish people had perished, or at any rate had left no historical traces. The inhabitants of the Judaistic southern kingdom, however, reached such a degree of national fixity that they not only survived the catastrophe of 586 B.C., but defied all the succeeding blows of fate; they have preserved their identity to the present day. The basis of this phenomenon lies in the relation of the people to religion. The unique feature was not that the national and the religious communities were identical—that was approximately true, if not quite axiomatic for any ancient people. Had that identity been the basis, the result might have been that Yahweh would have disappeared from history along with his people like the many *baalim*, and, in the end, like Zeus and Jupiter with the whole of Olympus. Rather, the decisive point was that, among this people, religion was an authoritative and urgent power in life in a unique manner. The northern tribes were suppressed at too early a date, and were also too strongly under foreign influences, for the consolidation of religious power among them. The southern kingdom made good use of the four additional generations of independence, and won a faith which as strong enough to gain victory over national death.

The Jew knew that God had chosen his people for Himself since the days of Abraham, and would redeem His promises to them. With the eyes of religion he regarded history as divine rule which, in the end, had to do only with Israel. The preaching of the prophets had lifted him above the primitive forms of such a faith in the future, and above its destruction by political and military calamities. He knew of his own sin and guilt, of God's anger and just punishment for the individual as well as for the people, and he also knew that God was not eternally wrathful with His own, and that His promises would remain undisturbed. This faith held the people together in the stress of exile; it brought them back, and enabled them to bear patiently the following centuries of foreign yoke. And that it did not deceive, had been wonderfully proved in the later course of history. When the time of distress was at its worst, and Antiochus Epiphanes desecrated both God, His law, and His holy temple, freedom was won by the sword of the Maccabees, and God's salvation was visibly poured out over His people. In those days, Daniel saw in nocturnal visions the meaning of history, and he set forth that meaning in the form of a dream revealed to Nebuchadnezzar.

Daniel is the first to have comprehended all earthly history as a great unity which moves towards a final goal according to a divine plan, and his understanding determined the thought and action of mankind for two millenia. The visions which he saw and described originate in Persian mythology,[1] but the explanation owed its origin to the spirit of Jewish religion. Four world empires follow each other in a diminishing order of value; the last is that of the Macedonians and is without inner unity or firm interconnection. Antiochus Epiphanes belongs to it, and he conducts a war of destruction against the "saints of the Most High" and desecrates the temple. But God Himself will intervene and destroy his kingdom. The "Ancient of Days" will ascend the throne, and on the clouds of heaven one will come like a son of man; he will receive power, honour, and royal rank from God, and all nations and tongues will serve him. "The kingdom and the rule and the royal glory under the whole heaven will then be given to the nation of the saints of the Most High, whose kingdom will be eternal and all powers will serve and obey Him." The "Kingdom of God" will be realized as Israel's rule over all the kingdoms of the world, and the Messiah sent by God will be king over His holy people.[2] World history cumulates towards catastrophe reaching its consummation by divine intervention, and issuing in a new kingdom which, in its glorious final end, will bring about the abundant fulfilment of the promises made to Abraham and his people. Thus in the earliest days of the Maccabean rising, the flame of national enthusiasm shot up, fed by unshakable belief in God's undeviating faithfulness, and it illuminated with a flickering light the apocalyptic picture of an earthly paradise.

[1] Ed. Meyer, *Ursprung*, ii, 189 ff.   [2] Dan., 7: 9, 13, 27

The unsuspected and unaccustomed political freedom of the following century stamped this hope ever more firmly upon the souls of the people and taught them to regard the disillusionments of the Hasmonæan rule and the slavery which came so suddenly in the Roman period, as the prelude to the last fight of all. The strain of the present must instigate the catastrophe which would introduce the revelation of the divine rule in the Messianic kingdom. In the days when Pompey established the Roman authority, new Psalmists arose who gave their people songs in the style and manner of the old "Davidic" psalm-book. We still have these Psalms under the name of Solomon in a Greek translation, and they are an invaluable record of the faith and hope of that period. In them we hear the voice of a devout man who cries to the Lord out of distress and sufferings brought on by war, who is ashamed of the sins and vices of his compatriots, and who recognizes God's judgement as just. All this finds its highest expression in the great Messianic Psalm 17:

Lord, Thou art our king for ever and ever, and our souls shall glory in Thee. What is the span of man's life on earth? All his life long he has his hope. But we hope in God, our Saviour, for the might of our God endures for ever with mercy, and His kingdom extends over the heathen.

Thou, O Lord, hast chosen David to be king over Israel, and sworn to him and his seed for ever, that his kingdom should not cease before Thee. But on account of our sins have sinners risen against us and set up a boastful kingdom on David's throne— i.e. the Hasmonæans—until a foreigner, Pompey, came and brought God's punishment upon them. He has also emptied the land of inhabitants, sent old and young into exile to the far west; he has dealt shamefully with the leaders of the people and treated Jerusalem like a conquered city. For among the people from the highest to the lowest, there was not one who did righteousness and justice, the king in misdeeds, the judges in disobedience, and the people in sin. Like birds frightened out of their nests, the friends of the "devout communities" fled from them and wandered about in the wilderness, in order to save their souls from evil—they were scattered over every country.

Lord, look down and raise up for them their king, the son of David, at the time which Thou hast seen, O God, that he shall rule over Thy servant Israel. Gird him with strength, that he may break in pieces the unjust ruler. Purge Jerusalem of the heathen who have trodden it underfoot. With wisdom and righteousness shall he drive out the sinners from the earth, with his threats he shall terrify them away from his sight, and scold sinners with the voice of their own hearts. And he will gather a holy people in a multitude about himself and rule them in righteousness; he will judge the tribes of the people that the Lord his God has sanctified. And he will not permit injustice to dwell among them any more, and no one shall live among them who knows iniquity. For he knows them, that they are all the sons of their God, and he will divide them by tribes over the land, and no stranger nor foreigner shall again dwell among them.

He will judge the nations and the heathen in the wisdom of his righteousness. And he will submit the heathen to his yoke and they shall serve him, and he will glorify the Lord in the sight of all men, and will purify Jerusalem in holiness, as it was in the beginning, so that the heathen will come from the ends of the earth to see his glory and as gifts will offer his sons who have suffered in a foreign land. They will see the glory of the Lord with which God has clothed it. But he rules over them as a righteous king, instructed by God, and in his days there is no injustice among them, for all of them are holy, and their king is the Messiah of the Lord.

He will not trust in horse and chariot and bow, nor heap up gold and silver as a war chest, and in the day of battle his hope does not depend upon great numbers. The Lord Himself is his king, his strength is that he hopes in God. He will make all the heathen afraid before him. For he will break the earth in pieces with the word of his mouth eternally, he will bless the people of the Lord in wisdom with joy. He is guiltless of sin that he might rule over great peoples, judge the governors, and blot out the sinners with the power of his word. He will not become weak in his days before his God, for God has made him strong through the Holy Spirit, and wise to give good counsel with power and righteousness. The blessing of the Lord is with him in power, and his hope in the Lord will not grow weak. Who can do anything against him? Mighty is he in his work, and powerful in the fear of God; he shepherds the Lord's flock in faithfulness and righteousness, and lets none of them suffer harm in their pasture. He leads them all by a straight path, and there shall be no pride among them for one to oppress another. Thus the king of Israel rules gloriously whom God has planned to set over the house of

Israel to lead it. His words have been purified in fire more than the best and most precious gold, he will direct the tribes of the holy people in the assemblies, his words are like words of saints in the midst of the hosts of the redeemed.

Blessed are they who shall live in those days, for they shall see the salvation of Israel in the assembly of the tribes. May God bring it to pass! O, that God would soon exercise His mercy upon Israel, and save us from the defilement of unclean foes. The Lord Himself is our king now and evermore.

That is the lively Messianic hope of the Roman era clearly and definitely described. The divine promise is to the house of David, the Hasmonæans are unjustified interlopers, and their deeds bear witness against them. Hence, in accordance with God's will Pompey drove them out. But in addition, the people themselves have become wayward, and have been justifiably punished by the Roman invasion. Jerusalem is disgraced, its people scattered in exile; even the devout had to flee into the wilderness from the unholy conditions in the land. If God will hear their prayers, and that at an early date, then the Messiah will arise who will drive the Romans from the country. This does not imply a war of liberation like that of the Maccabees; rather a divine miracle is expected which will sweep away the heathen from before the Messiah. Then Jerusalem will rise up anew in its former glory; the twelve tribes will inhabit Palestine again and have their former boundaries; the scattered people will return from the dispersion,[1] and will be offered as a present to Israel by the heathen who had hitherto oppressed them. And in the reconstituted kingdom, only Israel shall dwell—no heathen, no Greeks, no Samaritans; and this Israel shall not tolerate within itself sinners or half-Greeks. All shall be pure and holy, and live a happy life according to God's will under the righteous and holy Messianic king who has been chosen by Him. In this way, the royal rule of God, the "Kingdom of God" shall be realized in Israel. On the other hand, the heathen shall be subject to Israel and pay tribute to her; they will see in astonishment the glory of Jerusalem but have no share in it. Theirs are not the promises; the idea of a universal salvation was remote from the people of this age.

[1] Cf. Ps. Sol., 11: 2 ff.; 8: 34

The process of imagination had added a good deal in other directions to this kernel, e.g. that Elias or Moses would be the heralds of the Messiah; the glory of the new Jerusalem and the majesty of its future temple are painted in many colours, and the happiness of life in God's kingdom is depicted with pictures of the paradisal wealth of nature and of life. That means little. But there is significance in the question of what the religious communities to which these Psalmists belonged would deem as "holy" and "religious" or "devout".

It is clear that they regarded any intercourse with the heathen as the deadliest sin, and felt that the bulk of the people, and especially the ruling classes, had departed from God in the Hasmonæan epoch, and were now receiving their punishment from the Romans. Immorality, adultery, lying, deceit, and greed are the characteristics of this departure; sacrilege of the temple and disregard of the regulations for worship are the most definite witness of godlessness.[1] On the other hand, the "righteous" man is diligent in observing the law.[2] Sin does not increase in his house, for he is quick upon its tracks and expels it violently. Should an error be made at any time in ignorance, the devout man expiates it with fasting and mortification.[3] Then the Lord blesses him and gladly forgives him. He corrects him without shaming him, and keeps all grievous ill far from him.[4] He grants him definite prosperity, equally remote from grinding poverty and seductive wealth.[5] God has sealed him with His own seal,[6] by which he will be recognized and saved at the Last Judgment. Whereas the godless go to hell, the devout inherit eternal life.[7] The devout experience the righteousness of God towards themselves in the reward which is due to their righteousness; they can see it around them in daily life as well as in the larger course of history[8] where punishment sooner or later falls upon all sinners.

Such is typical "Pharisaic" religion. Even in the older Psalms, we find the circle of the devout who, in quiet inward communion with God, keep aloof from the loud and immoral ways of the daily round, and are repelled by the frivolity of "civilized" life. They have no desire to sit on a bench along with the godless

[1] Ps. Sol., 8: 10 f.; 4: 4-14; 2: 3 ff.; 1: 8 [2] 14: 1; 10: 5 [3] 3: 5-10 [4] 9: 12-15; 13: 6-9 [5] 5: 16-20; 16: 12-13 [6] 15: 8; cf. 10 [7] 3: 13-16; 13: 9 f. [8] 8: 7-31; 9: 3-9

and the scoffers, rather they will meditate day and night upon God's law. In the Maccabean insurrection, these Chasidim, i.e. the devout or religious, occasionally relinquished their aloofness; they took the sword and indeed fought even on the Sabbath day.[1] But when religious freedom had been won, they refused further support to the Hasmonæan dynasty; indeed, after John Hyrcanus, they became fierce and unrelenting opponents.[2] The law was the centre of their thought and practical life and, in continually renewed applications and metaphors, was lauded as Israel's most precious and sacred garment. Indeed, the emphasis veered from its moral to its ceremonial side, for it was the very prescriptions for worship and for cleanness which were felt as defence-works against the burning sea of heathenism round about. But a differentiation was made even within the ceremonial law. The heart of these devout people was not satisfied with the gorgeous temple worship; there were too many critical and sceptical words to be read in prophets and psalms about the value of the outpoured blood of goats. Rather the decisive factor was to be found in personal conduct in fulfilling all the prescriptions of the law. The religion of ritual piety was applied to the individual. Then, however, the strenuous effort to fulfil all the commandments perfectly led to casuistry, and this was continually refined until it spread its crippling net over the whole practical life of a devout person. From the time when he first awoke in the morning till he fell asleep at night, he was continually compelled to remember its prescriptions; his prayers were precisely regulated in wording, time, place, and bodily attitude. Everywhere he was surrounded by prescriptions for cleanness, and they determined the choice and preparation of food; the consecration of the Sabbath by abstaining from work was carried into grotesque consequences in detail. In the time of Jesus, there were two famous rabbis, Shammai and Hillel, and their disciples disputed[3] whether the evening prayer was to be offered in a standing posture or lying in bed; what was the appropriate order for prayers after a meal; whether the

---

[1] I Macc. 2: 41; Jos., *Ant.*, 12, 276 f.
[2] Jos., *Ant.*, 13, 288–292; Schürer, i, 271 f., ii, 473 f. Some passages *re* the Pharisees in Schürer, ii, 449–75. Billerbeck, iva, 334 ff.
Cf. the passages collected by Schürer, ii, 426, note 38

towel used for drying one's hand was to be placed upon the table or upon the cushion used as a seat.[1] Granted that on the Sabbath[2] no food might be cooked, but could one keep warm the water and food which stood on the hearth where the fire was still alight on the Sabbath evening? Yes, if it were a gentle fire of burning stubble, but if the fire was of burning wood, it must first be covered with ashes, otherwise there is danger that the food would begin to simmer—this was Hillel's view. In such cases, Shammai altogether forbade keeping food warm and only permitted water. Could those foods be put back to cook which had been taken away from the fire? Hillel said yes, Shammai, no. Might one eat an egg laid on a holy day by a hen which did not know the law? Shammai permitted it, Hillel did not[3]—and so on *ad infinitum* in all the spheres of public and private life. This mass of prescriptions was handed from one generation to another, and developed ever more highly until "tradition" outweighed the kernel of the Mosaic torah. It was particularly in these spheres that the scribism flourished whose aim in life was the systematic examination, in reality the further development, of the law. In so doing, it had created the material of the "Tradition" which was written down in the second century A.D. as the "Mishna" and in the fifth as the "Gemara". The law-book of Judaism known as the "Talmud" consists of these two sections taken together. The scribes mentioned by name in the present-day text of the Talmud go back in some cases to the Roman period.

From the end of the second century before Christ, we meet with the name of Pharisees, i.e. separatists, for the circle of the Chasidim already mentioned. It cannot be decided whether the name arose at some time during the Maccabean wars, because then they "separated" themselves from their former comrades, or because they help themselves apart from the masses;[4] perhaps the name was first applied to them by opponents and afterwards accepted by themselves. At any rate, the second view aptly describes their attitude in the community. Their separatism was to be seen on two fronts: against the socially superior aristocracy of the old priestly families, the

---

[1] Mishna, *Berachoth*, 1, 1: 8, 1 ff. [2] M., *Sabbath*, 3, 1
[3] M., *Jom. tob*, 1, 1 [4] E. Meyer, ii, 284. J. Jeremias, *Jerusalem*, ii, 115

Sadducees, and against the uneducated and religiously indifferent mob of the *Am ha-Arez.*

The Sadducees[1] derived their name from a certain Saddok,
and the only question is whether he was the High-Priest of
Solomon whom the Old Testament often mentions[2] and
reveres as the ancestor of an eminent priestly family,[3] or
whether a later Saddok, who was the head of a school, gave
his name to his adherents. The first view is to be preferred, as
the Sadducees were not a school but a caste and, in particular,
they were at home in the priestly families of the capital and
occupied the leading places in the body politic. Their political
activity brought them into contact with the forms of life proper
to the Græco-Roman civilization, and occasioned many accom-
modations of which the Pharisees severely disapproved. In the
Seleucid period, this development went suspiciously far and,
in the earlier Maccabean period, cost them all their influence.
But after the Pharisees broke with John Hyrcanus, they came
into control once more and, except for a short interval, remained there as long as the Jewish state existed. In the
Herodian period, to their chagrin, their adaptability had to
accommodate itself to the requirements of the Pharisees who
were the representatives of public opinion.[4]

Josephus frequently gives himself the pleasure of speaking
about the Jewish "Schools of Philosophers"[5] and in so doing
adduces all sorts of material in regard to Pharisees and Sadducees which smacks of philosophy, but which really renders it
more difficult to understand their real contrast. If the facts can
be reduced to a simple formula, we may say that the Sadducees
held to the traditional form of Judaism as found in the Old
Testament but rejected the new currents which had come in
after the Persian period together with the deductions from them
drawn by the Rabbinic schools. Hence they preferred to ignore
the personal immortality of the soul, and judgment after death,
together with the angels, devils, and intermediate beings of

[1] Billerbeck, iv*a*, 335 ff., 348 ff. Schürer, ii, 475 ff.
[2] 1 Kings 2: 35
[3] Ezek. 40: 46; 44: 15; also *Sirach* (Heb.), 51: 12, 9, and in the Damascus
document 6, 1–3; R. H. Charles, *Apocrypha and Pseudepigrapha of the Old Testament*
(1913), ii, 785–834
[4] Jos., *Ant.*, 18, 17; Schürer, ii, 487 f.
[5] Jos., *Bell.*, 2, 119, 160–166; *Ant.*, 13, 171; 18, 11–25

SADDUCEES: AM HA-AREZ 33

later apocalyptic; hence also they rejected the further development of the law in the tradition of the Pharisees.[1] They remained firm to the old law, and defended themselves against the Apocryphal books and the Talmud.

In contradistinction to the Sadducees, the Pharisees were at first, therefore, the vehicles of a freer and more vital religiousness which discovered new forms of expression for the ancient faith that Israel was the chosen people. But the ever increasing tendency towards correct fulfilment of the law led to a growing narrowness and a formalism, which allowed the depth of the prophetic tradition and the inwardness of the religion of the Psalms to fall into oblivion, and which conjured up the danger of arrogant self-righteousness. The frequency with which the Psalms of Solomon depict the righteous man and his excellence as recognized and rewarded by God, gives us a plain witness of it. But this meticulous observance of the law had another consequence, viz. the Rabbis, learned in the Scriptures, became the leaders of the Pharisaic communities, and determined the spirit that ruled in them. "Religiousness" became a technique with ever greater refinement and rested upon learning. One had to learn painfully how to be "righteous", and the more deeply a religious man penetrated into the secrets of Talmudic casuistry, the higher his religious perfection mounted. Religion became a matter of the trained intellect applied to conduct; whoever could not scale the ladder of knowledge could not reach the ideal nor even a tolerable degree of piety. The way to the righteousness which was acceptable to God, was closed to him.

From this standpoint, the scribe could only reject and despise these untrained and uneducated people, and he stigmatized them as *Am ha-Arez*, i.e. people of the land.[2] People who live nowadays in some metropolis of culture employ similar terminology, even if not directly in the religious sphere. Among the Pharisees, the epithet echoed to some extent their characterization of the heathen, but on the other hand, no aristocrat of Jerusalem had a charm against this title if he did not fulfil the requirements of the law. The differentiation went so far that the faithful Pharisee avoided mixing, or even contact, with the

[1] Jos., *Ant.*, 13, 297   [2] Billerbeck, ii, 494; Schürer, ii, 454, 468

Am ha-Arez, for it was impossible to know, with their defective observance of the law, whether they, or their clothing, or the articles touched by them, were ceremonially clean, or whether the produce which they offered for sale had been correctly "tithed". The devout person had this certainty only in connection with his compeers, his *Chaberim*, i.e. comrades[1] who had bound themselves together for the observance of the ritual and for Levitical correctness in regard to the dues: they and they alone constituted the true Israel in whom God took pleasure. In spite of all its earnestness of endeavour and its undeniable quality of ethical sensitiveness and conduct, this inner separation stamped its characteristic vices upon Pharisaism. That the *Am ha-Arez* responded with fierce hatred to the contempt of the Pharisees would be certain even if we did not possess the witness of the surviving Rabbinic literature.[2]

Besides the Pharisees and Scribes, Josephus mentions the Essenes as a third "School of Philosophers" and praises them for their ideal way of life.[3] Philo describes them in a spirited fashion in one of his Stoic tractates.[4] Otherwise we hear hardly anything about them, especially in the Rabbinic sources. Their name *Chasayya*, i.e. the devout, is Aramaic and corresponds exactly to the Hebrew *Chasidim*, and thus brings them into relation with the same sources as those from which the Pharisees had perhaps sprung. And it is in fact highly probable that we have here another shoot from the same root. The Essenes were a genuine order of monks who had their monasteries in the cities, and more especially in the villages, of Palestine. After the novitiate of one year and a probationary period of a further two years, the candidates judged suitable were accepted as full members, sworn to the manner of life of the society, and bound to keep their writings and teachings secret. Then at length they might share in the sacred meals which were regarded as the central act of worship. Everyone who entered the order, abandoned private property, and handed over his entire possessions to the society, and similarly all his future earnings.

---

[1] Billerbeck, ii, 501, 509 ff.; J. Jeremias, *Jerusalem*, ii, 116 ff.
[2] Billerbeck, ii, 518 f.
[3] Jos., *Bell.*, 2, 119–61
[4] Phil., *omn. prob.*, 75–91 (6, 21–26); also Bousset, *Judentum*, 456; Schürer, ii, 654. W. Bauer in *Pauly-Wissowa* Supp., iv., 426

In exchange, he received from the order all that he required for an ascetic life, in sickness and in health. Naturally, there were in this society no social differences, no masters and no slaves. The Essenes also withheld from marriage, and no women were admitted to the order; only a special sect among them tolerated marriage for the sake of propagation. Their food was confined to what was entirely necessary for the support of life, and their clothing was of white, i.e. colour of light. The most outstanding commandment of their manner of life was cleanliness and ceremonial washings were the means, employed every day, for avoiding uncleanness. All who abandoned the unclean outer world and entered the order must bathe; the same was required of the fully initiated Essene who had been in contact with a novice or probationer, to say nothing of a non-Essene. Before beginning the midday meal, each washed his body in cold water and then put on a sacred festival garment which, after the meal, was at once exchanged for working clothes. Moses and his law were held by them in the greatest honour, and they observed the Sabbath by strict abstention from work.[1] They rejected animal sacrifices and sent instead sacrificial offerings of money to the temple at Jerusalem:[2] their own sacred customs seemed to them to be better and to be true sacrifices.

They were mainly devoted to cultivating the land, and had no liking for commerce, the sea, or war.[3] They abhorred oaths because they spoke the exact truth without them,[4] and thus they appeared to both Josephus and Philo as patterns of all civic and philosophic virtues—the critical reader will do well to set aside the Greek emendations to both sketches. What remains is the life of a Jewish sect as described above, which had many points of contact with the Pharisees, but which is closer to the old roots. In abnegating sacrifices and emphasizing ethical conduct, they developed that religion of the prophets and of many of the Psalms which was repressed among the Pharisees. The esoteric writings and the names of angels of which Josephus tells us,[5] reveal living relations with popular apocalyptic and

[1] Jos., *Bell*, 2, 145; Philo, *omn. prob.*, 80 f. (6, 23). For the readings see Bousset, *Judentum*, 462. note 3
[2] Philo, *op. cit.*, 75 (6, 22). Jos., *Ant.*, 18, 19   [3] Philo, *op. cit.*, 78 (6, 22)
[4] *Ibid.*, 84 (6, 24); Jos., *Bell.*, 2, 135   [5] *Ibid.*, 2, 142

its Persian sources, and these latter are doubtless responsible for the traces of sun-worship which are to be found as isolated characteristics.[1] Baptism and sacred meals are the forms of worship upon which emphasis is laid, although it is doubtful whether they could be called sacraments. But we must remember that also among the Pharisees the ritual washings and the sacred meals of religious societies were greatly insisted upon, and were developed in their ritual. Although at first sight what we learn of the Essenes may seem strange, closer examination shows that they can be readily placed in the course of the religious development of Palestine as already known to us. What were the roots of their monasticism and asceticism is another question which need neither be raised nor answered, for our purposes.

The Essenes afford us an impressive proof that the religious currents of Palestinian Judaism are not exhausted by the artificial constructions which we find in the Rabbinic writings, and which even dominate Josephus's accounts. Only when we are clear as to how far this Essenism was removed from the victorious Pharisaism of the incipient Talmud, and as to the fact that, nevertheless, it enjoyed honourable respect and was widely spread in Palestine—only then are we able to understand the large and various possibilities of religious evolution in the Jewish spirit of that period. Moreover, the constraint of the common origin was more powerful, even in such disparate phenomena, than the wisdom of the schools will usually allow. And a comparison with the foundations of societies in the dispersion, such as we find in "Community of the New Covenant" in Damascus, or the Egyptian "Therapeutæ", deepens the impression of variety in the development of similar germs.

Further witness is borne to the spirit of Palestinian religion by a number of writings which arose in the pre-Christian period, and which enjoyed a more or less apocryphal existence for centuries. Many of them were taken over and edited by Christians, but were then forgotten until modern research brought them to light again from remote corners of eastern libraries. Here we include the books of Enoch, which were the work of several generations of strange prophets from the time

[1] Philo, 2, 128, 148

of the Seleucids to that of Herod. The books show a fantasy diligently at work trimming up and spinning out stories of early Bible times in a manner well known from the Jewish Haggada. Enoch who, according to Gen. 5: 24, had been taken up into heaven, imparted revelations of many hidden things: he had wandered through heaven and hell and reported what he had seen there, and he was able to give detailed information on physics, meteorology, and astronomy. The entire eastern fairy-land is laid under tribute to provide building material for the earth and the heaven which are called into being before our eyes, and the paths become plainly visible which join this product of Palestine to Persia and Babylon.

However, the chief interest of the prophets who wrote the Book of Enoch is in the outcome of this world, the end of time, the Last Judgment, and the future kingdom of God. Their eschatology is quite differently conceived from the Pharisaic nationalism of the Psalms of Solomon. Rather, Enoch joins immediately on to Daniel. He sees in visions the course of world history to its pre-destined end, which is implemented by an all-embracing flood of godlessness. God's anger is revealed in an inversion of the order of nature,[1] and in a judgment of the sword. After a series of miraculous and catastrophic events this æon declines to an end.[2] Accompanied by several thousands of holy angels, God comes to hold judgment;[3] the Messiah, the Son of Man who had been seen by Daniel on the clouds of heaven, will take his seat upon the throne and judge the wicked;[4] the dead will rise, and when the sinners have been destroyed, this world will pass away.[5] A new heaven will receive the "saints, the righteous, and the chosen", with in-effable glory, and they, along with the chorus of angels, will sing "Holy, Holy, Holy" to the Lord of spirits in the endless eternity of the new æon.[6] The Messianic idea and the hope of the promised kingdom are transposed into eschatological and apocalyptic spheres, and shape themselves in a variety of pictures which without inner, and often also without outer, connection with one another, light up and pass before the eyes of the seer in a swirling succession.

---

[1] Enoch 80: 2–6   [2] *Ibid.*, 91, 12–17   [3] 1: 9
[4] 45: 3–46: 8   [5] 51: 1; 91: 14   [6] 91: 16; 39: 5–13

The final aim of this kind of religion is the eternal salvation of the *individual* saint who has been chosen by God; the ancient note of the rulership of the whole chosen people dies away in the distance. The books of Enoch are the deposit of a fanatically religious cast of mind unique in kind, and directed towards the next world. It had much inward power of conversion, but no organizing capacity, and we naturally hear nothing of communities or sects of its adherents. But every attempt is useless to bring the world of ideas of the Enoch literature even into a loosely connected system: everything grows together in rank confusion, as in an oriental magic garden, intoxicating the visitor with varied colours and heavy perfumes.

There are several other similar books, putting now this and again that type of religiousness more definitely in the foreground; in one, ethical instruction is predominant, in another, Haggadic recounting of legend, or apocalyptic speculation on history. Taken one with another, they do us the service of bringing before our eyes the living religious activity of the Jewish people in their homeland before the beginning of our era.

No source, however, informs us of the simple people who, equally removed from scribism and from fanatical apocalyptic, strove well or ill to fulfil the moral requirements of God in the sense of the prophets, and to hope in God's grace after the manner of the Psalmists[1]; people who felt poverty and humble station to be the inheritance which gave them their expectation of God's special protection.[2] For He teaches the afflicted His way[3] and His Messiah will one day, at the Last Judgment, save the poor and the afflicted,[4] who although only a small number of saints, now sigh to Him under the oppression of the godless.[5] Thus in quietness and patience, they waited for the coming of the kingdom of God. They are not to be heard in political affairs, and they do not write books; learning is remote from them, and, as far as the Rabbis are concerned, they are lost in the multitude of the *Am ha-Arez*—who is there to tell of them? And yet it was from their midst that the change in world history took its rise, for Jesus was born and brought up among them.

[1] Mark 15: 43; Luke 2: 25, 38   [2] Ps. Sol. 5: 2, 13; 10: 7; 15:2
[3] Ps. 25: 9   [4] Ps. 72: 2, 4, 12, 13   [5] Ps. 13: 2, 4

Chapter Three

JOHN THE BAPTIST

IN THE DAYS WHEN HEROD ANTIPAS RULED IN GALILEE, (4 B.C.–A.D. 39) a man arose by the name of John. His clothing was woven of rough camel-hair, he had a leathern girdle round his waist, and he lived on locusts and the honey of wild bees. He preached that the kingdom of God was near at hand, and that now was the last opportunity for repentance; whoever repented of his sins and wished to amend his ways, might come to him and receive baptism in Jordan for forgiveness of sins. His call to repentance was very effective, and the crowds streamed out to hear him. He reproved them fiercely: You serpent's brood, who has promised that you shall escape God's threatening anger? Do you think that God will spare you because you are Abraham's children to whom the promises apply? Out of that stone God can create children of Abraham for Himself and present the promised grace to them. Only conversion and repentance will save you, and these must be made plain by your deeds. Already the axe is lying near the root of the tree; if the tree is rotten, the judge will hew it down and throw the timber into the fire. In terror, the people asked John: What are we to do? For answer, he said: Let him who has two coats give to him who has none, and let him who has food do likewise. The tax-collectors also came to him to be baptized, and asked: Master, what must we do? And he said to them: Take no more from the people than is ordered. Also the soldiers asked him: And what shall we do? And he said to them: Do not exercise force and oppression against anyone, and be content with your pay. Now is the time to repent: I am baptizing you with water. After me there is coming the man of authority, whose shoelaces I am not worthy to bend down and unloose: he will destroy you in the fiery baptism of the Last Judgment. The winnowing fan is already in his hand to cleanse his threshing floor. He will gather the wheat into his granary, but burn up the chaff in unquenchable fire.

Thus runs the popular tradition which is preserved in two

different recensions in the synoptic Gospels[1] and, indeed, so
excellently preserved, that very little critical work is required
to remove the few traces of Christian additions. At an early
date, Christian tradition made the attempt to understand John
as a forerunner of Jesus. It made his baptism parallel to the
Christian sacrament—which, as a baptism of the spirit, was
superior to John's baptism of water—and it discovered Jesus to
be the "stronger one" prophesied by John: this had its effect
upon the texts of our gospels. But these re-touchings remained
superficial and left undisturbed everything essential in the
material of tradition.

A clear and definite picture greets our eyes: an ascetic with
the fewest possible needs. Such were not unheard of in Roman
times: Josephus himself lived with one for three years.[2] But
John was a preacher of both repentance and divine judgment.
The Messianic hopes also spoke of a Messianic judgment, but
this judgment was to apply to the heathen, and to set Israel
upon the throne. Since the days of Amos, the prophetic spirit
had been turned against them, and had also threatened punishment to all sinners to be found among God's own people.
Popularly, the faith held to the idea of the advantage of the
chosen descendants of Abraham, who were marked by circumcision as belonging to God: it was against this faith that John's
fiery preaching was directed. What could be read in the
apocalypses, and occasionally heard in earnest Sabbath sermons,
operated with unique force when it echoed through the land
from the mouth of a prophet. For the message proclaimed that
the test was imminent: the Messiah was coming. But nothing
was said about Messianic glory and indescribable happiness;
rather the one who exercised the authority of the Lord, was
coming to hold judgment, he would light a fire for all sinners,
and destroy them. The prophet's preaching made them tremble
in their souls for fear of hell, and then showed them a way to
salvation that still remained open: immediate repentance and
amendment. The gospels and Josephus are unanimous in saying
that the decisive elements in John's message were simple and
complete righteousness in life, and keeping the divine, ethical
commands. According to the gospels, water-baptism indicated

[1] Mark 1: 2–6; Matt. 3: 1–12; Luke 3: 1–18   [2] Jos., *Vita.*, 11–12

forgiveness of sins and a repentant mind, but according to the, perhaps, rather artificial account of Josephus,[1] it did not signify the washing away of any sort of transgressions, but the sanctification of the body after the cleansing of the soul had been completed. In any case, it was to be distinguished from the ceremonial cleansing baths of the Jewish rite, and from the bathings of sects such as the Essenes; it was a single action which signified that the baptized initiate had gone over to the life of righteousness.

The Baptist did not come forward in accordance with any apocalyptic programme whatsoever. It was a new idea that there would be a final opportunity for Israel to repent,[2] and, similarly, that baptism sealed the act of repentance. We may call to mind Isa. 1: 16–17: "Wash you, make you clean, put away your evil doings from before my eyes; cease to do evil: learn to do well; seek judgment, judge the fatherless, plead for the widow." Here we have a baptism linked with ethical requirements which correspond to those of the Baptist, although the apocalyptic perspective is lacking. This may have been derived from Mal. 3, which prophesies of the angel who is to come before the Lord and "purify the sons of Levi, and purge them as gold and silver" (v. 3). Hence God requires conversion,[3] and, thereon, promises His grace. Before the day dawns, which "shall burn like a furnace", God will send the prophet Elias, who "shall turn the heart of the fathers to the children, and the heart of the children to the fathers; lest I come and smite the earth with a curse".[4] The faith in the appearance of Elijah—who is thus equated with the "angel"—as the herald of the Messiah, was entirely popular at this time,[5] and led to the consequence that John was regarded as an Elijah *redivivus*,[6] and Christians regarded this chapter in Malachi as a key for understanding John.[7]

How is this baptism to be understood? Josephus is a poor witness, for he has the obvious tendency of translating Jewish matters into terms of Greek philosophy and ethics, thus making them more to the taste of his readers. On this account, we would

---

[1] Jos., *Ant.*, 18, 117   [2] Cf., say, *Assumption of Moses*, 1, 18, "the day of repentance"
[3] Mal. 3: 7   [4] Mal. 4: 6   [5] Bousset, *Judentum*, p. 232
[6] Mark 6: 15; 8: 28   [7] Matt. 11: 14; 17, 12 f.; Mark 1: 2

be suspicious of his notice of the Baptist's preaching, were it not in full accord with the gospel tradition, where there is no question of moralizing tendencies and bias. But the case is different in regard to the baptism. When Mark characterizes it as a "baptism of repentance for the forgiveness of sins" (1: 4), that corresponds with the content of the rest of the tradition, and, in a certain sense, to the prophetic use of language; nevertheless, we learn really nothing thereby about the nature of this baptism. Was the baptism a symbol, as Josephus depicts it, or was it a sacrament which, when completed, effected a miraculous operation, and cleansed the sinner—like the baptism of the Christian church? Was it to be compared with the baptism of proselytes, which washed away the uncleanness from the heathen on entering Judaism, and grafted them with ceremonial purity on to the people of God? This last has been asserted,[1] and we are then presented with the strange paradox that John demanded that the Israelite, who was proud of his nationality, should submit to baptism, and be made clean, just as the unclean heathen must do, before he could come to God; which is too paradoxical to be convincing. It scarcely requires such roundabout arguments before it is comprehensible that John made his baptism the central action of his work. His point was by no means to gather his hearers into a new religious community, but to cleanse and redeem them before Judgment and the new era came. In this connection, the ceremony of washing sins away in water had long been customary in Israel, even more generally than among other peoples. But our sources make it in no way probable that sacramental ideas were bound up with John's baptism.

John gathered disciples round himself, and we hear that they fasted and, in this respect, were in agreement with the Pharisees.[2] In another passage, we are told that their master taught them to pray,[3] i.e. that they had received definite forms of prayer. But what else in this regard was thought, taught, or done, remains completely hidden from us. We only hear of the end.

---

[1] Cf. H. Schaeder in *Gnomon*, 1929, p. 367. J. Leipoldt, *Urchristl. Taufe im Lich d. Religionsgesch.*, 27

[2] Mark 2: 18   [3] Luke 11: 1

The growing power of the prophet over the people un-
settled Antipas, and he feared disturbance. Hence he had John
carried to the bloody prison-castle of Machærus—not far from
the east coast of the Dead Sea—and there secretly executed.[1]
Amongst the people, that graphic but dreadful story was told
which is preserved in Mark's gospel (6: 17–29) for the readers,
poets, and painters of succeeding ages. His school lasted for
some time after his death. This can be deduced from the
indirect polemic of the Fourth Gospel and from the legends of
the Baptist in the gospel message.[2] Quite soon, however, all
trace of them was lost and we hear no more of the disciples of
John.

Is that quite true? The numerous writings of the Mandæans
bear witness to the continued existence of the disciples of John
for several centuries and perhaps the baptist sect in southern
Babylonia at the present time, is the direct heir of John's work
in the days of the Herods. That is asserted nowadays by many
weighty persons, and anyone who regards the Mandæan literature as sources can draw an attractive picture of the spiritual
power which proceeded from John, and which influenced the
religion of Judaism, and especially that of Jesus and His
disciples. John's circle then appears as the nursery of an early
gnosis, which united Babylonian, Persian, and Syrian elements
in a many-coloured mixture on a Jewish background, and
grouped the whole round the ancient Iranian mythology of the
first man, that redeemer who descended from heaven in order
to awaken the soul bound and asleep in the material fetters of
this world, and to open up for it the way to heaven. This is very
intriguing, and gives quite unthought-of perspectives, leading
possibly to a new understanding of primitive Christianity;
nevertheless we must put it firmly and entirely on one side. It
can be shown[3] that the Mandæan literature consists of various
strata which come from widely different periods. And the latest
of these strata, belonging to the Islamic era—i.e. at earliest, in
the seventh century—are those which preserve the notices of
John the Baptist; they are modelled on the basis of the gospel

[1] Jos., *Ant.*, 18, 119
[2] M. Dibelius, *Jungfrauensohn*, 1–11. The notice in *Clem. recog.*, 1, 54, 60, is
valueless; nor do Acts 18: 25, 19: 1 ff. refer to the disciples of John
[3] *Sitzungsber. Akad. Berlin*, 1930, 596–608

records, and distorted till they are grotesque. In the same way, the many sallies against Jesus and Christianity are quite clearly directed against the Byzantine church, and have not the least connection with primitive Christianity. The fragments of the earlier strata belong to a rank oriental gnosis which has run to seed, and have no bearing on the historical John and his disciples.

Chapter Four

NOW AFTER THAT JOHN WAS DELIVERED UP, JESUS CAME into Galilee, preaching the Gospel of God, and saying, The time is fulfilled, and the kingdom of God is at hand: repent ye, and believe in the gospel. Thus our earliest record, in Mark 1: 14, tells of Jesus' first appearance; the new era in the history of the world was now beginning.

The question arises whether, and to what extent, the records telling of Jesus are, in fact, historical. Are our sources sufficient to give us a picture of the historical Jesus? Or must we be content with the spiritual conceptions elaborated by the primitive Church, and regard the "historical" Jesus as belonging to the sphere of the unreal, or at least the incomprehensible? That is the precipitate view advanced by some dogmatic radicals to-day. Both on the side against the Church and on that favouring it, there are several scholars who have wilfully taken the difficulty of the historical problem to be a proof of its impossibility; detesting historical research, they have abandoned it in favour of roaming at will in the fields of pure speculation.

But facts have their own importance and demand their rights from serious science; they fight their way through and, in the end, hold the field. It may be granted that our sources containing Jesus' words and deeds have been moulded by the Christian church: we can clearly perceive the work done on them by the earliest Christians, so clearly, indeed, that we can often find therein what is characteristic of the opinions and hopes of this very community. But in spite of all the transformation effected by tradition, we see in every direction the genuine rock of reliable information upon which the historian can build—if only he will deal with the sources of primitive Christianity by the same methods as all other existing sources. That means, however, that he must approach them as an expert and disinterested judge, not as a critic who is sceptical on principle. There is only one historical method; if we hear of special methods for religion, history, legend, form-criticism, and the history of worship, we must remember that these are not new methods, but new standpoints calculated to supplement each other and to refine the one historical method. Used in isolation, they can easily do harm.

We obtain our knowledge of Jesus almost entirely from the first three gospels. Mark's gospel is the earliest of these, and its author is probably Mark, the disciple of Paul, mentioned in 1 Pet. 5: 13, of whom Acts often speaks. The gospel was written shortly after A.D. 70, but made use of earlier writings; these however, cannot be restored with precision, and, indeed, are only sometimes clearly recognizable. Both the other evangelists used Mark as the basis of their record, and adopted almost the whole of his material, each of them naturally editing it in his own way in point of style and material. That the MS. of Mark of which they made use should show many variations from that which has come down to us, is not surprising and should not give occasion for seeking some other hypothesis.

However, both Matthew and Luke have employed another source which is clearly to be seen in the material they have in common apart from that of Mark, and which, within limits, can be reconstructed in these passages.[1] In the form in which it is available to us, this source also comes from the period after A.D. 70; it was written in Greek and it contains, in particular, sayings and speeches of the Lord. For this reason, we call it the "Sayings Source", and have good grounds for tracing it back to the apostle Matthew in its earliest Aramaic form. He is mentioned as the author of some such a piece of writing.[2] It appears to have been subjected to more definite changes in the course of its history than the text of Mark, and there is the difficult question whether the sayings-passages, which are preserved either only in Matthew or only in Luke, are derived from the document Matthew himself wrote. Luke in particular is characterized by extensive, valuable, and unique material, for which we should, perhaps, assume a special source. We must also reckon with the possibility that, in addition to these written sources, oral tradition played a part in the same

[1] Cf. Harnack, *Sprüche u. Reden Jesu*, 1907. Eng. trans., *The Sayings of Jesus*, 1910
[2] Euseb., *H.E.*, iii .39, 16 .by Papias

period, and added here and there stories separately current.

As a consequence, it appears that the written sources which are immediately accessible, or which can be easily reached by simple critical processes, originated in the seventies of the first century. From them we divine a literature earlier than A.D. 70, and this again rests upon the oral tradition of the first generation of disciples, and therefore appears, in the last analysis, as the foundation upon which all our knowledge of Jesus rests. Such a tradition tends to be a handing down of separate pieces, passed round independently, and put together by collectors who adopt a standpoint altogether foreign to the material itself. How to recognize the origin and understand the growth of this tradition when restored to its original elements, and how to appraise the quality of faithfulness in face of the tendency to transform and to add—these are the particular subjects of discussion to-day. In the records that lie before us, we can observe how the wishes, needs, and theological opinions within the Church added a continuation to a narrative, a saying, or a parable; and sometimes so altered it that the uninitiated did not recognize it again. Indeed, we can see religious fantasy calling some entirely new feature into life, and this, in turn, becomes subject to further development in accordance with the same laws. From what we actually see, we can deduce the early history of the rest of the material by presupposing that the same forces were in operation as at an earlier date; and we can then inquire what these forces may have effected by way of additions to, or transformations of, the history of Jesus in the period not covered by literary sources.[1]

In the course of these studies, analogies from allied spheres are frequently applied in order to gain a sharper focus. The numerous Rabbinic sayings offer a welcome parallel to the sayings of Jesus, for they were passed from mouth to mouth, and school to school, for centuries in the Jewish tradition, and finally they received a fixed written form in the Mishna and Gemara of the Talmud, or in commentaries on the Bible. This analogy is all the more valuable because they were not stored in the memory on account of "historical" interests, but either as

[1] Of fundamental importance is R. Bultmann, *Geschichte der Synopt. Tradition*, 2nd ed., 1931; cf. also Dibelius, *From Tradition to Gospel*, 1934

authoritative references for theological decisions, or as rules for the lives of the devout. Similar traditions of sayings may be observed amongst the monks of the fourth century, and these have been written down in the various collections of "Apothegms" of the fathers.[1]

The parallels are of value for understanding the tradition of sayings and speeches. In the same way, the legends of the saints afford instructive parallels to the way in which the accounts of the deeds and experiences of Jesus developed their present form and content. Of course, much skill is required for sorting out those texts which afford real parallels, i.e. those which have a sound historical foundation, from the host of merely imaginary or conventional records. For, here also, we have to do with an oral tradition which has been reduced to writing, but cannot be regarded as literature in the ordinary sense; rather, it corresponds to the style of popular books. This is the case with the gospels, and, in the shaping of the gospel tradition, the same laws have operated which usually govern the modelling of a popular account of the deeds or miracles of great men of God. It is useful to adduce examples here from other spheres of religion. The all-important thing is that the literary critic should retain a sound judgment of the possibilities, the probabilities, and the actualities, of the subject-matter at a time when he is absorbed in following the various transformations in the manner of its literary presentation. There are no infallible standards on which to base judgments, and all historical research is essentially an art which, like every art, depends for the value of its results on the qualifications of the student himself; but it can be developed by regular cultivation, rich experience, and ever fresh activity in various fields, until an opinion is reached that must correspond very closely with the facts.

Jesus grew up in the little Galilean village of Nazareth, where it is probable that He had been born. Joseph His father must have died early, for we only hear of Mary His mother. He had four brothers whose names have come down to us, James, Joses, Jude, and Simon, and also several sisters. By trade, He was a carpenter.[2] He was not confined to timber, saws, and

[1] W. Bousset, *Apophthegmata*, 1923   [2] Mark 6: 3

axes, however, for the spirit drove Him forth into the solitude. When the preaching of John the Baptist re-echoed in the land, He went as a pilgrim to the Jordan and had Himself baptized. Thereupon the spirit drove Him into the wilderness, where He wrestled in prayer with God, and strove with the devil. His wonderful personality was watched with many shakings of heads at home, and, in the end, He was pronounced mad. When He began to attract attention and the people crowded round Him, His family set out to take charge of Him, and to bring the disgrace to an end.[1] We find in Him the tragic quality of the lonely soul whom God has laid hold of by force, lifted out of the love and the friendliness of the world, and filled with deep anguish of spirit; but who, nevertheless, courageously confirms the divine imperative. There is the sound of an heroic inversion of all nature in His hard saying:[2] "If any man cometh unto Me, and hateth not his own father, and mother, and wife, and children, and brethren, and sisters, yea, and his own life also, he cannot be My disciple."

When John the Baptist was imprisoned and hidden from public sight, Jesus returned from the wilderness to His Galilean home,[3] and took up the preaching of him who had been silenced. But it sounded different in His mouth. He did not terrify His hearers by threatening them with the fiery flames of impending judgment; rather He spoke of God and the nature of His rule. For Him also, the transmutation of the age was at hand, and men of the present generation would experience the Kingdom coming with power.[4] Then all suffering would be assuaged, all tears wiped away, and he who, for the Kingdom's sake, had sacrified anything dear to himself, would be well rewarded.[5] But it was necessary to prepare oneself properly for this reign of God—and here the simple ethical preaching of John was not sufficient. The Kingdom of God attracted every one's desire to itself, just as treasure hidden in a field delights the lucky discoverer, as a precious pearl the merchant. All mankind must place themselves at the disposal of God's will and obey His call, leaving behind family, friends, and every possession: he who put his hand to the plough and looked back,

[1] Mark 3: 21, 31   [2] Luke 14: 26, modified in Matt. 10: 37   [3] Mark 1: 14
[4] Mark 9: 1   [5] Mark 10: 30

was not suitable for the Kingdom of God.[1] While it is necessary that we should do God's will on earth as it is done in heaven, we must recognize it as a mighty factor which threatens to disrupt every earthly relationship. "Think not that I am come to send peace on earth: I am not come to send peace but a sword." There will be disputes in the family, and enmity in the house—thus He preached;[2] and it was in accordance with His own experience. The people crowded to Him and listened open-mouthed; many ran after Him; a few remained with Him, and became His disciples. The first of these were two pairs of brothers, fishermen of Lake Genesareth, Simon and Andrew, John and James.

But he did more than preach; He also worked miracles, and testified thereby to the divine origin of His mission. The news of His deeds, spreading more rapidly than the content of His preaching, was told far and wide among the people. Cripples, epileptics, and madmen were healed at His command, and evil spirits vanished before the divine power. The lame and the blind, the deaf and the dumb, and even lepers felt His healing power. In one place indeed, He raised from the dead a twelve-year-old girl; in Nain, a young man. It serves no purpose to try, meticulously and pedantically, to determine the "historical kernel" of the various miracle-stories in the gospels, even if here and there it seems possible. No person of judgment to-day can any longer doubt that Jesus possessed miraculous power, and worked "miracles" as understood in the ancient sense; and to the historian, the extant records, just because of their popular character, flash light from very many facets, and are more valuable than dry official reports could be; for from them comes a reflection of His acts and deeds which pierces far into the deeps of human nature.

A prophet mighty in word and deed had arisen, armed with the miraculous powers of Elias—was he not the very Elias who was to be the herald of the Messiah? Or was Jesus the Messiah Himself who was to bestow the Kingdom of God upon His people? No! the other side replied, He is a false prophet, and has made a compact with Beelzebub, the prince of devils; that is why the demons must obey Him. But how could Satan

[1] Luke 9: 62   [2] Matt. 10: 34

destroy his own kingdom? objected Jesus; and if I really do cast out demons by the finger of God, then take notice thereby that the Kingdom of God has come to you.[1] In this way it would seem that His miraculous power was a glorious divine gift and at the same time a token that His gospel of the Kingdom of God was true. When in prison, John the Baptist heard of the deeds of this successor of his, and the popular opinion about Him, and sent to inquire of Him: Are you He that was to come, or ought we to look for someone else? For His deeds harmonized badly with the Baptist's prophecy of a fiery judgment. The answer resounded the words of Isaiah: The blind see and the lame walk, lepers become cleansed and the deaf hear, the dead rise, and the gospel is preached to the poor—the prophesied signs of the End are here; blessed is the man who takes no offence in Me.[2] At a later date,[3] Jesus asked His disciples: Who do men say I am? to which Peter replied: You are the Messiah. And Jesus knew that he spoke the truth.

The Kingdom of God was not merely knocking at the door; it was already present. It was like a bit of yeast in a bowl of dough which would soon leaven the whole batch. It was put in the earth like a mustard seed which began to sprout and to grow into a tree. And all this was a great divine miracle: he to whom God has promised the seed, sows it on the ground; it sprouts and grows of itself,[4] and brings forth blade and fruit— finally comes the day of harvest, the Last Judgment and the glorious End. In the present world, all sorts of weeds are still growing apace among the wheat, and even this is surely according to God's will; only at the Last Judgment will the chaff be burnt in the fire. There is no need for you to rise and look round for the Kingdom of God,[5] or to lie in wait in case some one says to you: here it is or there it comes; for it is in your midst. That was a new, astonishing, and estranging message, the paradox in Jesus' preaching, which would not sink into the people of His time, nor the scholars of to-day. It is true that Jesus used the colours of prophetic apocalyptic in preaching the Kingdom of God and its glory as promising salvation in a

[1] Matt. 12: 28; Luke 11: 20. Also Bultmann, *Tradition*, 2nd ed., p. 174
[2] Matt. 11: 2–6; Luke 7: 18–23
[3] Viz. after the death of John the Baptist, Mark 8: 27–29
[4] Mark 4: 26–29   [5] Luke 17: 20–21

future age whose commencement no one could calculate, because the Father had kept that entirely to Himself.[1] But this language was meant to describe the full revelation of the Kingdom, the final phases of which would be preceded by the signs foretold by the prophets; it was the coming of the Kingdom "with power". At this time, the Messiah would also appear on the clouds of the sky and set up His throne in the midst of a renewed Israel. But the Kingdom was coming with no less reality even in the present, and the Messiah was passing unnoticed through the land, illumined only by the splendour of miraculous deeds. He was thereby made recognizable, and He gathered the first subjects of the Kingdom round Himself. The new æon had already begun, before the old had collapsed —the media of time and space fail wherever a genuine prophetic message of divine reality is proclaimed.

Popular imagination took most delight in depicting the splendour and the joys of God's Kingdom on earth, and even Jesus' disciples would gladly have known the answer to the question as to who would sit at the right and the left of the Messiah at the future festival.[2] Jesus had more important matters to publish about the Kingdom of God. In the forefront was the teaching that the legal preciseness which was so keenly watched in Pharisaic circles would not be sufficient for one belonging to it; for God was not satisfied with the outer fulfilment of commands; but required the complete surrender of the heart in its deepest depths. Jesus took up again the Old Testament commandment[3] that we must love God with all our hearts, and our neighbour as ourselves, but He drew out of that commandment the final consequences of making religion an inward matter; the Sermon on the Mount contains a series of classic examples. In the command to love our enemies, He opposed natural feeling, and in the command to look for no reward and no revenge, as well as by prohibiting oaths, and divorce, He opposed the Mosaic law. In so doing, He knew Himself to be proclaiming God's will, and He troubled little about the indignation of the guardians of the Law. Fasting and ritual prayer counted for little with Him: a man must speak

[1] Mark 13: 32; this was Jewish teaching
[2] Mark 10: 37   [3] Mark 12: 29–30

with God in solitude. He regarded Sabbath observance as objectionable if it prevented neighbourly actions, or even only the usual eating and drinking. We find here and there many parallels to all this in the surviving sayings of the Rabbis, but they are no more than occasional ripples, which soon die away, and are lost in the sea of legal observances. With Jesus, life with God is like a broad river flooding all the land, and sweeping away every hindrance; there is nothing that would not be covered by its waves. From that life there springs everything which men call righteousness, virtue, good works.

The Jew regarded God as the righteous judge who dealt with men's deeds exactly in accordance with the written code. He also believed in a mercy which God evinced towards His favourites by forgiving their sins; and the Jew hoped that his own good work would receive a just reward, and his sins divine forgiveness. Even Jesus often spoke of reward in a popular, religious sense, and as if the self-denials and sufferings of this world would be recompensed in the Kingdom of God. But when He revealed the final secret of the Kingdom of God, the idea of recompense vanished into nothing. God was like the employer who at different times in the day engaged workpeople for his vineyard,[1] but who gave them all the same wages, and calmly set aside the complaints of the discontented by saying: You who were engaged first, have received what was agreed— are you envious because I have been generous to those engaged last? In the Kingdom of God, all righteousness is simply divine grace. And if you have fulfilled all the commandments, you have only done your duty; you have no claim on any reward, but are unprofitable servants. In the Talmud,[2] we find the answer given by Judaism to this conception of God—we have the same parable but another moral. Here, also, a vine-dresser had worked only two hours, and yet received a full day's pay. But the employer answered those who were discontented with this: This man did more in two hours than you in the whole day. In this instance, everything proceeded according to justice and merit. The contrast is quite clear: on the one hand is the Jewish conception of God with formal righteousness in the

---

[1] Matt. 20: 1–16
[2] *Jerus. Berachoth*, 2, 8 f., 5c; Billerbeck, iv, 492 ff.

human sense, and on the other, the God of Jesus, and a righteousness whose very nature is grace.

Moreover, it appears that the "righteous" are not those who
are the first to enter the Kingdom of God, but the despised and
the lost, the taxgatherers and the sinners, the poor and the sick.
In the Kingdom of God, there is more joy over one sinner who
repents than over ninety-nine "righteous persons" who, on
account of their very righteousness, never conceive that they
lack the best, i.e. knowledge of the nothingness of every human
being in the sight of the eternal God. The parable of the
Pharisee and the Publican brought that to classic expression
once for all. It was a new thing, and it came with a shock, that
Jesus' preaching of the Kingdom was directed towards sinners.[1]
Even nineteen hundred years later, we find this fact difficult to
grasp, although it was meant for us also.

The Old Testament religion sees God's blessing in riches as a
reward for good conduct upon earth, and is inclined to regard
poverty, illness, and suffering, as the divine punishment for
sin. The obscure and the simple knew better—that God had
promised His salvation to the poor and the pitiable.[2] And now
Jesus came, and blessed not only the poor and the suffering,
but also the sinners—for God is near them and calls them to
Himself. When the guests invited to the wedding feast failed to
respond to the invitation given by the divine host, the messengers went into the streets and lanes and invited the beggars
and the cripples, the lame and the blind.[3] Who is the better
son: The one who says, No! to his father's order, but repents and
does it, or he who says, Yes! and does not do it?[4] Thus the sinner
enters the Kingdom of God if he searches his heart and repents
—the very thing which the righteous man thinks he need not
do. In the same way, the poor man is nearer to the Kingdom
of God, for he is not blinded by the wealth and the cheap self-
righteousness of the giver of charity. He is not bound fast to the
present æon and its values by concern for material possessions,
and he has no treasure on earth, which fills his heart and closes
it to God. The rich young man would gladly have followed
Jesus, but he could not well abandon everything for the sake of

---

[1] K. Holl, *Ges. Aufs.*, ii, 9 ff.   [2] *Vide supra*, p. 38
[3] Luke 14: 16–24   [4] Matt. 21: 28–31

the Kingdom of God: it would not do; everyone could understand that, but—the pity of it! Hence: blessed are you poor, for
yours is the kingdom of God.

Jesus did not preach like the scribes, but like one authorized
by God—thus Mark[1] expressed the judgment of the hearers.
But for this very reason, i.e. because the accustomed teaching
was held in respect, no one wished to have anything to do with
Him. In Nazareth His home, He said bitterly that a prophet
counted for nothing in his native place; even in the larger
world round Lake Genesareth, He gained no hearing; He pronounced woe upon Chorazin, Bethsaida, and even Caper-
naum.[2] Therefore He avoided the towns and became the
preacher of the *Am ha-Arez*. Galilee was surrounded by pagan
districts, separated by Samaria from the Judaistic centre of
religion, and penetrated with foreign elements. Hence there
was no sympathy here with the strenuous legalism of the
Pharisees.[3] In this region, therefore, a hearing could be found
for a message which proclaimed that the Kingdom of God was
open to pagan or half-pagan taxgatherers, to despised sinners,
and to the poor and the pitiable; but closed to the Pharisees
with their display of righteous correctness, and to the rich
givers of charity. Here Jesus became a popular hero followed
by the masses; Herod Antipas regarded Him with considerable
doubt, and wondered whether He was the Baptist risen from
the dead; and therefore to be rendered harmless.[4] It was the
necessary consequence of His deeds and words that the Pharisees
should hate Him as one who contemned the Law, and should
persecute Him as a false prophet. There was no escaping a
decisive struggle if He was to be really the Messiah, and not be
content with the part of a forerunner.

Our sources speak unanimously of Jesus' Messiahship. Peter's
confession, "Thou art the Messiah", in Mark, harmonizes with
the indirect answer to the direct question of John the Baptist
preserved in "Q".[5] But we have no authentic tradition of a word
of Jesus Himself in which He claims this dignity as His own.[6]

---

[1] Mark 1: 22   [2] Matt. 11: 20–24; Luke 10, 13–15
[3] Cf. Walter Bauer in *Festgabe für Jülicher*, 16–34
[4] Mark 6: 14; cf. 8: 28; Luke 13: 31   [5] Cf. *supra*, p. 51
[6] The confession before the High-Priest (Mark 14: 62) is scarcely historical
cf. *Sitzungsber. Akad. Berlin*, 1931, p. 316

On the other hand our two principal sources have preserved quite a number of sayings in which Jesus describes
Himself as the Son of Man; and it can be clearly seen from the
context in Mark 8: 31 that this was understood in the Messianic
sense. Moreover, other passages show that the enigmatic title
means the future ruler of the Kingdom of God, for, according
to Dan. 7: 13, that ruler would "come on the clouds of heaven
like a son of man". In spite of the fact that no successful solution
has yet been found for the philological problems raised by this
term,[1] the general reliability of the textual tradition is as little
in doubt as the Messianic significance of the phrase. And it is
just as certain that "Son of Man" was not a current term for the
Messiah, for even the earliest Christians no longer understood
it, and avoided using it; thus it has remained a riddle to the
present day. We may take it as a reliable tradition that Jesus
was regarded as the Messiah by His disciples and by various
individuals among the people at large, sick and well, healed
and possessed. So, too, He regarded Himself as the Messiah.
And, just as He had given quite a new sense to the term,
"Kingdom of God", so too, He entirely transformed the meaning of "Messiah". He allowed the apocalyptic conceptions to
remain, and glow on the horizon; but He took the seeds of the
Kingdom, which were replete with divine power, and planted
them in the hearts of those hearers who repented and believed.
Jesus possessed an inner royalty, and was armed with miraculous powers given by His heavenly Father. After He had
received that Father's testimony,[2] He preached the gospel of
the new, divine community, and so brought the long-promised
salvation to His fellows.

Another, new element in the teaching which Jesus gave His
disciples was that the Messiah must die in order to complete
His work. It was most difficult to understand and they simply
did not believe it. No Jew had ever heard of a Messiah who
would have to die by the very nature of His office, and therefore this conception cannot have been applied to Jesus from
the outside. Rather, just as the message of the Kingdom and
the consciousness of His Messiahship received their characteristic nature from Jesus' experience of God, so it came home

[1] G. Dalman, *Worte Jesu*, 2nd edit., 191–219, 383–97   [2] Mark 1: 9–11

to Him, in His own soul, that His death was necessary for the accomplishment of His task; and this, in its nature, was an inner acceptance and affirmation of what His experiences of His opponents led Him to suspect as His personal lot.

We do not know how long Christ's public ministry lasted, for the single year into which Mark compresses his account is only a literary form and was not intended to be historical chronology. The Fourth Gospel quite obviously counts upon three years, but without our being able for this reason to regard it as a more reliable witness. It describes Jesus as attending the Passover in Jerusalem at least twice before He went there for the last time. The synoptics know nothing of this, and the saying from "Q", found in Luke 13: 34, is probably a quotation from the Book of Wisdom mentioned in 11: 49, and has no relevance to this question. Tradition tells of only one journey to Jerusalem, and Mark put His third prophecy of death, like a direction sign, at the head of his account (10: 32–34). Luke wrote down a valuable piece of tradition that had hitherto been circulating freely in the popular memory (13: 31–33): In that hour there came certain Pharisees, saying to him: Get thee out and go hence: for Herod would fain kill thee. And he said to them, Go and say to that fox, Behold, I cast out devils and perform cures to-day and to-morrow, and the third day I must journey; for it cannot be that a prophet perish out of Jerusalem.[1] Both these passages reflect the same sad echo: He is going to the capital to die there, for that is God's will. But Luke's record preserves a note on the historical circumstances. Antipas had sent some Pharisees with the message for Jesus to depart from Galilee. It was possible for Him to go either to Samaria or into gentile regions—but He had no call there. Hence He recognized that His hour had come, and He began the journey that was to prove fatal. His disciples were amazed, and the crowds were troubled about Him, for even they knew into what danger He was running.

The road led through Jericho, where He healed a blind man;[2] then He approached Jerusalem from the east. In the neighbourhood of Olivet, when exhausted by the journey, He appears to

[1] This must be the meaning of the traditional saying in Luke 13; 32–33
[2] Mark 10: 46

have borrowed an ass, an incident out of which later legends developed a Messianic entry into Jerusalem on the basis of Zechariah's prophecy (9: 9) which foretells of the gentle king riding on an ass into Jerusalem. According to the tradition preserved in Mark, Jesus then entered Jerusalem for the very first time, for that is the natural presupposition of the following remark, viz., that in the temple He looked round about upon all things, and then, because it was getting dusk, He went out into Bethany for the night.[1]

As has been the case with many other devout persons in later centuries, so it was with Jesus: His proper, religious feeling was most pronouncedly offended by the more than profane business carried on in the forecourt of the temple. He drove out the dealers with their sacrificial animals, and likewise the money-changers, broke up their stalls, and then closed the forecourt as a thoroughfare; this can only mean that He gathered the people round Himself to take forceful measures against the evil of sacrilege; uttering the denunciations of the prophets of old, He put Himself at their head.

That was a first sign of the storm in Jerusalem: the prophet from Galilee had raised a tumult in the temple, and that must have caused concern to the people in authority. Nevertheless, they did not attempt to overmaster Him by means of the police, but tried by various questions to entrap Him. Mark records a few disputes between Jesus and the Pharisees and Sadducees, which might well be ascribed to this period, the most illuminating being the question as to the payment of tribute money.[2] In Galilee, politics was not a matter of common argument, and the national insurrection in A.D. 66–70 found no echo in that province.[3] Jesus held quite aloof from political hopes, and the national Messianic ideal with its worldly complexion such as we know in the Psalms of Solomon appeared to Him on at least one occasion as a temptation of the devil. Opinion was different in Jerusalem, and liberation from the Roman over-rule was a national as well as a religious desideratum. When Jesus gave an equivocal answer to the question of tribute and showed Himself lukewarm, His standing in the capital was gone. His answer

[1] Mark 11: 11   [2] Mark 12: 13–17, also Jos., *Ant.*, 18, 4, *Bellum J.*, 2, 118
[3] W. Bauer in *Festgabe für Jülicher*, 22 ff.

avoided the trap and dealt with the crucial point of the problem. In effect, He said, "Since you have been obliged to surrender to the Romans the right of minting gold and silver money, it is foolish to ask whether one ought to pay taxes to these same Romans with foreign money." But as soon as the insurrection broke out in A.D. 66, the Jews once more coined silver money.

We have no idea how long Jesus was at odds with the authorities in Jerusalem. Not a syllable in Mark hints that Jesus—possibly in a pilgrim caravan—had come to Jerusalem just for the Passover; and we have already noted the passage in Luke saying that Antipas had banned Him, which makes it indeed unlikely. We may assume, therefore, that Jesus worked for a considerable period in Jerusalem, during which He gained numerous adherents among the people, and many influential enemies among the Pharisees and Sadducees. The members of the sanhedrin eventually decided to get rid of Him; it was to be done without causing a sensation, and before the Passover. Only two days were left.[1]

After He had prayed in a garden on Olivet, Jesus was arrested by night in the midst of His disciples, one belonging to the inner circle having informed the bailiffs of the place where He was accustomed to spend the night. At the arrest, the disciples fled, and only Peter turned back, and slipped after his Master into the courtyard of the High-Priest's official residence. There he mingled with the crowd and, by a couple of lies, managed to escape detection. But it is scarcely probable that we can depend upon his report, for from what we read in Mark about the night-trial before the sanhedrin, all signs indicate that we have a later Christian version here. Mark says that a night-sitting of the sanhedrin was held at once under the presidency of Caiaphas the High-Priest. The first charge was that Jesus had desired to destroy the temple and rebuild it in three days; but the reports of the witnesses did not agree, and Jesus maintained silence in spite of all the charges. Then the High-Priest put to Him the crucial question, which was one of conscience: Are you the Messiah, the Son of the Most High? And He answered: Yes, and prophesied that He would sit at the right

[1] Mark 14: 1

hand of God, and that He would return as the Son of Man upon the clouds of heaven. Thereupon the High-Priest condemned Him to death for blasphemy. It cannot be proved that this record contains more than a dim memory of the actual events.

But we can say, with some certainty, that the sanhedrin came to no legal condemnation on the count of blasphemy, for then they would have had to execute Jesus on their own authority by stoning. That was prescribed in the Law, and was accordingly carried out, as we see, e.g. in the case of Stephen. It is an error, which the gospels themselves share and have spread, that the Great Sanhedrin did not possess the power to pronounce and carry out capital sentences. Rather the undoubtedly trustworthy report of the course of events shows that the Jewish authorities, probably on quite good grounds, refrained from dealing with this matter in the form of a religious trial, and preferred to hand Jesus over to the Roman authorities as an insurgent.[1] The procurator, Pontius Pilate, is well known to us from other records.[2] He governed as Jewish procurator from A.D. 26–36, and was staying at that moment in Jerusalem, obviously because the people were streaming there for the Passover, and he wished to keep his eyes on the masses. Jesus was denounced to him as the "King of the Jews", which is as much as to say a Messianic agitator in the political sense. After a short hearing, Pilate had Him taken away, scourged, and crucified. That the lot of Jesus was seen in the light of Old Testament prophecy, and was reflected in the hearts of His own people, is shown with moving power in the Passion story of the gospels.

On the thirteenth or the fourteenth of the month of Nisan, in the afternoon in any case before Passover eve,[3] Jesus died on the cross. A devout member of the sanhedrin took the body down from the cross and put it in a tomb hewn in the rock. We hear no further of the disciples. Prophecy had been fulfilled: the shepherd was killed and the sheep were scattered. The Messianic dream was at an end.

---

[1] This can be plainly seen in Mark 15: 1. For the whole, cf. *Der Prozess Jesu* in *Sitzungsber. Akad. Berlin*, 1931, 313–22

[2] *Prosopographia imp. Rom.*, iii, 84

[3] E. Schwartz, *Z.N.W.*, 7, 23. Wellhausen, *Mark*, pp. 108–10

Chapter Five

THE FIRST CHURCH

THOUGH CRUCIFIED, DEAD, AND BURIED, JESUS DID NOT remain in a state of death. He appeared to His disciples and was seen alive by them. First to Peter, then to the Twelve, then to more than 500 brethren at one time, afterwards to James, and later to all the apostles—that is the record of the oldest and most certain tradition preserved for us by Paul in I Cor. 15: 5–7. Mark 16: 7 contains a further clear indication that the first appearance of the Risen Lord to His disciples took place in Galilee: there Peter saw the Master again, there the Twelve came together and were entrusted by the Risen Lord with His mission. Accordingly they went to Jerusalem. Here He appeared to the five hundred, and this led to the founding of the Church,[1] as told in the traditional record of the first Whitsuntide. But Jesus appeared also to His brother James, and thereby gained him for the Church where he at once received an honourable position. Finally, there was a closing appearance to all the leading persons of the Church: it was the ultimate confirmation of their office. Thereupon the Lord went to heaven. Phantasy and apologetics expanded, multiplied, and altered these appearances, added the proof of the empty grave, and brought into existence the later forms of our gospel texts.

Earlier generations of scholars have made strenuous and zealous efforts, either to "explain" the resurrection of Jesus, or else to defend its inexplicable and miraculous character; as if it would be of real advantage if we could see more clearly through the details and the historical connection of the events, or could prove their uniqueness. All the events of history take place in the phenomenal world, and can only be conceived by us in terms of natural causation. But every attempt to comprehend the deepest nature and meaning of history, whether in general, or in individual instances, leads us into regions which lie beyond these boundaries, into the metaphysics of the philosopher and the theologian. Of course it is only in these

[1] K. Holl, *Ges. Aufs.*, ii, 47, 49, 53 ff.

deeps that the springs flow from which any interpretation of history draws life and gains value. All criticism of the gospel records, and all attempts to discover the native facts, can only be carried out on the basis of our ordinary experience of the way things happen: and they usually lead to very diverse hypotheses of visions; with which the inquirer must be content. But the verdict on the true nature of the event described as the resurrection of Jesus, an event of immeasurable significance for the history of the world, does not come within the province of historical inquiry into matters of fact; it belongs to the place where the human soul touches the eternal.

The Messiah had to reveal Himself in Jerusalem, for it was here that the Master's death had in fact taken place—hence here also must He return in glory, riding on the clouds of heaven, in order to set up God's kingdom in all its might and splendour. Even in apocalyptic hope, Jerusalem remained, as it had ever been, the central point of divine action, the capital of the new, as of the old, Israel; and from it the disciples must not depart.[1] Here the mother-church of primitive Christianity was constituted of native Jews who were adherents of Jesus, i.e. those who explicitly believed that the promised Messiah had appeared in the person of Jesus of Nazareth and that He had only revealed Himself in humility and died on the cross in fulfilment of the divine will and prophetic foretelling; He would soon come again and bring God's kingdom to the earth.

These believers in Jesus belonged to those quiet, religious people who gladly gave themselves the name of "the poor", as found in the Psalms, and who treasured with faithful hearts the sayings of the Master about the blessedness of the poor. At the same time, however, they knew themselves to be the saints,[2] the faithful who were beloved by God, the remnant of the people separated off for that Last Day of which the prophets and the apocalyptists had spoken. Both names meant the same thing and described those whose hope and expectation was that the existing, sad condition of the lowly and needy would soon end, and that they would be rewarded with overwhelming glory. The eschatological expectation of this original church,

[1] Acts 1: 4
[2] Cf. Lietzmann, *Komm.* on Rom. 15: 25. Excursus

composed of Jews, is reflected in the shining allegories of the Revelation of John.

Its members were Jews: they wished so to be, and so to remain: they attended worship in the temple, and Solomon's portico was their favourite meeting place.[1] They remained faithful to the Law, and zealously insisted that Jesus had not come to end the Law, but to fulfil it; and had warranted that heaven and earth would pass away before a letter, indeed even a fragment of a letter, would pass away, and everything be fulfilled. In addition, they accepted the scribal and Pharisaic exegeses of the scriptures.[2] What differentiated them from the Pharisees was, partly their certainty that the Messiah, whom the remaining Israelites still expected as about come, and partly their faith that He would soon reappear in glory. This conviction and this faith were not mere abstractions, but of vital force. Their experience, when the Risen Lord had appeared to them, still made their hearts throb if they looked with much yearning for His final return, visible to all the world; yet they also knew that He, who had risen from the dead, came close to His own, though invisible, whenever two or three were gathered together in His name.

It was at this point that their table fellowship won its deeper significance.

Whenever the disciples gathered for a meal in accordance with Jewish custom, and one of them pronounced a blessing over the bread, they recalled the happy days when the Master had formerly blessed and broken the bread for them. He returned to them, and they became conscious of His presence. The story of the disciples of Emmaus echoes this sense marvellously. Again, the knowledge of the presence of Jesus and the secret happiness of possessing the highest divine grace made the simplest meal in the rudest hut a foretaste of the heavenly banquet which the Lord would celebrate with His own at the Messianic table. Hence, in the first church, the bread was broken "with gladness and praise",[3] and the yearning prayer "Marana tha", i.e. "Come, O our Lord" alternated with the

[1] Acts 5: 12; 3, 11; cf. John 10: 23
[2] Matt. 5: 17–18; 23: 3
[3] Acts 2: 46 f.

Messianic "Hosanna"; present and future were woven into a single fabric.[1]

In this way the first church was held together by the fact that all its members shared the experience of the presence of the Risen Lord. A rite of initiation was also observed. No account is given of its origin; the first records assume it as well known, and in final form; Matt. 28: 19–20 is a theological explanation, added at a later date. The accounts in Acts as well as the Pauline letters, assume that the Christian is baptized on being received into the Church, whereas the tradition in the gospels does not reflect such a mode of initiation into the circle of Jesus' disciples. The remarks in John 3: 22 and 4: 1 f. are valid and historical reports of Jesus' custom, and perhaps indicate the direction in which we must look for a solution of the problem. Jesus Himself had been baptized by John, and He esteemed John's baptism highly. It appears also as if many of John's disciples had gone over into Jesus' following. Hence John's baptism was taken up into primitive Christianity[2] in its original significance of a washing away of the uncleannesses of the old æon, a cleansing necessary for the entry into the new Messianic world. The recognition that Jesus was the "Coming One" expected by John, was all that one needed to transmute baptism, as practised by John, into a Christian rite of initiation into the Church. Acts[3] records a very instructive story on this point: Paul met a number of Christians in Ephesus who had been baptized with John's baptism. He then taught them that they must be baptized in the name of Jesus; only when they had complied was the Holy Ghost given them, and only then did they receive the gift of prophecy. But they had already been "disciples", i.e. believing Christians (19: 2). In other words, we have here a glimpse of an earlier condition such as we must regard as the first, tentative effort to order the customs of the Church. At a later date, the more exact, liturgical, and definitive formula was added. Simple baptism in the Johannine mode, "for repentance and forgiveness of sins", was no longer sufficient; the name of Jesus must be named over the candidate.[4]

---

[1] Lietzmann, *Messe u. Herrenmahl*, p. 250
[2] Ed. Meyer, iii, pp. 245 ff.   [3] Acts 19: 1–5
[4] Otherwise Acts 8: 16 f. Here even baptism in the name of Jesus is not enough. The apostles must also "lay on" their hands.

These Ephesian Christians were no more disciples of John than was the Apollos who had been mentioned a little earlier;[1] he also had received only the Johannine type of baptism, but his work was that of a Christian missionary impelled by the Spirit.

There is probably some justification, from the gospel texts, for holding that John's following exercised even further influences on the first Christian church. We learn from Luke 11: 1–4 that John taught his disciples to pray,[2] and that, consequently, Jesus' disciples desired similar instruction from their own Master—whereupon Jesus gave them the "Lord's prayer". But we have to recognize that the text of Luke at the beginning of the prayer, as preserved in the principal manuscripts, is very uncertain, and in any case widely different from that in Matt. 6: 9–13, which was adopted for the liturgy of the Church. The most conservative inference from these facts is that, in the earliest tradition, the Lord's Prayer was not repeated in a definite and fixed form of words. This means that Jesus Himself cannot have prescribed and commanded a final and authoritative form; nor has any invariable form been handed down. Rather, it would seem that the original form of the Lord's Prayer consisted of the very simple petitions which underlie the Lukan text. Eschatological petitions for the coming of the Kingdom of God, expressed in phrases influenced by Jewish prayers, have been added. The kernel, which includes the petition that God will forgive us in proportion as we ourselves forgive others, breathes the very spirit of the Sermon on the Mount, the addenda express the Messianic yearning of the Church quite in the mood of the Master's preaching. There is nothing to suggest that the content of the Lord's Prayer[3] had been modelled on the prayers of John's disciples, for these are altogether unknown to us. The fact that a liturgical prayer was authorized and introduced into the Church, however, arose from the desire to do the same as the Baptist's disciples; and this fact is clearly expressed in the gospel tradition.

In addition, the Jewish custom, especially of the Pharisees, of fasting devoutly twice in the week (Luke 18: 12), was observed

---

[1] Acts 18: 24–28   [2] Cf. Wellhausen, *Comm.*, *ad loc.*
[3] M. Dibelius, *Joh. d. Täufer*, p. 42 ff.

among John's disciples, and was taken over by the first church. The change is explained in Mark 2: 18–20; the joy of the wedding feast was over, for the Bridegroom had been taken from His people.[1] Now was the time for repentance in expectation of the End, and it was well to fast. The Jews fasted on Mondays and Thursdays, so did John's disciples, and so must the Jewish-Christian first church have done. They also observed the Sabbath, as implied by Matt. 24: 20. The prayer to be saved from flight "in winter" as it stands in Mark, is supplemented in Matthew by the addition, "and on the Sabbath". This addition reflects tendencies within the Church, and shows that it observed the Sabbath in the Jewish way, and would not allow it to be desecrated by journeying, even in time of stress. The spirit of freedom as preached by Jesus had obviously suffered, but this was not perceived at the time. The majority had not actually known Him, and they gradually transfigured His impress. Thus it came about that the traditional observance of the Sabbath, doubly holy in Jerusalem, outweighed any memory of Jesus' own attitude. Moreover James, the leader of the church, belonged at bottom to those who were strangers to Jesus, and strove for the ideal of a Jewish "righteousness". One legend, accepted in the Church, which was written down by a Christian of the Antonine period[2] represents James as a devout man held n high respect by the Jews, and as a true, oriental ascetic who, by his lengthy prayers, had grown callouses "like a camel's" on his knees. One of the most trustworthy narratives of Acts[3] depicts the Jewish-Christians in Jerusalem as "all zealous for the law"; four of them had sworn an oath according to the Old Testament rite[4], and Paul had to join them, and undertake to defray the entire cost of the sacrifices necessary to free them from their oath, in order to allay suspicion about his own orthodoxy.

The leader of the first Church was James. He had been gladly given this honour, immediately on joining the Church, obviously because he was Jesus' brother. After James' death, a cousin of Jesus was chosen to be his successor, and, even at a later date, blood relations of Jesus enjoyed special regard in

[1] M. Dibelius, *Joh. d. Täufer*, p. 39   [2] Hegesippus in Eus. *H.E.*, ii, 23, 4–18
[3] Acts 21: 20–26   [4] Num. 6: 18–20

the Church.[1] In Acts, "presbyters" are mentioned along with James at the head of the Church, but we know nothing more about them.

In Jewish communities, it is customary for a sort of committee of eminent "elders" to constitute the advisory council.[2] This was the case even in Old Testament times, and has continued throughout the centuries. Hence it is not surprising to read of such a council of elders also among Christian believers. Whether their number was defined—say twenty-four, as in the Revelation of John—or indefinite, cannot be said.

But what was the position of the original Apostles? May we still regard them as the real founders and the recognized authorities of the Church? Most certainly; and their importance is clear enough from the way in which Paul had to struggle at a later date. They were indeed not only the guarantors and vehicles of the tradition, but also they had been appointed to sit on twelve thrones, under the presidency of the Son of Man, and judge the twelve tribes of Israel in the Messianic Kingdom (Matt. 19: 28). According to Rev. 21: 14, John saw their names written upon the twelve foundation stones of the walls of the heavenly Jerusalem; nevertheless, near the throne of the Lamb, twenty-four "elders" were seated on twenty-four thrones.[3] These inconsistencies are the reflection of opposing tendencies in Jerusalem at an early date.

The Twelve appear to have been a closed circle from which only Peter and John the son of Zebedee stood out as individuals. These two, together with James, constituted the "pillars" of the first Church, as Paul once called them,[4] making use of a title which he himself had not originated. What they decided ior the Church was regarded as binding upon the original Christians. In Acts 3 and 4, Peter and John appear as great miracleworkers, and are the apologists of the Church. At a later date, they were sent to Samaria to regularize Philip's missionary work.[5] That fact makes their outstanding significance quite clear. But Acts, being written from the opposite standpoint to that of Revelation, leaves James quite in the background. The

---

[1] Heges. in Eus. *H.E.*, iii, 11; 20, 1–6; 32, 6. Cf. Julius Africanus, *ibid.*, i, 7, 14
[2] *Z.W.Th.*, 55, 116 ff.   [3] Rev. 21: 14; 4: 4; 5: 8
[4] Gal. 2: 9   [5] Acts 8: 14

differences remained, and often made themselves felt.[1] Eventually, however, the further spread of Christianity, and the destruction of Jerusalem, settled the issue. The Twelve came to be regarded as the founders of the Church universal, while James and his successors were held supreme in the original church and its posterity.

If we look at the circumstances here described, it might appear as if the first Church entered, by force of circumstances, into a Judaizing reaction which would necessarily end with a complete disavowal of the true spirit of the Master. Indeed we shall see that this was the lot which befell a part of it. But other forces remained alive and pressed in the other direction, forces which were grasped by eager and capable men.

We have seen that the Church faithfully retained the Jewish customs of fasting and Sabbath observance. But it was a new departure, and one of special importance, when the Church began to celebrate Sunday as the peculiar day of the new society. It was regarded as "the day of the Lord", and on it believers assembled to break bread, i.e. for the "Lord's Supper". How did the first day of the week come to be called the Lord's Day? The term was used in 1 Cor. 16: 2; Acts 20: 7; Rev. 1: 10, and in the *Didache* (14). The author of the Epistle of Barnabas, writing about A.D. 132, gives as the reason (15: 9) for this celebration of the "eighth day" that the resurrection of the Lord took place then. All this accords with the relevant passages in the gospels.

The choice of this day has been explained by some scholars by parallels from other religions, or they have suggested that it was selected in order to have a special day as a special mark of the Church.[2] But we find few traces of such an interest; rather it seems to have faded away among the churches described above. On this theory, indeed, the observance of Sunday as the Lord's Day would have originated among the Hellenistic Christians, and those who so observed Sunday must have been brought into opposition to James' group. But we do not find the faintest suggestion of that sort, for, apparently from the very beginning, Sunday was the holy day of the week for all Christians alike. If so, the obvious reason is in all probability the

[1] Ed. Meyer, *Ursprung*, iii 225   [2] Ed. Meyer, iii, 243

real one, viz. the first appearance of the Risen Lord took place on the first day of the week, hence on a Sunday. It is, in fact, the day on which the church of the Apostles began its new life. We may easily infer that they also expected that the Lord would come again in glory on a Sunday; and if this is so, we have discovered a sufficient reason for the Sunday celebration of the communion of the Lord's Supper, with its Messianic expectations and the "Marana tha". But here, too, was a starting point from which to show that the Church was distinct from Judaism, and for settling on Sunday as the Christian holy day in contradistinction to the Jewish Sabbath. The process began as soon as strict ritualism gave place to a more liberal conception, and as the newness and uniqueness of Christianity came to be more fully understood.

A further differentiation developed readily from this stage. If the Lord had appeared to Peter on a Sunday, it followed that He had risen on a Sunday: the gospel records depict that already. But according to Hos. 6: 2, the resurrection took place "on the third day" after death; hence the death of Jesus must have taken place on a Friday, and it would appear appropriate to respect the day by fasting. The Jewish fast day was Thursday. Thus there seemed to be a parallel shift of a day: the Christian Sunday was observed instead of the Jewish Saturday, and the Christian Friday instead of the Jewish Thursday. Then, by carrying the parallel further, the second Christian fast day would have become Tuesday instead of the Jewish Monday. But the fact that actually Wednesday was chosen is a proof that the displacement was not made for its own sake, but that it was connected with something specifically Christian: in this case, the only reason can have been that Jesus' passion began on a Wednesday, i.e. the day when He was arrested. A Church Order dating from the third century, the *Didascalia*, preserves this basis.[1] Paul did not require his own churches to observe any special days, nor did he even give Sunday a Sabbath character.[2] But the course of evolution was away from this kind of Puritanism, and it brought into being a new division of the week, in which there was a remarkable assertion of

[1] *Didascalia*, c. 21, p. 107, 25 Flemming. Holl, *Ges. Aufs.*, ii, 210
[2] Rom. 14: 5; cf. Col. 2: 16

Christian self-consciousness as distinct from Jewish ceremonialism, and, indeed, the claims of Jewish forms of worship as a whole. The week was completely rearranged, and this from a purely Christian standpoint; whoever accepted the new arrangement could not, in fact, also retain the old one, for only Tuesday would have remained as an ordinary day. In theory, perhaps, the Sabbath could have remained as the day of rest alongside of the Sunday, the day when the Lord's Supper was celebrated. In fact such was the case for a while,[1] but gradually the Jewish Sabbath gave place to the Christian "Lord's Day". Prohibitions dating from the beginning of the second century betray the last traces[2] of the struggle between the two kinds of week, but no direct evidence whatever has survived. It is noteworthy that, in the controversy with gentile Christians, the question of Sabbath observance played no part.

The record in Acts shows clearly, in spite of all the influence of literary tendencies, that new elements soon arose alongside that of the natives of Palestine (the "Hebrews") who constituted the Judaizing strain in the original church. These elements brought about an advance, and therefore to some extent a return, to the historical Jesus. They were the "Hellenes" or "Hellenists", not merely Jews of Greek speech, but those who had grown up in the Greek diaspora, and had now settled in Jerusalem. As a rule they would belong to some corresponding union or society in their synagogue at Jerusalem, as in Acts 6: 9. These Jews also spoke the Aramaic current in Palestine, as in the case of Stephen and Paul,[3] and as is assumed in general in Acts. The carefully edited record in Acts 6: 1–6 shows that there was a tendency in the first church to regard them as of a somewhat lower grade, but that they successfully resisted. To care for their interests, they chose their own council of seven; significantly enough, all bore Greek names. Their members also included the proselyte Nicolas of Antioch who had once been a pagan. It may be that, among other duties, these seven were made responsible for looking after the Hellenistic widows as Acts records, but they regarded missionary work as their main

---

[1] Ebionites in Euseb. *H.E.*, iii, 27, 5, and footnote 2, p. 69, *supra*

[2] Ignat., *Magn.*, 9, 1. *Oxyr. Logion*, 2. *Didache*, 14, 1; 8, 1

[3] Acts 7 and 21: 40

duty.[1] Stephen, their leader, preached a great deal in the diaspora-synagogues of Jerusalem, and gained adherents to the Church. Philip went as a missionary to Samaria, and later evangelized the strip of coast land between Ashdod and Cæsarea. At that time he lived with his four daughters in Cæsarea;[2] finally he went to Hierapolis, where he died.[3]

Acts 6 and 7 records the martyrdom of Stephen in a passage affected by certain literary mannerisms, like all martyrologies, but obviously retaining much historical veracity. It shows, in particular, that the Hellenists held the temple worship in low esteem and disregarded the Jewish, ritual requirements. This led to a charge being preferred before the sanhedrin against Stephen, which ended with a finding of blasphemy. He was stoned to death.

At the same time, however, there was a spontaneous persecution of those who shared his views. Many were imprisoned, the majority fled the city and scattered throughout Judea, where they quietly worked for their Master. The apostles remained in Jerusalem—so the record says.[4] That probably means that the persecution was directed only against the Hellenists, who were hostile to the Mosaic law, whereas the true, Palestinian Jews remained unmolested. The inner division in the Church had now become outwardly visible, and the question arose whether James and the original apostles were able to reclaim the loyalty of those who had become separated.

We are still dealing with the earliest beginnings, where only isolated events can be grasped; and only disconnected, overdrawn records, expanded by legend, are at our disposal. The period is of fundamental importance, but its history cannot be traced authentically. Yet we can recognize the effective forces, and the direction in which they were working.

From the very beginning, the original church was a missionary church; she followed up the preaching of Jesus, and won converts for the Kingdom of God. But she laboured only among the lost sheep of the house of Israel and avoided roads that led to the Gentiles or to the towns of the Samaritans.[5]

[1] E. Schwartz, Gött. Nachr., 1907, 280 f.   [2] Acts 8: 40; 21: 8
[3] Polycrates of Ephesus in Euseb. H.E., iii, 31, 3 (where he is confused with the apostle)
[4] Acts 8: 1   [5] Matt. 10: 5

Perhaps she followed the example set in the lifetime of the Lord,[1] and sent out her missionaries in twos, without money or food, with only one garment, with sandals and staff, as pilgrims always going from place to place. And if any place did not receive them, they shook the dust from off their feet, "as a witness to them", and travelled further. Their hope was high that they would not have come to the last of the towns of Israel before the Son of Man should appear.[2] But we have no further details of the progress of the mission, and only incidentally are we told of churches in Judea, Galilee, and Samaria.[3] The last named had been founded by the Hellenist, Philip, who only later received the approval of the original apostles. Peter is the only one of the Twelve whom we actually see working as a missionary, but, perhaps, even that is to say too much, for we hear of him really only as an inspector of the mission field. Along with John, he visited the churches founded by Philip in Samaria, and later journeyed through the coast land via Lydda, Joppa, and the plain of Sharon, to Cæsarea,[4] i.e. Philip's area over again. Afterwards we meet with him in Antioch and the west. Paul characterizes him[5] emphatically as the apostle entrusted with the mission to the Jews. But the missionary work of the first church was confined to Jewish Palestine. The persecution connected with Stephen, with its far-reaching effect of scattering the Hellenistic section of the church, brought new regions into the Christian orbit for the first time. We have already seen how Philip worked in Samaria and on the coast. Others went to Phœnicia, Cyprus, and Antioch. Acts seems to be correct in asserting that this mission, conducted by the Hellenists, was confined entirely to the Jews. In Antioch, however, a new feature developed. Among the Hellenistic refugees were a few people from Cyprus and Cyrene who did not confine themselves to these limits, but preached to the Gentiles and had astonishing success.[6] The Gentile mission was born, and the confines of the Law were broken.

The church at Jerusalem had maintained the connection with the Hellenistic branch after it had separated off. The inner

---

[1] Mark 6: 7–13; Luke 10: 1–16; cf. E. Meyer, iii, 260   [2] Matt. 10: 23
[3] Acts 8: 5; 9: 31; Gal. 1: 22   [4] Acts 9: 32–10: 1
[5] Gal. 2: 7   [6] Acts 11: 19 f.

contradiction or antithesis, which had certainly existed hitherto, was not strong enough to destroy the feeling of the common bond of faith in the Lord, and this fact was of decisive significance for the whole history of the Church. Wherever a Hellenistic mission was founded, and new Christian churches were called into being, emissaries of the original church came on the scene to test the quality of the new brethren, and to regulate intercourse with them. In the original Christian consciousness, there was in fact only one single Church of "disciples" of the Lord; its locus was temporarily the earthly Jerusalem, until, at the parousia of the Son of Man, the heavenly Jerusalem would come down and be the dwelling-place of those who belonged to Him. Those who were compelled to live outside Jerusalem belonged equally to the Church at Jerusalem; for all the far-flung hosts of Christians were branches of the one all-embracing central body. All stood under the authority of the apostles to whom the Lord Himself had given the right of pronouncing the final verdict on all questions relating to the proper form of worship.[1] In missionary praxis this meant that Peter, who alone was really active, possessed the highest authority throughout the whole of the daughter churches. The structure of the Church depended upon him in the earliest period,[2] and the grafting of the newly-arisen churches on the total organism depended upon his recognition of them.

There was a second consequence of the central position of Jerusalem. Granted that no communism ruled in the capital such as has been deduced from certain exaggerated expressions in Acts, yet, in the spirit of discipleship to Jesus, there was an appropriate far-reaching mutual readiness to help, which showed itself occasionally in the selling of property for the benefit of the charitable funds.[3] In order to understand this phenomenon there is not the slightest need to suggest that all earthly possessions had lost their value on account of the expectations of the parousia. It was taken for granted in this host of brethren that none should suffer from need. The church was anxious to continue performing these acts of kindness, and soon regarded them as a great privilege. The principle came to be recognized that an itinerant evangelist could claim hospitality

[1] Matt. 18: 18   [2] Matt. 16: 19   [3] Acts 2: 44; 4: 32–35

from the churches as recompense for preaching—that he should reap material things for having sown spiritual things, as Paul expressed it.[1] And, similarly, it came to be generally recognized that the church of the spiritual capital had a right to be supported by her daughter churches. It would be one of Peter's concerns on his journeys of inspection to arrange these financial matters. Thus, perhaps at first only half-consciously, though later systematically arranged, there grew a complete parallel to the temple-tax which was sent to Jerusalem by Jewish communities in the diaspora. By the compulsion of historical development, though without being actually intended, there grew in a few years, from the little group of enthusiasts in Jerusalem, a great fellowship whose links reached as far as the Mediterranean and the capital of Syria, and which was organized in spite of many inner conflicts, as a brotherly unity. James ruled in Jerusalem, but the original church laid claims upon the diaspora, where Peter exercised the headship of the apostolic college, and was the rock on which the Church was built.

[1] 1 Cor. 9: 11

Chapter Six

THE JEWISH DIASPORA

IN THE ELEVATED MOOD OF THE MACCABEAN PERIOD, THE Hebrew Sibyl, disguised in the dress of Greek prophecy, foretold the fate of the Jewish people. It bewailed the Babylonian imprisonment, when wife and child languished as slaves of the enemy, and all possessions were lost; then it continued[1]

> Thou fillest every continent and state;
> And all men learn thy usages to hate.

In the reign of Augustus, Strabo set it down in plain prose that, by his time, Jews "were to be found in every city, and that in the whole world it was not easy to find a place where they had not penetrated and which was not dominated by them".[2] Documents, literary notices, and excavations agree in supporting these statements; and modern reference books contain innumerable passages recording the existence of Jewish colonies in the late Hellenistic and Roman periods. If, however, we look more closely, we see indications of a most dreadful catastrophe. The entire rich culture of Hellenistic Judaism, which had been carried by many millions through the whole of the post-classical ancient world and far beyond the eastern border of Mesopotamia, had been systematically annihilated, with terrible consequences. Talmudic Jewry destroyed its Greek-speaking sister, pulled down her buildings, and ploughed up her sites. What records we possess are due to excavations, or to accidental finds, e.g. the shattered remains of synagogues and burial places with a few inscriptions, and occasional scraps of parchments or papyrus. Besides these, there are certain, disconnected notices in ancient writers. We only possess literary materials of greater extent in as far as the Christian Church adopted them, viz. the Old Testament in Greek, Josephus, who was esteemed as an historian, and Philo, as a model exegete. In addition, there were all sorts of apocrypha which could be made to serve their own ends when edited by the Christians.

[1] Sibyl, 3, 271   [2] q d Jos., *Ant.*, 14, 115

Of the wealth of their own life, which the lively Jewish spirit must have developed in the many different surroundings; of the development of theological thought and of public worship; of the inner life of the communities of the diaspora, their constitution and their social connection—of all these and many other matters we know practically nothing. Whole centuries of Jewish history have been silenced by their own people. Thereby also our chance of understanding the spread and inner development of Christianity in the first period has been greatly hindered. Our only recourse is to attempt to reconstrue events from the few surviving data, and this in circumstances where even the richest sources would scarcely be sufficient fully to satisfy our inquiries.

From 722 B.C. onwards, great political catastrophes with compulsory transportations of populations continually fell on Palestine, and, in addition, the uncertainty of affairs in their native land, strains and stresses occurring periodically in smaller tidal waves, drove thousands and tens of thousands of Jews to emigration; how many people followed them voluntarily in these circumstances cannot be estimated. But it is certain that, at the beginning of our era, surprisingly large numbers of Jews were to be found throughout the whole ancient civilized world, and also beyond its borders. It is, of course, a gross exaggeration when Philo,[1] on one occasion, asserts that their number was not much less than that of the indigenous population. Nevertheless, a critical examination of figures which have been handed down to us gives an astonishingly high result.[2] In both Egypt and Syria, there may well have been 1,000,000 Jews; in Palestine 500,000; in the rest of the Roman empire at least 1,500,000. If there were 55,000,000 inhabitants in the empire, at least 7 per cent of them must have been Jews. This proportion holds good even if, with other scholars, we raise the absolute figures. Modern records offer no simple comparison, because religious statistics ignore the converted Jews; nevertheless it is very instructive to learn that in Germany about 1 per cent, in Frankfort-on-the-Main 6·3 per cent, of the population, just before the outbreak of the war of 1939–45, were Jews. It is an unsolved enigma how this gigantic growth of Judaism in the

[1] *Leg.*, 214 (6, 195)   [2] Harnack, *Expansion*, i, 9–13. Juster, i, 209–12

diaspora had taken place. Recently an attempt has been made to solve it by supposing that other Semites, and in particular the Phœnicians (who were once very widely spread, and who gradually fade out altogether from the landscape), were to a large extent absorbed by the Jews.[1]

This great multitude of people was not a mere pell-mell of numbers, nor a matter of isolated individuals like (say) Germans to-day in North America, but a national unity with a religious identity, and some general kind of organization.[2] By far the greater majority regarded Jerusalem, not only as their ideal home, but also as the centre of their religion and politics. This was seen in two ways: (1) annually, many thousands of Jews went to Jerusalem for the feast of the Passover, and to offer their sacrifices;[3] (2) much more clearly was it seen in the carefully observed custom that, even in the diaspora, every Jew, of 20 years and upwards, paid annually a double-drachma (about 1s. 6d.) as his temple due. In the various cities, collecting chests were set up with this object, and at specified times correspondingly large sums of money were brought to Jerusalem by delegations sent for the purpose.[4] A number of official regulations are known from the time of Augustus, which guaranteed to the Jews the right to make these collections and transmissions of money.[5] Whether the supreme collegiate council in Jerusalem, the sanhedrin of the seventy, possessed more than a moral authority, to which one could appeal in difficult cases in regard to religious questions and closely connected juristic problems, is a matter that must remain undecided. Positive notices in this respect, about the circumstances in the first century, have simply not come down to us. It is true that Acts 9: 2 says that Saul received full power from the High-Priest to arrest suspected Jews in Damascus and bring them to Jerusalem; all the same, there is scarcely room for doubt that this record is not correctly worded, at least in the juristic sense.[6] There can scarcely have been any jurisdiction of the sanhedrin in the diaspora. Nevertheless, all Jews were conscious of their obedience to the one law, as recorded in the

---

[1] F. Rosen, *Juden u. Phönizier*, 1929   [2] Cf. esp. Philo, *in Flaccum*, 45 f. (6, 128)
[3] Philo, *de spec. leg.*, 1, 69, 76–78 (5, 17 f., 19 f.)   [4] Cicero, *pro Flacco*, 28, 67
[5] Jos., *Ant.*, 16, 163–173. Schürer, ii 314   [6] Juster, ii 145 n. 5

Old Testament and the Tradition, and that law determined the legal relationships of Jews to one another all the world over.

According to ancient law[1] in general, the Jews of the diaspora were "foreigners" everywhere, and enjoyed the usual legal protection of those who were regarded as settlers. This protection also afforded them freedom to regulate their own affairs in their own way. Hence they organized themselves into religious societies centring on the synagogues, and appointed their own officers to settle their legal disputes. The community had a council of elders with "archons" at the head, and an "archisynagogus" as a religious president.[2] It was recognized both as a religious and a political body, and more than one imperial decree confirmed it in due form. In addition there were places, neither few nor insignificant, where the municipal rights of citizenship were granted to Jews. This was particularly the case in Syria, where Seleucus I, in founding his cities, had obviously settled large numbers of Jewish emigrants, and had granted them privileges accordingly.[3] The facts were similar in Asia Minor and Egypt; at least that is what the Jewish writers assert, above all Josephus. But in the case of Alexandria, of which the same statements are made, extant documentary evidence proves them to be false.[4] There, the Jews strove for the rights of citizens, but neither possessed nor obtained them; and we must therefore go cautiously in dealing with the other notices of the same sort.

In any case, they did not cease, when they became citizens, to cling to their own communities with their special status. The idea of fusing themselves with, and melting into their Gentile environment lay quite remote from them. They managed to keep themselves apart from the religious obligations of the Hellenistic citizens, from sharing in the observance of the municipal cultus, and from everything connected with it. Hence the rights of citizenship meant, in their case, an increase in legal protection without the burden of new duties.

The position remained the same when a Jew became a

[1] Juster, ii, 1 ff., 111 ff.   [2] *Ibid.*, i, 409–96
[3] Jos., *Ant.*, 12, 119. Schürer, iii, 122. Juster, ii, 2–18, 30–32
[4] H. Idris Bell, *Jews and Christians in Egypt* (1924), 8–10

Roman citizen. The innumerable freedmen liberated from Pompey's cargoes of prisoners, and the continually reinforced supplies of those who came later, automatically received this honour by the act of enfranchisement. But Roman citizenship was also granted as a genuine honour to single individuals or to entire groups, who had proved amenable to Roman policy. This was not an insignificant matter to a Jew, but it did not therefore alienate him from his people and their legal system if he wished to remain loyal to them. But, in relation to the local authorities, he obtained considerable protection from his citizenship, for he was raised, as a privileged person, above the mass of the population, guarded from dishonourable punishments, and, on a capital charge, was subject only to the imperial court in Rome; in short, he was not liable to the caprice of provincial officers. The Jew obtained this prerogative without being required to share in the corresponding duties in the sphere of the imperial cultus,[1] which would have been inconsistent with his strict monotheism. The Jews sought and found a substitute for that cultus in other forms of expressing loyalty, and went as far as offering daily sacrifice for the emperor in the temple at Jerusalem.[2] The regard paid to their religious scruples was sufficient to have them excused from appearance in a court of justice on the Sabbath; and, in isolated cases, Jewish soldiers were dispensed from military service on this day.[3] Of course they keenly desired general freedom from liability to military service, but this they never attained; in Cæsar's time alone was this privilege occasionally given to those Jews in the province of Asia who possessed Roman citizenship.[4]

Amongst the occupations[5] followed by the Jews of the diaspora, the most important was farming. Strikingly numerous pieces of evidence are extant from Egypt and Asia Minor in regard to Jewish settlements, as well as about property owners, farmers, and day labourers of Jewish nationality. In the west, notices about Jewish farmers are not numerous until the fourth century A.D. On the other hand, commerce is strikingly

---

[1] Juster, i., 339–53   [2] Jos., c. Ap., 2, 77. Bell., 2, 197, 409
[3] Jos., Ant., 16, 27. 45. 60. 163. 168; 14, 226. Juster, ii, 121; i, 358
[4] Jos., Ant., 14, 227 f., 230, etc. Juster, ii, 265–79   [5] Juster, ii, 294–310, 31–205

small; only in the great city of Alexandria does it seem to have developed early to any significant extent, and here we also find great Jewish banks at an early date—and even warnings against loans from Jews.[1] We hear more frequently of Jewish industry or trade, and weaving in various branches, especially in connection with dyeing, which was indeed a Jewish speciality and remained as such for centuries. We have unfortunately no available records in regard to the economic rôle of the Jews in Rome. The epitaphs give scarcely anything of value, and the rabble of beggars at the *porta capena*, of which Juvenal speaks,[2] is no more typical of the occupations of Judaism at Rome than is his doddering, old-woman soothsayer.

Thus Judaism was very closely united within itself, and at the same time sharply differentiated from the world. Nevertheless, in a remarkable way, it made the greatest efforts to spread its views, and to gain adherents to its religion from among the pagans. Jesus and Horace agree in declaring proselytism as a characteristic of the Jewish nation. "The Pharisees compass sea and land in order to make even one proselyte" (Matt. 23: 15); and Horace (1 *Sat.* 4, 142) attacks one who despises poetry and threatens to overwhelm him with the whole mass of poets, "and we, like the Jews, will compel you to come over to our side". How is this to be explained?

From the days of Deutero-Isaiah, the idea had never been extinguished among the Jews that they were intended to be the light of the Gentiles, and to proclaim salvation to them; their conversion would complete the glorious revelation of the Lord.[3] This idea continued to live in the Psalms and in apocalyptic literature, and when, in the Hellenistic period, Judaism came into contact with Greek culture, two things must have become evident. The first was the ceaselessly progressive decay of "idol worship"; the second was the relation of Jewish monotheism to the modern currents in the prevailing religions, together with the many contacts between Jewish morality and the requirements of the current ethical preaching of the popular philosophers of the Stoic school. Both these features gave educated Jews the proud conviction that the time had come for

---

[1] U. Wilcken, *Chrestomathie*, n. 55–62   [2] Juv., 3, 14; 6, 543
[3] Isa. 49: 1–6; 60: 1–6

their religion to shine before the Gentiles,[1] and that God would give them the promised success. From this standpoint we can understand why Hellenistic modes of thought penetrated into Jewish Wisdom-literature. The two streams readily mingled, especially as Hellenistic ethics had already absorbed many elements of the "wisdom" of the orient. Moreover, there arose a Jewish polemical literature against image worship and idolatry, which united arguments, inherited from the distant days of the prophets, with the proofs used by the Greeks since Xenophanes. The essential bases of Jewish religion were felt to be monotheism, a theological axiom; the spiritual quality of worship without images; and law-abidingness in the sense of an ethical attitude in the whole of one's life. Moreover, everything of a ceremonial character, together with the formal acts of worship, was deemed to have been taught by God, and therefore to be worthy of receiving honour. In this way, a process of spiritualization penetrated almost all classes of the relatively small circle of Jews of Greek education in the diaspora, but must have risen only rarely to the height which we find in Philo of Alexandria. Yet in all its phases, it was both the dynamic and the means of propaganda in the Hellenistic world. Judaism overstepped its national confines, and felt itself called to be a universal religion.[2]

The Old Testament was translated in Alexandria into Greek, but this was for use in public worship.[3] It was not a book for an educated public. Hence Hellenistic Jews now appeared who wrote the history of their people in a manner that accorded with prevalent taste. At first, this was done carefully in harmony with the Bible and acknowledged traditions, but after Eupolemus and Artapanus,[4] all the Hellenistic arts were employed in order to give shapeliness, colour, and even unrestricted range to one's own imagination, down to the impudent falsehoods of "Hecatæus".[5] The ultimate aim, in every case, was to show that Moses and his people were the original source

[1] Bertholet, *Die Stellung der Israeliten und der Juden zu den Fremden*, 257–302
[2] Philo, *vita Mosis*, 2, 20 (4, 204). Jos., *c. Ap.*, 2, 280–82
[3] Strack-Billerbeck, iva, 407
[4] Fragments of these writers have been preserved by Alex. Polyhistor, cf. *Fragm. hist. Graec.*, ed. E. Müller, iii, 211–30
[5] Müller, ii, 393–96, but cf. H. Lewy, *Z.N.W.*, 31, 117–32

of all civilization, including the celebrated learning of the Greeks.

Nor could the Old Testament scriptures be used forthwith even for purely religious propaganda, for they stood in great need of commentary if they were to be comprehensible to men of the period. At least, only the later Wisdom literature, which bore the names of Solomon and Jesus Sirach, would be immediately appreciated by a Hellenistic mentality. But the writings that were really successful were conceived from the Greek standpoint. A celebrated name as the author of a book would awaken confidence, and the form of the writing must be made to correspond. Thus, in the second century B.C., didactic poems were written in hexameters, and were given out to be the prophecies of a mythical Sibyl. These poems represented a category of literature presumably cultivated by other men of eastern origin. Here Chronus and Zeus, Solomon and Alexander, the Trojan war and the Babylonian captivity, were cleverly conjoined. Homer was condemned as an ancient prevaricator. The history of the world was regarded apocalyptically, and ended in the royal Messianic kingdom of peace in paradise; even the Greeks would be gathered into it. Ancient wisdom was commended under the name of Hystaspes, the Persian, or Orpheus, the Thracian. A modern supplement was added to the praiseworthy didactic poem of Phocylides of Solon's time; and, after the manner of the usual anthologies, a collection of forged quotations was prepared with special skill. These cited the most celebrated writers from Orpheus, Homer, and the dramatists, onwards to the popular, comic poets and the preachers of practical philosophies of life, e.g. Philemon, Menander, and Diphilos, as witnesses to Jewish doctrines.[1] Really, it was propaganda for the Old Testament when, under the name of a certain Greek called Aristeas, a "letter" was published which gave the astonishing information that King Ptolemy Philadelphus had caused the holy book to be officially translated and that an astounding miracle had placed it beyond doubt that God had co-operated in the work.

No estimate is possible as to the value of this kind of activity. It is undeniable that the Jewish mission, as a whole, attained

[1] Schürer, iii, 595–603

a very considerable success, as is plentifully testified by both Jewish and pagan writers.[1] Juvenal[2] describes the development in Hadrian's time, viz. the father rests on the Sabbath day and eats no pork; the son has himself circumcised and becomes a fanatic. Seneca coined the biting epigram[3] during the reign of Nero, that the customs of this accursed people had spread over every country: "The conquered have given their laws to the conquerors." Epitaphs agree with this in mentioning relatively numerous proselytes.[4] Everywhere, the Jews were successful in grouping round their synagogues a circle of "God-fearers", who were attracted by the spiritual excellencies of the Mosaic religion, and turned, with inner conviction, to its monotheism and its ethical teaching. They attended the meetings for worship, and naturally entered into personal association with this or that member of the church. In this way, the Sabbath became to them a sacred day; Jewish table customs and food laws attained practical significance, and became, in effect, a religious usage. After appropriate teaching,[5] even if this did not rise to the very fine distinctions made by Philo's allegory, the religious usage, nevertheless, gained a deeper sense and exerted power over the soul. From this wide circle, there then separated off the small number of those who ventured to take the decisive step, and, by circumcision and the levitical bath of purification, joined themselves completely to the community of Israel; these were the "proselytes" in the strict sense of the word. They took the law upon themselves in its entirety, and thereby became Israelites, and might hope to share in the promises of the chosen people. Of course they could never become "Sons of Abraham"; in prayer[6] they might well address "the God of the fathers of Israel", but not, like the real Jew, "the God of our fathers". Thus they were only later members of the nobility by letters patent, alongside of the old, original aristocracy of the blood, and on occasion they must have felt the difference.

The Roman state was not well-disposed to such conversions, and was not inclined to extend to converted Romans the

[1] Schürer, iii, 164 ff. [2] Sat., xiv, 96–106
[3] Preserved in Augustine, 1 civ. dei, vi, 11 [4] E. Diehl, Inscriptiones, ii, pp. 497–99
[5] Jos., Ant., 18, 81 [6] Mishna, Bikkurim, 1, 4. Schürer, iii, 187

privilege of freedom from religious duties of an official character, such as was granted to born Jews. Hence, at times, there were punishments on account of "atheism", and we have isolated notices to the effect that the persons concerned belonged to the Roman nobility.[1] Under Hadrian, circumcision, which had hitherto been tolerated, was placed under general prohibition,[2] and at the same time conversion to Judaism was strictly forbidden. In all such cases the state prosecuted, not only the guilty proselytes, but also punished the leaders of the Jewish propaganda.[3]

On a general view, it would therefore seem that the Jews possessed very many more enemies than friends in the world.[4] Even if they should appear welcome settlers to diadochoi who were founding cities, and to politicians who were concerned with economics; and even if they enjoyed imperial favour, nevertheless, the populace could not tolerate them in all the provinces of the great empire. Just because they did not feel themselves to be simply a part of the great whole, as did the other peoples, but separated themselves off, and carefully guarded their special character, they were everywhere regarded with a mistrust which developed into hate, a mistrust which the masses, like children, feel towards anything strange in their midst, if it seeks to assert itself. However much the Jewish writers might commend their religion as enlightened philosophy, men in general, including those of the highest education, were convinced that the Jews prayed to the clouds and the sky, were committed to a barbarous superstition,[5] and were hostile to every form of civilized culture. There were many other similar opinions in Alexandria. They used to tell there of the history of the Jewish people as a combination of the shameful and the ridiculous; and also of secret information in regard to their worship: in the temple at Jerusalem there was a golden ass's head to which they paid divine honours—or was it a statue of Moses riding on an ass, and holding the book of the law in his hand? In any case, the Jews were ass-worshippers,[6] and what

---

[1] Juster, i, 256–59
[2] *vita Hadriani*, 14, 2 (in the *script. hist. Aug.*) also Juster, i, 264, n. 2.
[3] Jos., *Ant.*, 18, 83–84   [4] Heinemann in *Pauly-Wissowa*, suppl., v, 3–43
[5] Cicero, *pro Flacco*, 28, 67 f. Juvenal, xiv, 97. Hecatæus fr. 13, 4 in Müller, *Frag. hist. Græc.*, ii, 392   [6] Jos., *con. Ap.*, 2, 80. Posidonius fr. in Müller, *op. cit.*, iii, 256

was worse, every year, or at least every seven years, they captured a Greek, killed and sacrificed him in accordance with their ritual. Then they ate his heart, and thereby swore an oath of everlasting hostility to the Greeks.[1] It was self-apparent that such people had to be rendered harmless even when the authorities protected them for some unknown reason. This explains why, when a suitable opportunity occurred, popular feeling against the Jews was unleashed.

At least from the end of the second century B.C., the Greeks in Alexandria lived in hostility towards the Jews who had been granted equal rights by Alexander, and who, in order better to preserve their national characteristics, were segregated, by the Ptolemies, into a special quarter of the town, where they developed their own communal organization.[2] In those days, the Ghetto was a privilege! The latent tension was released violently for the first time[3] after Caligula had come to the throne (A.D. 38); up to this time, Flaccus had been a most excellent prefect, but now being uncertain of the attitude of the new rulership, he did not feel it wise to keep the reins tight. When Agrippa I, the newly appointed king of the Jews passed through, the Alexandrian mob seized a welcome occasion for tumultuous demonstrations, and cunningly demanded also that statues of the emperor should be set up in the synagogues.[4] At the same time, loud complaints were made about the unjustified spread of the Jews in the city: in particular, two of the five quarters were really Jewish, and, even in the other three, there were many Jews. On the other hand, this widespread Jewish population raised a vigorous agitation for recognition as full citizens of Alexandria.[5] Thereupon Flaccus ordered them to be restricted to one quarter, and he also reduced their municipal rights. A riot of the mob ensured the carrying out of the edict; the Jews were driven out of the four quarters, and concentrated in the fifth. But large numbers found no room there, and camped helplessly on the shore and in the cemeteries

[1] Jos., op. cit., 2, 94 f. Damocritus fr. in Müller, op. cit., iv, 377
[2] Claudius in Jos., Ant., 19, 281; Jos., Bell., 2, 487. Bell, Jews and Christians, p. 16 f.
[3] The source is found in Philo, in Flaccum (6, 120 ff.). Bell, Jews and Christians: the letter of Claudius, cf. 16–21
[4] Philo, op. cit., 25, 41 (6, 124. 128)
[5] Bell, op. cit., p. 25: 5, 89; cf. pp. 13. 16

close to the city.[1] Whoever ventured to appear in the cleared quarters of the city was seized and put to death in the most brutal manner. Still further to placate the people, thirty-eight elders of the Jewish community were scourged in the theatre, Jewish houses searched for weapons, and other cunning devices thought out.[2] This, of course, did not help Flaccus; he fell into disgrace, and paid the death penalty. But the Jews who meantime had been reinforced from Egypt and Syria,[3] effected hardly more than an armistice under Pollio, his successor, for the emperor seemed to find in their denial of his divinity an incomprehensible spiritual defect.[4] At length, the emperor Claudius commanded the prefect to bring both parties to peace; at the same time, he re-established the Jews in all the municipal rights they had previously enjoyed, and in their religious liberties.[5] But the antisemites did not give way; a delegation went to Rome and accused King Agrippa, and further disturbances took place at home. Claudius was then enraged. The leaders of the Jew-baiters, the Alexandrian gymnasiarch Isidorus, and Lampon, who had come to Rome as the delegation accusing Agrippa, were executed, and an imperial edict[6] ordered peace in the firmest tones. The Alexandrians, however, honoured these men with pride as martyrs to their well-being and the freedom of the city; and they published the documents of their trial as something to their honour.[7]

Thus hostility remained, and when the outbreak of the Jewish rebellion in Palestine (A.D. 66) greatly inflamed their passions once more, terrible Jewish pogroms took place in Alexandria; 50,000 were killed in the city and 60,000 in the rest of Egypt.[8]

As for Palestine, the Jews in Cæsarea first rose against the Syrians, and the frequent disturbances and local conflicts ended in a general slaughter of the Cæsarean Jews, of whom more than 20,000 were killed at one time.[9] This led to an insurrection in the interior of the country; the Jews broke into Syrian villages

[1] Philo, in Flaccum, 54–6 (6, 130)   [2] Op. cit., 64–75, 86 (6, 132 f., 136)
[3] Bell., 25, 96. Philo, legum, 129 (6, 179)   [4] Phil., op. cit., 367 (6, 222)
[5] Jos., Ant., 19, 280–5. Bell., 25   [6] In the papyrus ed. by Bell, 23–6
[7] Phil., in Flacc., 20; leg., 355 (6, 124; 220). Lietzmann, Greek Pap., 2nd edition (Kleine Texte, No. 14), 21 f.
[8] Jos., Bell., 2, 487–98   [9] Ibid., 2, 266–70, 457

and towns and took their revenge. But the Syrians defended themselves, and then there was more slaughter of Jews in Scythopolis, Ascalon, Ptolemæus, Tyre, Hippo, and Gadara. Josephus is emphatic that peace was maintained only in Antioch, Sidon, and Apamea.[1] But in Antioch, animosity became so sharp that force was used more than once, and the Sabbath rest and obligatory sacrifices were prohibited; and this led to bloodshed. It needed the authority of Titus to put a stop to the angry demands for withdrawing municipal rights from Jews.[2] After Nero, a new wave of hatred for the Jews welled up in the Roman world, and was re-echoed more particularly in Seneca and the satirists. The sketch of Jewish history introduced by Tacitus into his *History*[3] breathes the complete contempt of a cultured Roman for this most despicable of all slave races, a race which hated gods and men, and which was given to an absurd and unclean superstition.

In spite of all the close connections maintained with Jerusalem and all the common feeling, the Judaism of the diaspora had, in the course of time, come to differ in character from that of the people of the native land. The most striking instance was the fact that they had forgotten the language of Palestine, and accepted the Greek of everyday use. The change was due to the history of the Jewish people, who had long abandoned their mother-tongue even in Palestine. When the exiles returned from Babylon, they brought with them the current Aramaic language, and retained it for a millenium. Hebrew remained the sacred language of scholars for religious usage, and the discussions in the Mishna were written down in Hebrew even in the second century A.D. But the Talmuds of the fourth and fifth centuries, being in Aramaic, show that Hebrew was obsolete even in the theological schools.

Valuable documents of the fifth century B.C. belonging to the Egyptian diaspora and written in Aramaic have been found in Elephantine. An interpolation in the text of Isaiah (19: 18) mentions five Egyptian towns in which "the language of Canaan" was spoken. In the Ptolemaic period we still find traces of Aramaic in upper Egypt[4] and in Alexandria;[5] but

---

[1] *Ibid.*, 2, 458, 461, 466, 477–9   [2] *Ibid.*, 7, 43–62, 100–11. *Ant.*, 12, 121
[3] Tacitus, *hist.*, v, 5, 8   [4] Schürer, iii, p. 49   [5] Lid barski, *Ephem.*, iii, 49

about this time, Greek began to be used by Jews, both as the language of the administration, and in everyday life. In the latest period of the Ptolemies, the Jews of Onias not only wrote Greek epitaphs for their dead, but also bewailed the loss of the departed in elegiac poems formed on Hellenistic models and mentioning Hades as well as Moira. In the entire remainder of the Mediterranean world, the memorial tablets of the Jewish diaspora are almost exclusively in Greek. Here and there is a Hebrew phrase, e.g. *shalom*=peace, or *shalom al Israel*=peace be to Israel, upon a gravestone, but inscriptions genuinely composed in Hebrew or Aramaic are very rare. The common opinion that the adjective, "Hebrew", points to communities speaking Hebrew or Aramaic, is mistaken. The door-post of a synagogue has been found at Corinth[1] bearing the name of the congregation: "Synagogue of the Hebrews." But these Hebrews did not speak Hebrew, for the inscription is in Greek! Outside Palestine, only the Rabbis knew any Hebrew—but no one knows how many they were, nor how much they knew. The remote region of the Crimea is alone in preserving Hebrew inscriptions of the first to the fourth century A.D.[2]

This change of language, both at home and in the diaspora, was not without far-reaching effects upon public worship. The ancient custom of reading the Hebrew scriptures in the synagogue necessitated a translation into the Aramaic which the people understood, the original text and the translation followed one another verse for verse. Dubious passages were not translated, but read only in Hebrew.[3] Originally the translations were extemporaneous, but naturally they soon assumed forms fixed by tradition. Out of these forms grew the Aramaic Targums, which were at last put into writing in the Talmudic era, i.e. about the fifth century. Moreover the liturgical prayers, which Jewish prayer books even to-day preserve in their original Hebrew form, were said by the people in the vernacular. The Mishna[4] expressly permitted it, and a shrewd Rabbi rightly told an objector that it was better to do so, than that the people should not pray at all.[5] Nevertheless, this

---

[1] Deissmann, *Licht v. Osten*, 13   [2] P. E. Caspari, *Quellen*, iii, 269
[3] Mishna, *Megilla*, 4, 4, 10   [4] Mishna, *Sota* 7, 1. Schürer, iii, 140 f.
[5] Talm. Jer., *Sota*, 7, 1 f. 21 b

reply seems rather to evade the real point, and Charlemagne gave a better reason for using German in the Lord's Prayer.[1] An Aramaic targum was current in Palestine, side by side with the original Hebrew, and a Greek translation in the diaspora for public worship in the synagogue.[2] Known and preserved as the Septuagint, or LXX, the latter originated in Alexandria. The first part to be translated was the most important, and it took premier place also in public worship. This was the Pentateuch, the Greek version of which was current as early as the end of the third century B.C. The prophets and the other books followed gradually and by various translators. Soon after 116 B.C., a grandson of Jesus Sirach was familiar with the whole of the Old Testament in Greek.[3] At the time of the early Roman empire, as is shown by the use made of it by Philo and Paul,[4] the LXX was the universally recognized Bible of the diaspora, even for the purposes of divine worship.

In Alexandria,[5] an annual festival was held on the Pharos island, when the people gave thanks for this translation. There seem to have been several translations of isolated books current at the same time,[6] but they disappeared early almost without trace. It was the rivalry of the Christian Church which had made the LXX equally its own, that gave rise, after the second century, to newer and more literal translations for Jewish use. In the nature of the case, it is doubtful whether the original Hebrew was read alongside the translation; possibly custom varied. By the time of the emperor Justinian, greater emphasis was placed on the reading of the original in public worship, and the question was discussed whether any translation at all could be read aloud along with it. These facts show that the influence of the Judaism of the Talmud had grown, but do not prove what was the custom elsewhere in the Empire centuries earlier.

Not only were the Scriptures read in Greek, but also the same language was used for the prayers and the confession of faith, i.e. the "Shema", in the public worship of the synagogue. The sources testify to this fact in regard to Cæsarea, the quasi-gentile capital

[1] Capitulare, 28, 52   [2] Schürer, iii, 140, 426. Billerbeck, iv, 407
[3] Sirach, Prolog. Wilcken, Archiv. f. Pap., iii, 321
[4] Perhaps the headings of the temple-psalms in the LXX also belonged to the Greek synagogue. Cf. Schürer, ii, 351, and Rahlf's edition of the Psalms, 72
[5] Philo, vita Mosis, 2, 41 (4, 209)   [6] Cf. Handbuch on Gal., 5, 1

of Palestine,[1] and naturally the same holds good for the diaspora in general. Only just recently have scholars traced out a little Greek prayer-book of the Jewish synagogues[2] that dates from the second century A.D., and that is enshrined in a Christian liturgy of the fourth century. This discovery is very suggestive. It is only a drop out of the ocean, but it makes quite clear how little is really known about worship in the synagogues of the Greek diaspora. We may take it for granted that this worship, not only changed in the course of centuries, but also differed in different places; and moreover that there were many different degrees of Hellenization.

Besides reading and prayer there were exegesis and preaching, of course in Greek. The collective term, *deuterosis*, was given to the traditional elements here. The term is a liberal translation of the Hebrew *Mishna*, i.e. repetition, and it included everything deduced from, or built on the Law or the historical records of the sacred text: hence the Halakha or specialized legal casuistic, and the Haggada, the Biblical legends. Even Augustine testified[3] that this *deuterosis* was passed on only by word of mouth, not written down—showing that the diaspora followed the example of Palestine. It follows that there was a Greek Halakha and a Greek Haggada; or, to put it otherwise, the diaspora possessed a Greek Midrash and a Greek Talmud. Traces of both often occur in Paul, Philo, Josephus, and the Apocrypha—but no actual documents, and it is scarcely probable that much was written down. Indeed, everything of this kind disappeared when the Judaism of the Greek diaspora ceased to be.

Very little evidence has survived affording a true idea of the cultural life of the Hellenistic diaspora. Most information refers to Egypt. The LXX translation was made here, and it was here that Pseudo-Aristeas was at home. III Maccabees, perhaps IV Maccabees, and the Wisdom of Solomon were written in Egypt, and here Philo laboured. Other regions afford little information about Judaism, whereas, in regard to the contemporary beginnings of Christianity, it is precisely Egypt that is quite blank. Nevertheless Alexandria distributed its

---

[1] Talm. Jer., *Sota*, 7, 1, 2, 21*b*. Schürer, iii, 141   [2] *Const. Apost.*, 7, 33–8
[3] *C. adv. leg. et proph.*, ii, 1, 2; 8, 580*e* Bened. Philo, *vita Mosis*, 1, 4 (4, 120)

Greek Bible throughout the whole of Judaism, and, except Jerusalem, was apparently the only spiritually productive centre of Israel. This fact makes it possible, within bounds, to generalize the phenomena obtaining there.

The translation of the Bible into Greek opened the door to the Hellenization of the Jewish religion. Greek conceptions inevitably entered, along with the Greek vocabulary, into the sphere of thought of the synagogues, and the philosophical connotations of innumerable terms led to further philosophizing developments of Old Testament trains of thought. Analogous processes took place in regard to religious terminology. It was an unplanned, but unavoidable, consequence of translation from one language to another, and it came forward most prominently in Alexandria. A school of exegetes arose there[1] who approached the Pentateuch from the philosophical standpoint, and who had learned, from the Stoics, the method of allegorical interpretation. These men found philosophical truths expressed in the early stories of the Bible. Thus Adam was understood as *nous*, i.e., reason was the foundation of mankind. His "helpmeet", together with the beasts of the field and the birds of heaven, represent the emotions. Eve was the antithesis to reason and also its necessary sensory complement. The snake was the symbol of desire or love, which brought the two opposite poles together, and effected the unity of man.[2] Sarah and Hagar signify virtue and sound education, but the latter must first be taken to wife, i.e. be united with him who was to have children by the former.[3] When we are told[4] that Jacob fled from Esau to Mesopotamia and entered the house of Bethuel (Gen. 27: 42–28: 5), the meaning is that the upright man ought to plunge into the stream of life, and guard himself there, in a practical way, in order that he may find a quiet harbour in the house of wisdom. The latest researches have succeeded in sorting out from Philo's writings fragments of such teachings of the Alexandrian Jews, and in recognizing an early writing of Philo's about the eternity of the world[5] as the notes

---

[1] W. Bousset, *Schulbetrieb*, 43–56, 74–83
[2] Philo, *leg. all.*, 5–9, 36–8, 71 (1, 91, 97, 104)
[3] Philo, *congr.*, 6, 9–11, 23 (3, 73–7), Bousset 98–100
[4] Philo, *fuga.*, 25–52 (3, 115–21). Bousset, 128 f.
[5] Philo, vol. vi, 72–119. Bousset, 134–37

of a lecture of the kind we have just described. This older tradition appears to be quite intoxicated with the intellectual and spiritual verve, the complete candour of Hellenism, whereas Moses and the Bible are, by contrast, but little emphasized. Jews of this type capitulated completely to the Greeks in the things of the mind—probably without drawing any consequences at all affecting religion in public worship or private life; for they were unaware of having made any real departure from the essence of their own religion. They believed that, with the aid of the newly acquired philosophical means, they were merely enabled to reach a profounder, and therefore a more accurate, conception of the meaning of the Mosaic law. These men felt that it was a point in favour of the new understanding that it harmonized with the teachings of the Greek sages. That the Greeks should have learned from Stoicism how to illumine their own religion in the same way; that the revivified Platonism of the following centuries should have employed the same weapons to defend the Homeric faith, and should have read philosophical wisdom into the Egyptian cults—all this was in accordance with the trend of the times.

Philo of Alexandria was the only one of the Hellenistic Rabbis to give a genuinely literary form to his lectures. Moreover he was in full earnest, and very loyal to Judaism. When the Jewish persecution under Flaccus threatened to outlaw and destroy his people, he regretfully, but nevertheless firmly, sacrificed his contemplative leisure, and joined a diplomatic delegation to the imperial court, although it offered little prospect of success, and might easily have meant death. Obviously the Alexandrian Jews wished to present the most cultured and learned of their number to the emperor. But Philo was a Jew, not only on account of his patriotic feelings, but also by religious conviction. To him, Moses was the source of all truth and wisdom, and the Law was the inexhaustible spring from which he was never tired of drinking. His writings show that "he had meditated upon the Law day and night". And even if he traced deeper secrets beneath the plain meaning of the words, secrets which contained the real sense of the sacred Scripture, he felt that nothing of this detracted, in any way, from the sacred authority of the text, as it actually stood. He warned his readers[1] that none of the customs of the Fathers was to be dropped, "which greater men than ourselves established". Ritual was for the body, just as the deeper sense was for the soul. But, immediately he began to explain the Law, he followed the method of Hellenistic allegory in its entirety. The "great", and "most holy" Plato was, for him, the master whom he cited ever and again; but he referred frequently to Aristotle, Heracleitus, the Pythagoreans, Epicurus, and especially the Stoics, as his authorities. What Moses had taught had been accepted by the Greek philosophers, and explained by them in greater detail; in the last analysis, Greek philosophy was doctrine about God, the world, and man. The Mosaic law was in harmony with the nature of the universe, and he who lived by that law, determined his actions according to the will of nature and was therefore the true citizen of the world: he lived by the same standards as ruled the entire cosmos.[2] In other words, the genuine Jew corresponded to the ideal of the Stoic sage.

In this way, Philo read Plato's theory of ideas, the Pythagorean symbolism of numbers, and the Stoic teleology, into the Biblical story of creation. So also he found that the "unwritten laws", i.e. the fundamental types of virtue,[3] were described in the accounts of the Patriarchs, and he appraised their lives as examples intended to encourage the readers. To him, Enos was the man of hope, Enoch. Translated by God into a better life he represented repentance, amendment, and conversion to the study of philosophy. Noah was the "type" of an "upright man". But these three constituted only an immature striving of mankind, and the three great patriarchs were the first athletes wrestling against hostile passions for the sacred guerdon, with the full strength of grown men.[4] Virtue either sprang from study—as with Abraham, or was innate nature,—as with Isaac,—or the result of practice,—as with Jacob. In this way, the three patriarchs represented the three types of philosophical virtue. Philo's life of Abraham, written from this standpoint, has been preserved. It describes his passage from the astrology of the Chaldæans, through the sphere of sensory knowledge, to

---

[1] *Migr. Abr.*, 89 f. (2, 285 f.)   [2] *Opif. mundi.*, 3, 143 (1, 1, 50)
[3] *Abr.*, 3–5 (4, 2); *decal.*, 1 (4, 296)   [4] *Ibid.*, 48 (4, 12). *Jos.*, 1 (4, 61)

true divine wisdom. The "political man" is added as a fourth type, the sage who undertook the practical realization of the ideal in actual life. The example of this kind of man with his versatility and changeability, was Joseph with his coat of many colours.[1] Then, in another series of books, Philo discussed the details of the Mosaic law, and deduced their general, ethical principles from the Decalogue, which was held as fundamental. He also spiritualized the entire corpus of the ceremonial law, utilizing traditional explanations, and making it philosophically comprehensible.

His biography of Moses is also to be included in the works where he continued to keep in close contact with the literal meaning of his text. Here he showed how the records, when historically understood, and the commandments when genuinely applied, could only be comprehended from a higher standpoint. But in another series of writings he leads us into the temple of his speculations proper. In the *Allegories of the Law* and the appended tractates, all relation to historical event disappears. Adam and Eve, Cain and Abel, Noah, Abraham, Jacob and Esau, Sarah and Hagar, are, for this allegorical interpretation, only "types" of forces in the human soul, and these influence each other by their operation in different directions and by their complementary character. Their reciprocal relationships show the philosopher how to understand the life of the soul, the way to virtue, and communion with God. Even here, Philo, though a Jew, shows that he is in agreement with the spirit of his age, and that, in the end, all philosophy finds its goal in practical life, and its crown in ethics.

He founded this ethic on the Platonic antithesis between spirit and matter, and made much use of Stoic ways of thought, and its ascetic tendencies. God was approached by way of victory over the emotions and conquest of the sensual passions; the freedom of the soul consisted in liberating her from the prison-house of the body which bound her in chains. But at this point other voices were to be heard among doctrines of the philosophic schools. Philo spoke in the tone of a mystagogue to a small group of initiates,[2] when he confided to them the secret

---

[1] *Jos.*, 31–4 (4, 68)   [2] *Cherub.*, 42–50 (1, 180 f.)

of the immediate divine origin of good in the human soul;
when he urged the soul to leave reason behind, and enter a
Bacchantic frenzy; to get beyond itself and the consciousness of
the ego, and, in "sober intoxication", in the frenzy of heavenly
love, to let itself be lifted up to what truly existed.[1] Here Philo
was no longer a disciple of Greek philosophers, but one of the
Hellenistic mystics, whose esoteric teaching of the God-born
soul languishing in fleshly bonds had penetrated him to the
heart. From those mystics he had also learned that the mystes
could again discover the way to the divine, original spring if he
stripped off what was earthly, and let the divine spirit rule in
him. More than once[2] he calls his readers to make the venture
of flying up to heaven, as he himself had so often been inspired
to do. His idealized description of the order of the Therapeutæ[3]
reached its climax in a nocturnal ceremony which conferred the
rapture of ecstatic enthusiasm upon the ascetic who had been
trained in abstemious living and continual meditation.

His philosophic system provided the basis of this ethic. God
was absolute existence and unity; he could not be comprehended by human organs of perception, and could only be
described with negative predicates. By His nature, He was the
causative principle, and thus active and creative. At the other
pole a passive principle existed in matter, over which He
showed His power when He created the world.[4] Yet the
Highest had no direct contact with unclean matter, but made
use of intermediary and incorporeal powers, called "ideas".[5]
Together, they constituted an intelligible world, an ideal
pattern or model according to which the world of the senses
had been made by the creative activity of these self-same
powers.[6] The world of ideas might also be understood as a
unity: for it was the logos of God,[7] the original Idea as such,
which united in itself all the various and innumerable ideas.[8]
The logos, the shadow and image of God, His creative organ,[9]
stood between God and the world: not uncreated like God, nor

---

[1] *div. heres.*, 69 f. (3, 16 f.). Bousset, *Judentum*, 450 f. Reitzenstein, *hell. Myst.*,
66 f. *Poimandres*, 204. Hans Lewy, *Sobria ebrietas*, 73 ff.
[2] *Cherub.*, 27 (1, 176); cf. *migr. Abr.*, 35 (275)   [3] *vita contemp.*, 83–9 (6, 69 f.)
[4] *mundi opif.*, 8 f. (1, 2)   [5] *spec. leg.*, 329 (5, 79)   [6] *mundi opif.*, 16 (1, 5)
[7] *Ibid.*, 25 (1, 8), *somn.*, 45 (3, 266)   [8] *sacri. Abel.*, 83 (1, 236)
[9] *leg. alleg.*, 3, 96 (1, 134); *spec. leg.*, 1, 81 (5, 51)

a creature like us.[1] Philo makes use of Biblical terminology in describing the logos as the first-born of God, as the archangel, as wisdom, the high-priest, the advocate who intercedes before God for created beings.[2] Incidentally, he evolved a further system of another five powers, or *dynameis*, which originated from the logos—creative power, royal authority, mercy, commandment, and prohibition.[3] He not infrequently makes brief references to these attributes or powers, although elsewhere he formally enunciates the doctrine that the logos is the union of two prime forces: goodness and authority.[4] It is gratuitous to attempt to find a system in his fanciful speculations on hypostases. The conceptions exist side by side and occasionally intermingle, without losing their peculiar qualities. In particular, the relation of these trains of thought to the theory of ideas is nowhere explained, and this in spite of a few attempts to solve the problem, by suggesting the equation, "The logos equals intelligible world and prime idea." Further on, the innumerable separate *logoi* appear as the Biblical angels,[5] also called dæmons by philosophers. Incorporeal souls inhabit the space between heaven and earth;[6] some descend and become incarnate, others take the opposite direction and fly up to the æther. The best and purest of these souls separate themselves from the rest as the servants and messengers of God, mediating between Him and mankind. But whether, and in what way, these angel-logoi are to be described as ideas, is not explained; both streams of thought remain side by side because they flow from different sources.

It might seem as if the central thought and teaching of Philo could be completely explained from the two roots of Greek philosophy and Hellenistic mysticism; the latter rests upon an oriental foundation, and the Jewish element could then be regarded as its outer form. But this explanation would not penetrate to the final depths. For in spite of all his speculations, ethical deductions, and mystic enthusiasms, Philo remained at bottom a convinced Jew whose lips had been touched by the

[1] div. heres., 206 (3, 47)   [2] Ibid., 205 (3, 47); vita Mosis, 2, 134 (4, 231)
[3] fuga., 95 (3, 130)   [4] Cherub., 27 (1, 176)
[5] sobr., 65 (2, 228); conf. ling., 28 (2, 235); migr. Abr., 173 (2, 302); somn. 1, 115, 148 (3, 229, 236)
[6] somn., 1, 134-41 (3, 234 f.); gigant, 6-16 (2, 43 ff.)

God of the Old Testament. He spoke of Him as the Father, in another and more vital manner than did the philosophers; he praised His mercy and grace; he knew that He and all that belonged to Him were holy. He spoke in a tone other than that of the Stoics, about sin and sinners, and he knew the religious significance of repentance. In continually changing phrases, he spoke of the faith which one must offer God as a spotless and most lovely sacrifice, and as exemplified by Abraham.[1] Quite in the Old Testament manner, he felt the nothingness[2] before God of everything human and earthly, and knew Him to be the giver of all good: He had sowed the seeds of good in human souls, and the blessedness of ecstasy was in the end, His highest gift of grace.[3] Philo's God was not the ideal construction of the philosophers, but the Eternal, the Ineffable of the Old Testament and the synagogue; and his logos was, in the last analysis, the personified creative Word of Genesis, and the Wisdom of the writings of Solomon.[4]

Philo was a solitary thinker, and was proud of being such. His writings were intended only for a small circle of readers of a similar degree of culture, and naturally found no echo in the larger circles of the diaspora. They would have disappeared without trace had not the Alexandrine Christians esteemed them, and preserved them in the theological libraries of the following centuries. They are only characteristic of the Judaism of the early empire in as far as they show to what extent philosophical and religious elements of Hellenism could be appropriated by a highly cultivated Jew, without his being conscious of turning aside in any way from his national religion. We must seek other sources for the atmosphere and thought of the Judaism of the Greek diaspora, although these sources usually point to Egypt as their homeland.

The letter of Aristeas is the first writing to catch our eye, and, lately,[5] convincing reasons have been adduced for placing it in the period about 140 B.C. In the form of a letter, it gives a pretty legend in regard to the origin of the Septuagint, the

---

[1] *Cherub.*, 85 (1, 191). *Abr.*, 262–69 (4, 57 ff.). *div. heres.*, 90–5 (3, 21 f.)
[2] *mut. nom.*, 54 (3, 166); *somn.*, 1, 60, 212; 2, 293 (3, 218, 251, 305)
[3] *leg. all.*, 1, 48, 82; 3, 219 (1, 73, 82, 162)
[4] Cf. E. Schwartz, *Gött. Nachr.*, 1908, 537–56
[5] Bickermann, *Z.N.W.*, xxix, 280–98

sacred translation of the Pentateuch. It explains the special merit of this translation as due to the scholarly interests of Ptolemy II and his councillor, Demetrios of Phaleron. A fanciful description of Jerusalem, its temple, and the overawing nobility of its cultus produces even on the gentile reader a most charming impression. The "six-times-twelve" translators, who had been requested to act by Ptolemy, and authorized by the High-Priest, arrived at the Alexandrian court; here they were received with high honour and invited to be guests at a banquet. They began to discuss philosophy;[1] the king proposed a different question to each of the seventy-two elders, and, in each case, received a sagacious answer. The problems of a ruler, as well as the various virtues, were discussed philosophically with profit. The religious principle of all Jews, that man must do everything as in God's sight, echoed, like a refrain, in every one of their learned answers. God stood as a most exalted example before human eyes, and He alone could give the power necessary for every good. The king's legation in Jerusalem had already been instructed by the High-Priest himself in regard to the deeper meaning of the Jewish ceremonial law:[2] it was primarily intended to separate the monotheistic Jewish people, by their strict morals, from polytheistic peoples, in order that they might maintain their own faith in its purity. But the commandments of purification had a further, symbolic meaning, and were the embodiment of ethical teaching. If, however, the question was raised in regard to the deepest nature of the true worship of God, the sages answered[3] that one did not truly honour God by gifts and sacrifices, but by purity of soul and the pious faith that everything was created by Him, and maintained according to His will.

The religion of the prophets was thus transformed by Aristeas under Stoic influences into a universal humanism. The ceremonial law was spiritualized, polytheism repudiated, and monotheism made fundamental. The essence of religion appeared to be the recognition of the creative and providential omnipotence of God and the exercise of the moral virtues. The typically Jewish element is to be found in the fact that these

[1] *Aristeas epist.*, 187–300   [2] *Arist.*, 128–71   [3] *Ibid.*, 234

virtues could be gained and made operative not by human
strength alone, but only by divine aid. We find a similar
attitude in the Wisdom of Solomon, which is probably more
than a century later, and which linked on to the Hebrew
Wisdom-literature of the post-exilic period. Here again we see
the idol-worship of polytheists attacked in traditional forms,
from a standpoint where the influence of Stoic modes of
thought can be traced.[1] In addition, there is a polemic similar
to that which is usual in prophetic literature, and which is
directed against the godless who oppress the righteous and the
religious with brute force.[2] But these wicked men imagined in
their hearts that death was the end of all, and, therefore, that
it was fitting to enjoy, without restraint, the pleasures of a short
life.[3] They deceived themselves, for God had created man for
immortality, and death had only entered the world by the
devil's envious malice.[4] After death, the righteous were at
peace and near God, and would sit in judgment over sinners;[5]
the Lord of all would crown and protect them with His right
hand. Through the conception of personal immortality, the
eschatology of the prophets was developed into a doctrine of
recompense which included a theodicy.

A second principal objective of the book now appears in the
doctrine of the personified wisdom, the *sophia*. She mediated
between God and man,[6] confirmed the rulership of kings,
granted all knowledge to man, imparted every virtue to him,
and raised him to immortality. She sat on the throne with God,
was the reflection of His eternal light, a model of His goodness,
a breath of His divine might.[7] She, and she alone, taught how
to know the will of God, and led man on the true path to
salvation;[8] she also faithfully protected the fathers of Israel.[9]
Thus she appeared to be a divine property, but she was still
conceived quite personally as a "hypostasis", as an envoy and
servant of God and as the good spirit of mankind, exactly as
in the earlier wisdom literature of Proverbs[10] and Jesus Sirach.[11]
Similarly, approximating to an hypostasis, was the "word" of
God, the logos, which saved all, which, like a warrior from the

---

[1] *Sap.*, 13–14   [2] *Ibid.*, 2, 12–20   [3] *Ibid.*, 2, 1–11   [4] *Ibid.*, 2, 23–24; 1, 13 f.
[5] *Ibid.*, 3, 1–5, 23   [6] *Ibid.*, 1, 6–11   [7] *Sap.*, 9, 4; 7, 25 f.   [8] *Ibid.*, 9, 13–18
[9] *Ibid.*, 10, 1–21   [10] *Prov.*, 8–9   [11] *Sir.*, 24

throne of the heavenly king, sprang down upon earth and, with
the sword of the commandment of God in his hand, filled the
land of Egypt with death. The parallel is plain when it is said
of God that he created the world by His logos and man by His
sophia.[1] In full analogy, the sophia is also characterized as
the 'spirit (*pneuma*) of God," or made parallel to it: "the
sophia is truly the spirit that is friendly to man;" it is the spirit
of the Lord; it fills the world and searches the hearts of men.[2]
There is no recognizable difference between sophia, logos, and
pneuma. They are only different terms for the same being, a
being which is conceived as a property of God, but which is
separated from God Himself when personification is complete.
Here we see the broad basis upon which Philo erected his
philosophy of hypostases. In the Palestinian literature of the
following period, analogous phenomena are just as evident, and
they appear in ever new forms, owing to the reluctance to
mention God directly, and especially to take His name on one's
lips. In this way, the names of His properties became words
replacing "God". But at the same time, the properties themselves were conceived as active heavenly persons who mediated
the unapproachable and unsearchable being of the Eternal.

IV Maccabees also originated in Egypt. In the form of a Stoic
diatribe with a learned cast, it discusses the thesis that, in a
religious man, reason should control all emotion. After an extraordinary mixture of philosophic phrases and Old Testament
examples, the author passes to his real thesis. He tries to prove
his proposition by the story of the martyrdom of the seven
Maccabean youths and their mother, and he gives a detailed
account of the brave speeches of the martyrs, and the shocking
tortures which they withstood unmoved. In the appropriate
place[3] he points out and emphasizes the conflict between a
confessor's courage, on the one hand, and brotherly or motherly
love, on the other; and declares that even this latter is excelled
by a godly reason. It is a tractate full of warm feeling, and
reflects great national pride in these heroes, and, in spite of the
pedantic logic with which the philosophic point of view is
maintained, it breathes, in essence, the religion of the Judaism

[1] *Sap.*, 16, 12; 18, 15; 9, 1, 2   [2] *Ibid.*, 1, 4, 5, 7; 9, 17
[3] 4 Macc. 13: 19–14, 1; 15, 4–24

of the diaspora. The martyrs bravely died and expiated the sins
of their race; and they brought to those belonging to them
liberation from the stress of persecution. Now they stood near
God's throne in the choir of the patriarchs, and had received
pure and immortal souls from God.[1]

Jewish legends without philosophical garnishments are
recorded in the third book of Maccabees, where reactions to the
anti-semitism of the later, Ptolemic period may be clearly
recognized.[2] But the High-Priest's prayer[3] is valuable for the
study of religion, because obviously it represents the form of
prayer used in the synagogue at Alexandria. God is invoked as
the King of heaven and the Lord of creation, as the Holy One,
the Only, the Almighty who created the world, and who, as
righteous ruler, punishes the wicked. Then follow examples
from the Old Testament, the giants, the Sodomites, Pharaoh.
God had chosen Jerusalem as His holy city, and given it the
promise of His special protection. And God was faithful. The
stress of the present time—i.e. the pretended desire of Ptolemy
Philopater to view the temple—was only the consequence of
the Jews' own sins. "Wash away our sins now, and let Thy face
again shine upon us." The High-Priest prayed in this fashion
for the people, and in this fashion must innumerable prayers
have been offered in Greek synagogues in times of persecution.
In spite of their Greek dress, these are purely Jewish modes of
thought.

If we now consider other prayers, we see at once that an
essential part of synagogue worship must have consisted of
praising God as the almighty Creator of the world; and also that
it was characteristic of Jewish prayers to cite God's ways with
His people. We only need to read Psalms 104 and 105, which
follow one another because of similarity of content. These Psalms
constitute some of the best examples of this way of praising
God in the Hebrew synagogue. The conviction that the sins of
the people had brought all the misfortunes upon them in the
course of their history, is expressed in Psalms 78 and 106 in
a great many different ways. And in the midrash contained in
the second half of the Wisdom of Solomon,[4] the national and

[1] 4 Macc. 17: 18–22; 18: 23   [2] Bickermann in *Pauly-Wissowa*, xiv, 797–800
[3] 3 Macc. 2: 1–20   [4] *Sap.*, 10–19

religious basis of this Jewish philosophy of history becomes clear, for here is a Hellenistic midrash born of a genuinely Palestinian spirit.

The prayers already mentioned[1] are extant in two parallel redactions.[2] They praise God as creator. They reveal the spiritual nature of the Greek synagogue, and enable us to compare it with the older Palestinian mode. For the latter, Psalm 104 is the classical witness. God's mighty acts in creation are hymned in marvellously vivid language: His omnipotence sets boundaries to the sea, His goodness cares for man and beast; He gives life to all, He takes it back and creates new life; His majesty makes the earth tremble, and the devout singer praises the Lord throughout his life. That is simple Old Testament piety with a plain, straightforward way of thinking. On the other hand, the Hellenist offering prayer viewed creation as purposive in structure and arrangement from the beginning. It was created as a cosmos from the start, and the "spirit of life"—a Stoic expression—hovered over the waters. Then the various acts of creation were recounted as in Genesis, but always in such a way as to emphasize the blessings enjoyed by man and beast. Those things which the Psalmist said simply, and for their own sakes, are mentioned in these prayers as examples of a profound principle. God proclaimed the creation of man to His sophia with the words: "Let us make man"; then He created man, the citizen of the world, out of the four elements and with the five senses subordinated to the dominance of reason. When man transgressed the commandment, God did not completely repudiate him, but promised him resurrection after death.

The difference from Psalm 104 is obvious, and comparison immediately brings the Hellenistic elements into the light of day: (a) the Stoic idea of the organized cosmos purposive in all details, and penetrated by the "spirit of life" of the godhead; (b) man as a creature endowed with senses, whom reason rules "as charioteer"; (c) his body consists of four elements; and (d) he is a "citizen of the world". When we add the belief in a resurrection and the hypotasis of sophia, we have all the

[1] *Vide supra*, p. 90
[2] *Const. Apost.*, vii, 34 =viii, 12, 9–20; Bousset, *Götting Nachr.*, 1915, 451 ff.

elements characteristic of this kind of prayer. Moreover, nothing here is new, for every trait occurred in the literature of the diaspora already discussed. What we then deduced from the writers is sufficiently confirmed by the prayers of the synagogue. The religion of Greek Judaism is in essence identical with the old religion as found in the tradition of the Fathers, but it is markedly penetrated, and in certain places overwhelmed, by Hellenistic modes of expression and thought.

The remaining prayers in this collection confirm our conclusions. God is worshipped as the Almighty, and as the Saviour.[1] Just as in Philo, He can only be described in negatives:[2] all "rational and holy nature" does Him homage;[2] sophia is His daughter;[3] man is a "citizen of the world",[4] a rational being[5] endowed with a body purposively formed,[6] and with an immortal soul;[7] resurrection is promised to him after death,[8] and therefore he will attain eternal life.[9] His present life is for him a "racecourse of righteousness";[10] only faith, of which Abraham's is the model, can penetrate to heaven; it fills the soul with the hope of rebirth, and precedes knowledge, or "gnosis".[11] These Hellenistic terms are accompanied by the traditional formulas of Biblical religion, and also the typically Jewish view which regards the history of Israel as the revelation of God's choice, discipline, and mercy. What is dealt with in Psalms 105, 106, 78, has parallels, not only in numerous separate passages,[12] but also in the broadly-planned second part[13] of the great prayer, whose first part contains the cosmic hymn of praise on the pattern of Psalm 104. The spirit of the Wisdom of Solomon was active in the Greek synagogue.

[1] *Const. Apost.*, vii, 33, 2   [2] *Const. Apost.*, 35, 9   [3] and [4] 35, 10   [4] 34, 6; 39, 2
[5] 34, 6; 38, 5   [6] 38, 4   [7] 38, 5; cf. 33, 3   [8] *loc. cit.*   [9] 39, 3
[10] 33, 3   [11] 33, 3, 4   [12] 33, 4–6; 37, 2–4; 38, 2; 39, 3   [13] viii, 12, 21–26

Chapter Seven

PAUL

AS ALREADY DEMONSTRATED, ACTS SHOWS THAT AFTER THE persecution of Stephen, the Hellenists were the first missionaries in the diaspora; and that it was among them that the idea of a mission to the Gentiles became fact. The Syrian metropolis of Antioch is mentioned as the scene of this new departure which was to be so very significant for the history of the world. Further, we said that the first church in Jerusalem heard of it and sent thither, as their trusted representative, a Levite from Cyprus, who bore the Palmyrenian name of Barnabas, and who had already made himself very acceptable to the community.[1] Barnabas rejoiced in the growth of this Hellenistic church and remained with them a whole year as teacher and preacher, after which he sent for an assistant, named Paul, from Tarsus. Thus it was Barnabas who, in fact, introduced Paul, the world-missionary of Christianity, to his life's work. Who was this Paul?

He was born in Tarsus as the son of a Benjaminite Jew who had the distinction of possessing Roman citizenship.[2] We have no information how the father obtained this standing; he may have been the freedman of an eminent Roman, or, already a freedman, he may have earned the interest of the Romans, and so have received the honour of citizenship as a gift. A tradition preserved by Jerome[3] says that his parents belonged originally to Gishala in Northern Galilee, and removed to Tarsus in consequence of warlike disturbances. This tradition is not improbable since Paul on one occasion[4] described himself as a "Hebrew", i.e. probably a man of Palestine. In any case, one may conclude that the boy grew up in a well-to-do household. Besides his Hebrew name, Saul, he bore the honourable Roman cognomen, Paul; it is still undecided whether this name was chosen because of its similarity of sound, or in memory of a former patron of the family.

---

[1] Acts 4: 36; 11: 22–25   [2] Rom. 11: 1; Phil. 3: 5; Acts 22: 3,28
[3] *Comm. on Philem.*, 23. *Vir. inl.*, 5   [4] Phil. 3: 5

It is certain that the young Paul received a good education and learned some handicraft besides the usual subjects taught at school. He entered into a sort of apprenticeship with a tent-maker.[1] Perhaps even at this stage he had it in mind to follow the calling of a rabbi, which indeed presupposed sources of income from a subsidiary occupation.[2] He appears to have come to Jerusalem at an early age, for, according to Acts, he says he was brought up there, and was a pupil of the celebrated rabbi, Gamaliel, who was an eminent "Tannaite" of the first generation.[3] Paul himself asserts that he was a wholehearted Pharisee, unconditionally faithful to the Law, and, on this account, had hated and persecuted the newly uprising sect of the Christians.

In the Jerusalem church, his active share in the stoning of Stephen was not forgotten,[4] and, according to Acts, he himself told how he had travelled to other towns in order to continue there the persecution of the Christians.[5] He had been com-missioned by the sanhedrin to go to Damascus, scarcely in order to bring the Christians, whom he found there, in bonds to Jerusalem—for the sanhedrin were not competent to order this[6]—but in order to encourage the Jews to repel the new danger in the name of the sanhedrin.

On this journey, the hand of God was laid upon him; in broad day the Risen Jesus, whom he was persecuting, appeared to him in a blinding light and called him to be His apostle.[7] Thereupon he went into the wilderness, as behoved a man who had been called of God; the barren steppes of the Arabian kingdom of Nabatea stretched out to the south-east of Damascus. Here he thought out the significance of his experi-ence, and at last turned back to Damascus.[8]

There he began preaching Jesus as Messiah, to the astonish-ment of the Christians, who were at first dubious; and to the confusion of the Jews, who plotted to kill him. The latter gained for their plans an Arab sheik who was subordinate to the

[1] Acts 18: 3   [2] Schürer, ii, 379
[3] Acts 22: 3. Schürer, ii, 429 f. Strack, *Einl. in d. Talmud,* 120
[4] Acts 7: 58–60; cf. 26: 10   [5] Acts 26: 11, 12
[6] Acts 9: 2 = 22: 5. Juster, ii, 145, n. 5
[7] Gal. 1: 16; 1 Cor. 15: 8 f. Acts 26: 13–16; 9: 3–6, 22: 6–10. Hirsch, *Z.N.W.,* 28, 305 ff.
[8] Gal. 1: 17

Nabatæan king, Aretas IV, and who officiated in Damascus as the Nabatæan "ethnarch". They intended to fall upon Paul outside the city, and for this reason kept a close watch on the gates. The Christians heard of the plan and by night lowered Paul in a basket over the walls.[1] He escaped unhurt to Jerusalem at a date fully two years after his conversion.[2] This visit was probably in A.D. 35. In the capital, he desired particularly to make Peter's acquaintance. After doing so, he remained with him for two weeks. At that time he also saw James, but no other apostle, nor did he appear in the church. He must therefore have remained hidden from sight in the greatest secrecy, as is quite comprehensible in the case of a convert in the city where there was still a vivid memory of his work as a persecutor. During this fortnight he had his only opportunity of gaining authentic information about the earthly work and life of Jesus from Peter, his most eminent disciple. Hitherto, he can only have heard accidental and much perverted rumours. Perhaps also he had certain memories of his own, belonging to his previous residence in Jerusalem.

Paul soon left the capital, and went into the regions of Syria and Cilicia, but did not visit the churches of the Jewish Christians, to whom only the rumour of the conversion of their former enemy had penetrated.[3] There now followed thirteen years of missionary work about which we have no further information.

The records of Acts are not clear on this point. They describe details with obvious faithfulness, but give us no picture of the whole. In any case, Barnabas sent for Paul from his home town of Tarsus, whither he had gone from Jerusalem.[4] On Paul's arrival in Antioch, they worked together there for a full year.[5] Accompanied by John Mark a cousin of Barnabas, the two undertook a missionary journey to Pisidia and Lycaonia.[6] The exact period of this journey cannot be determined, and it is possible that other work was done of which we have received no tradition. The only certain fact is, as Paul emphatically declares in Gal. 1: 17–24, that, during all these thirteen years, he never visited Jerusalem.

Meantime, a problem had become acute which had already

[1] Acts 9: 19–26; 2 Cor. 11: 32 f.   [2] Gal. 1: 18   [3] *Ibid.*, 1: 21–3
[4] Acts 9: 30   [5] *Ibid.*, 11: 25 f.   [6] *Ibid.*, 12: 25–14, 28

existed in germ in the Hellenistic church at Jerusalem, and which had grown to gigantic proportions on account of the mission to the Gentiles, viz. the question as to the operation of the ritual law in the case of new converts who had formerly been Gentiles. As long as the believers in Christ remained, and felt themselves, still to be Jews, the adoption of the ritual law offered no problem; a pagan who had been won for Christ entered the circle of disciples by circumcision and by baptism understood in a Christian sense. But when, under the pressure of the new teaching, the operation of the Law was strongly disputed even amongst Hellenist Jews as is described in Acts,[1] it is not surprising, with the increasing strength of the Hellenistic Gentile mission, and apart from the question of circumcision and other ritual observances, that the observances of further prescriptions for cleanliness in regard to foods should have been felt unnecessary. What was new in Christianity received proportionately fuller recognition, as traditional Judaism necessarily lost significance. Regardless of consequences, Paul had drawn this conclusion for practical life, and had effected the "freedom from the Law" in his missionary churches more logically than was practised in Antioch, the Syrian metropolis. Conflict with the traditionalists at Jerusalem could not be avoided, and it is only astonishing that a dozen years passed before the antitheses compelled an attempt at a solution.

Paul and Barnabas went up to Jerusalem and negotiated with James, Peter, and John, the "pillars" of the first church. They secured recognition of their Gentile mission as free from the Law, i.e. baptized pagans need not be circumcised. The first church, on its side, declared that, as in the past, its mission would be to Jews only. The church at Jerusalem would receive financial support from the Gentile daughter-churches. This was the only obligation laid upon them.[2]

It was with this clear and happy message that the two leaders of the gentile mission returned to Antioch, but it was soon to become evident that a complete solution had not been reached. Obviously the greater majority of the church at Antioch were Gentile Christians; and the standpoint of freedom from the ritual requirements, now recognized even by Jerusalem

[1] Acts 6: 11–14; 7: 48, 53   [2] Gal. 2: 1–10 as against Acts 15

as fully justified, was dominant to such an extent that even
the Jewish-Christian minority, on occasion, dispensed with the
food laws. Especially was this important when it was a question
of eating in common with the other brethren, i.e. of celebrating
the Lord's Supper. In this way, a friendly agreement was
reached in the Pauline sense, and, when Peter appeared in
Antioch, he adopted the local custom without more ado.

But other people, commissioned by James, appeared in
Antioch and they were not so tolerant. They thoroughly dis-
agreed with the view that born Jews might disregard the Law
in any way, and they appealed to the consciences of the local
Jewish Christians. Thereupon, Peter himself became doubtful
and drew back; and even Barnabas, Paul's former travelling-
companion, began to avoid table-fellowship with the "unclean".
The logical result was, plainly, that the Lord's Supper could
not be observed in common, and the two sections of the church
became distinct and separate communities. It was evident to
all eyes that the agreement at Jerusalem had not answered the
crucial question of the churches of the diaspora, nor settled
which section in mixed churches was to have the say. Paul had
solved this problem, implicitly, in the gentile-Christian sense;
but now the representatives of James came, and gave the
opposite answer in no uncertain voice, in so far as they required
the gentile Christians to observe the Jewish food requirements
before table-fellowship would be permitted. Peter and Barnabas
recognized this requirement as justified. Thereupon, Paul rose
up in passionate anger on behalf of his contention, and attacked
Peter in front of the assembled church. But the other side did
not give way, and from that time forward Paul took his own
path separately from that of Peter or Barnabas.[1] All this
involved Paul in much hatred and strife.

How did this dispute at Antioch arise? The possibility is that,
soon after the departure of Paul and Barnabas, the "Apostolic
Decree" was drawn up in Jerusalem, and was made known to
the most important churches by a circular letter. The text is
contained in Acts 15: 23–29, though obviously in an edited
form; and Judas and Silas, who are mentioned in it as messengers, must be the representatives of James mentioned by Paul;

[1] Acts 15: 39

their arrival started the dispute. The decree confirmed the view that the gentile Christians were not required to become Jews in all respects; they were required to abjure illicit sexual intercourse in every form, and also to use only *kosher* meat at meals. This was all that was meant by the formal language of the prohibition *re* meat that had been offered to idols, or blood, i.e. meat which had not been drained; or meat from strangled animals, i.e. not ritually killed. This meant, again, that all meat sold in the public market was excluded, and that only a Jewish butcher, or, if he sold nothing to Christians, a Jewish-Christian slaughterer, could be employed for providing meat. This legal requirement was no trivial matter, and there is no room for wonder that Paul should have repudiated it warmly, especially when broadcast in the churches behind his back. Only towards the end of his life, when he again visited Jerusalem, was he given any direct official information. Thus it would seem that he never agreed to this requirement, not even at a later date when it brought his Corinthian church into confusion. He pushed unruffled along the straight road of freedom from the Law.

He now carried his missionary work into the larger world, he alone being the responsible leader. Compared with himself, even the most capable companions appeared to be, at best, only valuable assistants. His sphere was Asia Minor and Greece—but the old questions continually menaced his work. Wherever he went, the "Judaizers" followed. In accordance with the policy of maintaining unity, they explained to the newly converted Gentiles the necessity of eating only kosher meat, according to the Apostolic Decree; and also, contrary to its letter, but quite in accordance with the spirit of Jewish-Christianity, they taught the soteriological significance of circumcision. These emissaries were in continual contact with Jerusalem, and they made it seem credible to the churches that James and the original Apostles stood behind them. Moreover the shadow of Peter was continually falling upon the path of Paul, whose relationship with the original Apostles at last broke down completely; for, when the agreement he had reached at Jerusalem was subsequently revised by the Apostolic Decree with all its consequences, he could not but regard it as a breach

of covenant. Apparently he must have said as much in Antioch
when face to face with Peter, although he says nothing to that
effect in his letters. He did not write a single syllable about the
Apostolic Decree or its authors; and, apart from the passage in
Galatians, he says nothing about his relationship to the original
Apostles. He could not dispute their authority, nor could he
praise their conduct or their attitude towards himself. He therefore had to be content to combat in principle the influences
issuing from Jerusalem, and to rebuke, as firmly as he could,
the emissaries who were ruining his churches. He never wrote
a single word about those who gave them authority; nothing
about James in Jerusalem; nothing about Peter in Corinth and
Rome. He ignored them. But looking more closely, and reading
between the lines of his letters, we perceive behind the "servants
of Satan", the "false apostles", and the "spurious brethren",
the shadows of the great figures in Jerusalem.[1] Paul stood alone
among the Christians whom he had converted, and very
dangerous opponents worked behind his back.

Acts gives us a fairly detailed account of the outer course of
Paul's missionary work. There are indeed larger gaps than the
text itself lets us suspect; nevertheless, the book is of inexpressible value. It records a far-reaching campaign, "the second
missionary journey",[2] which took him through the middle of
Asia Minor, along the Macedonian coast-lands, and into the
heart of Greece. He was not successful in gaining a toothold in
Athens, but he founded a church in Corinth. Here he remained
for eighteen months, when the hostility of the Jews, perhaps in
the summer of A.D. 51, compelled him to return to Antioch. In
spite of many inner difficulties, the Corinthian church remained
faithful, and has maintained an unbroken history until the
present day.

The "third journey",[3] which began soon afterwards, was at
first a renewed visitation of the churches in Asia Minor founded
on the previous occasion. The journey ended in Ephesus, which
Paul made the headquarters of his missionary work for two
complete years. From here he visited Corinth again; and finally,
when he had to leave Ephesus, he added a journey of inspection

[1] 2 Cor. 11: 13–15, 26; Gal. 2: 4   [2] Acts 15: 36–18: 22
[3] *Ibid.*, 18: 23–21: 14

throughout the whole of Greece. But he soon came to the conclusion that he had discharged his task in the east, and he directed his glance towards Rome, and, indeed, beyond it, to Spain.

Already, the gospel had penetrated thus far. A gentile Christian church had been founded in Rome, not by Paul, but, possibly, by men connected with the church at Antioch. The danger was that this church, like so many others, would be manœuvred into opposition to Paul. It is not improbable that Peter was responsible for this danger, owing to his resentment at the rebuke he had had to swallow in Antioch. He had visited Corinth,[1] and gained adherents who made things difficult for Paul. Quite probably, he had gone thence to Rome and had persuaded the church to the way he preferred. Paul attempted to hinder this from Corinth. He wrote powerfully to the Romans, and made them acquainted with his entire programme. He did this as a preliminary measure because he intended first to go to Jerusalem with the gifts which his churches had duly collected. Afterwards, he would come himself to Rome. But things happened otherwise than he hoped, if not otherwise than he feared.[2] It is true that he attempted to overcome the mistrust of the original church at Jerusalem by correct observance of the Law, but unfortunately he was recognized in the temple by certain Jews of Asia Minor, and was at once accused of having brought into the sacred area a non-Jew among his companions. For so doing, the penalty was death.[3]

Paul was dragged out of the temple and was in mortal danger, when the Roman commandant seized and held him in the hope that he had arrested an Egyptian leader of a band, who had been diligently sought for. The commandant must have been astonished to find that the trouble was due to an uproar among the Jews themselves, and on religious grounds, and moreover that the prisoner was a Roman citizen. The further course of events cannot be clearly seen from the only apparently exact narratives of Acts.[4] In any case, the commandant held Paul in a sort of protective custody, in order that

[1] 1 Cor. 1: 12; 9: 5   [2] Rom. 15: 31
[3] Inscription in Dittenberger, *Or.*, n. 598, Juster, ii, 142 f.
[4] Juster, ii, 143f.

the Jews should not destroy him,[1] and eventually handed him
over to the procurator in Cæsarea. Even here no decision was
reached; he was neither handed over to the Jewish court, nor
set free, nor judged according to Roman law, but kept two
years in prison. A decision was only reached when a new
procurator appeared in the person of Festus, who suggested to
him that he should go before the sanhedrin in Jerusalem.
Hitherto Paul had always submitted himself, as a faithful Jew,
to the judgment of his own people, and had accepted their
verdicts; indeed on five occasions,[2] he had suffered without
demur the punishments decreed by them, but now he refused
the suggestion and desired to be sent as a Roman citizen to the
imperial assize.[3] Thereupon Festus did his duty and dispatched
him to Rome.

Paul arrived there after a long and varied journey, and, when
he left the ship, was greeted by Christian brethren on Italian
soil. He then lived in Rome for two years in relative freedom,
though under police supervision, and was able to have unhindered intercourse with the church, and to preach. What
happened after that we do not know. It is possible that he was
set free, and was able once more to set out on his journeys, and
to continue his work. He may have visited Spain, and may also
have seen the east again. This may be a legend, but it is certain
that he suffered martyrdom in Rome under Nero[4] and was
buried on the side of the road to Ostia.

Paul did not initiate missionary work to the Gentiles; even
without him, Christianity would have extended round the
Mediterranean; but he gave the religion of Jesus the form in
which it was capable of conquering the world, without receiving
damage to its own soul. He had never sat at the feet of the
Master, but nevertheless was the only one amongst the Apostles
who really understood Him. Body and soul he was a Jew, but
the spirit of the diaspora had extended his horizon. He weighed
the meaning of the history of his people, and boldly construed
it as issuing in the revelation of the universal religion of the
heavenly Lord; the history of the world since then has confirmed his judgment.

[1] Acts 23: 12–35; cf. 23: 10   [2] 2 Cor. 11, 24
[3] Acts 25: 10 f.   [4] 1 Clem. 5: 7

To appraise the achievements of Paul's life, we must take yet another fact into account, viz., as far as we can follow his life, he was a sick man. Probably in outward appearance the exact opposite of a handsome figure such as Dürer depicted, he carried a "thorn in the flesh" and "the marks of Christ" in his body.

His work meant that, physically, he "died daily" with Jesus, i.e. he constantly overtaxed his strength in order to be equal to the problems with which his calling faced him. Of recent years, certain "modernists" have made a fanciful attempt to maintain that Paul was an epileptic, but without grounds. However, his nerves were overstrung, and they plagued him with hallucinations which brought bitter suffering to him and others. He did not complain about this, but was proud, even in weakness, to labour for Christ. The Lord Himself had once said to him, "Let yourself be content with My grace, for My power is made perfect in weakness." Thus his theology of the cross[1] was born out of his own experience, and he himself knew what it meant to die with Christ.

Now we must turn to his teaching. How and what Paul had preached to the Gentiles, we can only say in general outlines, for no source depicts Paul as a missionary seeking to win unconverted Jews, or pure pagans. His letters were addressed to churches already in existence, and they assumed that the truths essential to Paul's theology were already known to those churches. And letters, even when they are dictated, give us by no means a reliable idea of the spoken word. Apparently Paul himself had heard on one occasion from his opponents that his personal presence was quite different from his letters[2]—a judgment which may also hold good for his missionary preaching in comparison with what he says in his letters. When we remember, moreover, that the Apostle only took to writing when he had to answer quite definite questions, or to overcome practical difficulties, and never for the purpose of giving a connected account of his teaching, we see further grounds for the manifold uncertainty and defectiveness of our knowledge.

---

[1] 2 Cor. 12: 7; Gal. 6: 17; 2 Cor. 4: 10. 1 Cor. 9: 27. *Handb.*, excur. on 2 Cor. 12: 10

[2] 2 Cor. 10: 10

There is the further fact that Paul is an individual thinker who goes his own way and writes in his own highly individual style. In spite of all his learning, he does not speak "like the Scribes", but with the rare power of a prophet whose eyes see beyond the men in front of him, into the deeps of eternity. He understood human nature in his fellows, without their being able to comprehend him for themselves. None of his hearers and readers fully understood Paul—and so it is to the present day.

His letters are very revealing, and show his heart while he was dictating. He discusses a point quietly, calmly, and clearly: then he tries to draw an elaborate inference. He begins, becomes entangled in the sequence of his phrases, pursues a subsidiary line, introduces an incomplete picture, and finally sticks fast. He begins again, but once more his thoughts, in their multitude, overwhelm the words which come slowly limping after, and which get entangled once more in sentences doing violence to normal construction. The reader guesses what he means to say, but it is not down on paper. Then finally, though by no means always, the form is made to suit the content. Yet it is the same Paul who can fill his words with magic, and let his feelings stream into the hearts of his readers, or up to the throne of God. This was the case when he was wrestling for the souls of the vacillating Galatians, or when, in writing to the Corinthians, he indited the exalted hymn of love; and to the Philippians, that of Christ the Lord. Passages like these exhibit Paul as a master of language who, by the grace of God, controls the whole register of the human instrument; or, again, he is like a rare and attractive wild plant growing in the conventional and well-kept garden of contemporary Greek writers.

Let us attempt to draw a picture of his world of ideas. He knows God by what he learned at home from his parents, at school, at the synagogue, and from the rabbis; and he has read God's revelation of Himself in the Old Testament. As a Hellenist, he knows that even pagans, after earnest meditation upon the universe, are able to infer the invisible nature of its Creator,[1] and, from moral promptings in their breasts, to recognize the will of the divine Law-giver; but he is proud that only Israel had received the full and direct revelation and the

[1] Rom. 1: 20; 2: 14 f.

written Law, letter for letter.[1] Moreover, it is not sufficient merely to hear and to study this Law, but to practise it, and indeed to keep it in its entirety.[2]

God is righteous—i.e. He punishes the transgressor of His Law, and rewards the obedient or righteous. His wrath against pagans was revealed, similarly, when they departed from the truth. He had turned from them and abandoned them to the greatest moral confusion, which increased to the degree in which the knowledge of God of these idol-worshippers was darkened. But the Jew had reason also for looking at, and testing, his works as to whether he himself really obeyed God better than did the despised pagans, for the Day of Judgment awaited at the end of time. Then God would repay each according to his works, rewarding the doer of good with honour and eternal life, punishing the disobedient with His wrath—Jews as well as Gentiles, without respect of persons. This conception of God went far beyond the prevailing Jewish view, and meant a close approximation to the teaching of the great prophets; but it was a faith which Paul shared with the best of his Jewish fellow-believers. Yet it was understood by them in a totally different way, and this really neutralized it completely, because Paul comprehended the righteousness of God and the meaning of sin from a new standpoint.

The parables of Jesus, as we have already seen,[3] depict the righteousness of God in a way which roused the vigorous opposition of the Talmud. To people who like to draw up a formal account with God, it is provoking if the righteousness characteristic of human ways of thinking be set aside and replaced by a grace which gives freely. Paul, too, understood the divine righteousness in this way, only he expressed it in complicated forms of thought. That it was God's purpose to save men was, for him, the indisputable foundation of all religion. Earthly experience showed him, what he could also prove from the Scriptures, that all men without exception were sinners, and therefore no one, whether Gentile or Jew, could fulfil the Law. None of the children of men is righteous; sin separates them all from God. Therefore, if righteousness, in a legal sense, corresponded with the nature of God, only wrath and punishment

[1] Rom. 2: 27   [2] *Ibid.*, 2: 13; Gal. 5: 3   [3] *Vide supra*, pp. 51 f.

would remain for men. In that case, however, where would be God's redemptive purpose, revealed in the promises of the Old Testament and just as indubitably in His punitive righteousness? Hence God must be able to take sinners to Himself, and yet be righteous in so doing. It follows that His righteousness is different from the human virtue which bears that name; it is revealed when God, of His free grace, accepts the sinner, and "makes him righteous", giving him that characteristic as a gift which he cannot earn by his own achievements.

But there is a condition, viz. the sinner must "believe", i.e. in full recognition of his own insufficiency and helplessness, he must surrender himself entirely to divine grace and, setting aside every doubt, be certain that God makes him righteous, and will give him eternal life. The question arises whether this only means replacing the idea of divine righteousness by that of mercy? Would it not be simpler to say that God is not "righteous" in the human sense, for then no man could escape judgment, but rather that He is merciful? This way of stating the case really meets all the requirements, but Paul would have regarded it as serious blasphemy to deny God the property of righteousness,[1] and so he sought and found a way of uniting his profound, religious experience with a theory of righteousness which satisfied formal logic. God's righteousness must indeed demand punishment and expiation from the sinner; this expiation was made to God when the innocent and sinless Jesus voluntarily bore the punishment of sin, and suffered death. He suffered death as a vicarious, expiatory sacrifice on behalf of sinful mankind. Thereby He reconciled God, satisfied His righteousness, which had demanded expiation, and opened in this manner the way of mercy which can bring to the Christian believer the necessary righteousness. Thus God *is* righteous and *makes* righteous.[2]

The idea of expiatory death for another was crudely expressed in the animal sacrifices of the Old Testament ceremonial law. As we have already seen, Hellenistic Judaism raised the idea to the height of the voluntary sacrificial death of the Maccabean youths for the sins of their people.[3] Paul carried the thought

[1] Rom. 3: 5   [2] Rom. 3: 23–26, 5, 8–9; Gal. 3: 13
[3] *Vide supra*, p. 101

to a sublime height, and used it to reconcile the idea of divine righteousness and that of a sinful mankind.

The supra-mundane and supra-human process involved was, however, not a course of events which takes place in accordance with the inner necessity of the divine nature as Anselm, the Schoolman, teaches, but a free action of God's grace. Paul was well aware that there was no "sufficient ground" for God's action which could offer mankind an excuse for bargaining with God. He knows that he himself was saved by the incomprehensible mercy of God, and he looks shudderingly into the abyss into which His unsearchable will flings the clattering potsherds of the vessels of His wrath.[1] God accepts whom He will and rejects whom He will, and the lot of the babe in the womb is already settled according to God's free choice. As always, where ideas of predestination meet with practical religious needs, these theories did not cramp Paul, but only strengthened his joyous consciousness of the divine election,[2] although his successors, for centuries, were reluctant to discuss the subject. But, even for Paul, the doctrine of divine predestination was not the last word. In the greatest deeps of his soul, he glimpses the holy secret of an all-embracing divine love which would, at last and in the end, redeem the rejected, a love which had concluded all under disobedience in order to have mercy upon all.[3]

For mankind, there was only *one* way to this God and His grace, namely Jesus Christ. This Man had lived His brief life in Palestine as an itinerant teacher, had died, in the end, a criminal's death on the cross. But He had arisen from the dead. He had appeared to His disciples and lastly also to Paul; He still lived and laboured near and with God, and would soon come again. That was the personal message and experience of Paul, but he also sought to explain the secret of His person. He was the Son of God in quite a different sense from any other human being. At one time, He had lived in divine form with His Father,[4] and was equal with God; but then, at the Father's command, He had descended from heaven, and taken human form, in order to redeem mankind. An inescapable fate

[1] Rom. 9: 10–29 [2] Rom. 8: 28–39
[3] *Ibid.*, 11: 32 [4] Phil.2: 6–11; cf. Rom. 8: 3

burdened mankind, for in their flesh dwelt the power of an evil
dæmon, sin, which was contrary to God, and compelled men
to conform to its overpowering will. Even if they should in-
wardly catch sight of a better self, no matter how much that
self might strive and struggle after the good, it was all in vain.
One man after another fell as a sacrifice to Death, and was
accounted according to God's irrefragable law, as the wages of
sin.[1] Then God's son came upon earth, born of the House of
David.[2] He took on a body of flesh like ours and one in which
sin dwelt and was active.[3] He submitted to the Law which
applied to all men,[4] but shattered the power of Sin; He did
not do its will, but remained sinless,[5] and thus overcame it
in His flesh.[6] Nevertheless, obediently to the will of the Father,
He bowed to His human destiny. Being sinless, He was not
subject to death, yet He accepted death voluntarily and died
like a sinner, indeed like a criminal—and the evil spirits of this
world triumphed. But they did not suspect what lay in God's
purpose,[7] for the sacrifice was made for the sake of mankind.
Sin was conquered on its own ground and therefore death could
no longer retain its booty. Jesus, though crucified and buried,
rose again to new life.[8] His work had been completed and now
God set Him upon the heavenly throne at His right hand, and
gave Him the name above every name, the name of *Kyrios*, i.e.
the Lord, before whom everything bows whether in heaven,
or on earth, or under the earth. This is the cosmic drama of
salvation which was carried through by God, Christ, and the
heavenly powers against Sin and Death, with all their dæmonic
assistants. In spite of all prophecy, the earth below guessed
nothing of what was happening there.[9]

Only with the revelation of the risen Christ was redemption
proclaimed to man, and the way pointed out by which that
redemption could be accepted; for, in the end, the individual
man had to be brought into relation with all that had been
done in heaven. We have already shown that Paul characterized
faith as the means by which man grasps divine grace. In so expressing himself, he formulated the process of salvation from

[1] Rom. 7   [2] *Ibid.*, 1: 3   [3] *Ibid.*, 8: 3   [4] Gal. 4: 4
[5] 2 Cor. 5: 21   [6] Rom. 8: 3   [7] 1 Cor. 2: 8   [8] 1 Cor. 15: 3, 4
[9] *Ibid.*, 2: 8; Col. 2: 15

the psychological standpoint. The decisive factor, according to Paul, was the total surrender of self, as distinct from trusting in one's own works; but faith was only the subjective form of perception, viz. the apprehension of an objective process or a positive change which was taking place within the man himself.

The natural man lived in the earthly sphere under the burden of sin and death, in such a way that his "flesh" was predominant. The Lord, however, was a divine being, i.e. He was spirit, pneuma, and He penetrated with this heavenly material each one who trusted himself to Him. A Christian received the spirit and thereby in full reality shared in the Risen Lord. His body became a member of Christ[1] and the sum total of Christians can be described as a single unity, as the body of Christ whose head is the Lord.[2] Hence, he who becomes a Christian enters into a mystical fellowship of the spirit; he is actually "in Christ", as if in a heavenly fluid. This spirit overcomes sin in the flesh. The victorious warfare against sin, which once took place in the person of the historical Jesus, is repeated anew in every Christian to whom the spirit has been given. In effect, every Christian becomes anew a "Christ upon earth". The spirit seizes control in man, breaks the power of the passions of the flesh, and levels the road towards a life according to God's will. The Christian lives "in the spirit" and not "in the flesh". He fulfils the requirements of the divine law,[3] a thing for ever impossible to the natural man. But this fellowship with Christ is also the fellowship of His sufferings. The way of the Lord had led through suffering to resurrection; and, in the same way, the Christian here on earth takes part in the sufferings of Christ in order afterwards to share His glory.[4] From this point of view Christ is the first-born of many brethren whom He will transfigure like Himself.[5] The Christian experiences the divine blessing in the sense of power in the struggle against sin; the proud feeling of freedom from its dæmonic compulsion; the joyful possession of all the virtues well-pleasing to God; the voluntary and victorious bearing of all sufferings in

[1] 1 Cor. 6: 15, 12: 13   [2] Rom. 12: 5; 1 Cor. 10: 17; Col. 1: 18, 24
[3] Rom. 8: 3 f., 13: 8
[4] *Ibid.*, 8: 17; 2 Cor. 4: 10, 13: 4; Phil. 3: 10; Gal. 6: 17   [5] Rom. 8: 29

happy consciousness of fellowship with his Lord. On the other hand, he lives in the hope that complete redemption, i.e. entire liberation from the body, the joyful experience of heavenly glory, awaits him in the future.[1]

The process of redemption is therefore something which God effects in man whereby he is transformed from a being fettered by earthly conditions, or "of the flesh", into a spiritual, pneumatic being on the model of Jesus Christ. This process only ends with the final separation from the body, the entry into heavenly glory, and the gaining of a transfigured body. That is redemption in the fullest sense of the word. But we may ask how it begins, and how the individual sinful man is brought into this pathway of salvation.

The first step is the preaching of the divine message, the proclamation of the divine invitation to men[2] to be reconciled with God, and let themselves be redeemed.[3] They are required to believe without condition and without limit. This faith, however, is not simply an emotional attitude developed in the deeps of the soul, but at the same time an impulse of the will which leads to action, a will which seizes the saving hand of God. Action must follow decision; the newly converted believer joins the church of Christ, and is made a Christian by baptism. There the miracle of a divine mystery is fulfilled in him.[4] He sinks beneath the water and so dies, yet he dies no ordinary human death, but the death of Christ. The death once suffered upon the cross on Golgatha for the sins of the world is accounted to him; it becomes his own death, a death which he now suffers for his own sins. Thereby he pays the due price of sin and thus is set free from it. Through this miracle, God makes him righteous; he no longer possesses sin. This may be regarded as the negative side of the process of becoming a Christian, of being "baptized into Christ", literally, "submerged in Christ".

The positive side is that he "puts Christ on"; he is introduced into that spiritual body of Christ[5] which is constituted by the entire Church. In other words, the heavenly substance of the spirit is granted to him. The sinner dies in baptism: the Christian who rises from the water is a new creation,[6] "the old

---

[1] Rom. 8: 23, 13: 11   [2] *Ibid.*, 10: 17; Gal. 3: 2   [3] 2 Cor. 5: 20
[4] Rom. 6: 2–11   [5] Gal. 3: 27 f.; 1 Cor. 12: 13   [6] 2 Cor. 5: 17; Rom. 6:4

has passed away, lo! it has become new". He is now "in Christ".

Hence Paul can also say that, just as in baptism we share in the death of Christ, so in coming up from the water we share His resurrection. Paul formulates our experience of sharing in Christ's resurrection, however, in the sense of a goal to be aimed at, i.e. we must now live in the new life, and we are able to do so by the power of the spirit. We are mortified to sin and have suffered death; our new life in the spirit is to be lived in the service of righteousness,[1] and issue in eternal life in the fellowship of the Risen Christ. In this way, baptism brings about the birth of the Christian as a new being free from the natural bonds of earthly life, and united by the spirit with the Risen Lord. The first element is faith, the second is baptism, the third is the spirit. Thereby the man is justified and placed on the pathway to redemption. But the man who is reborn lives, as long as he is in the flesh, by faith and not by sight.[2] Faith is always the attitude of the Christian, and this term is used by Paul to describe the essential character of the Christian state.

Paul's doctrine of baptism contains an explicit, sacramental mysticism which cannot be understood directly on the basis of Hellenistic Judaism, although the latter reveals certain similarities. We shall deal with this subject later; just now it is of decisive importance for understanding Paul that we should determine the ethical level of his theory. This theory depends on his conception of God, and regards redemption as man's liberation from all the powers which prevent our fulfilling God's will, and living according to His commandments, until finally we can abandon the last fetters of the flesh and triumph in fellowship with our Redeemer. For Paul does not regard salvation, *soteria*, as already fully ours; rather it is a promise for the future which faith now seizes upon.[3] At the beginning of this process of salvation, is the decisive act of justification and new birth through the spirit in baptism. The Christian is now righteous, dead to sin, and free from its power.

---

[1] Rom. 6: 18–23; 8: 9–11   [2] Gal. 2: 20; 2 Cor. 5: 7
[3] Cf. Rom. 8: 24; Eph. 2: 5 8 is the only exception, a fact which is, at the same time, a proof that the letter was by another writer.

If we have followed Paul's theory so far, we shall have understood him to imply that to the Christian, as a new creature,
sin is no longer possible. If, in the earlier stage, that of the "old
Adam", the dominant factor was sin, now it is the spirit; and
if at one time the evil power irresistibly compelled us to sin,
now we shall look to the divine power of the spirit, and
ascribe to it that sure guidance by which the Christian may
attain perfect sinlessness after the example of Christ. We shall
see that, in later ages, this conclusion was drawn by many. But
Paul did not do so. It is true that he describes the status of a
Christian as a new man, justified, sinless, and filled with the
spirit—as we have already explained. He strongly insists that
the Christian is dead to sin, but nowhere does he say that sin
is dead. It is still there, working in the world of unredeemed
men with unbroken power, and waiting in ambush for the
opportunity of winning back the lost territory. The experiences
of life, the battles which the new convert must fight for a
moral foundation, showed Paul clearly enough that sin still
played an evil rôle in the Christian churches. Deeply pained,
he perceived that, in spite of their Christianity, the Corinthians
lived in bickerings and strife; to their disgrace, he drew the
conclusion that they were still "of the flesh", and deserved
censure "as men",[1] and this in spite of the fact that they had
not been denied the possession of the spirit.[2] This could only
mean that they gave way to the power of sin in the flesh, that
they were not successful in the struggle of the spirit against the
flesh, as Christ was, but must recognize defeat.

We are now in a position to understand how it is that Paul
could describe a Christian's freedom from sin and his spiritu-
ality as saving facts and yet, in the same breath, he could urge
Christians not to allow sin to rule in them, but to place their
bodies at the service of Christ;[3] and how he could discuss the
duty of not living according to the will of the flesh.[4] Indeed he
exhorts his churches, clearly and unmistakably, to let themselves be led by the spirit of God, and through the spirit to put
to death the carnal, i.e. sinful, passions.[5] Sin is not dead in the

[1] 1 Cor. 3: 3 f.; cf. Rom. 8: 12 f.   [2] 1 Cor. 3: 16; 6: 19, and indeed 5: 5
[3] Rom. 6: 12-14, 19; 1 Cor. 6: 20   [4] Rom. 8: 12
[5] *Ibid.*, 8: 13 f.; Gal. 5: 16 f.; Col. 3: 5-10

flesh any more than it was dead in the body of Jesus when He lived on earth; rather it must be put to death in each individual by the spirit dwelling in him just as it dwelt in the body of Christ. In this way the Christian life, as actually found in the individual, remained only an imperfect copy of the ideal which had been realized in Christ; that life constituted a struggle to be well-pleasing to Christ.[1] All that Paul could say of himself was that he had not yet attained the perfection of the Christian life, but that he was making every effort to reach the prize. Both in the recognition and the conquest of sin, there is a progressive movement from the small to the great, and there are degrees of perfection.[2]

We are now in a position to understand Paul's doctrine of a judgment which all Christians must undergo and which will judge them according to their works.[3] They must show themselves to be free from guilt, and their hearts will be tested as to whether they are able to stand innocent and pure in God's sight.[4] This is not to contradict, but to assume the doctrine of justification by faith alone. The works of the reborn man are done through the spirit, and not by the flesh. From another standpoint, this life in the spirit is to be regarded as the life of faith, i.e. life in faith that we possess the righteousness which comes from God.[5] That is how we must understand the celebrated saying of the Apostle that everything which is not of faith is sin.[6] He could have said, alternatively, that what does not come from the spirit is sin. The Last Judgment decides whether the Christian has really been justified in the spirit by faith, or whether he has remained in the flesh as a sinner. This is not casuistical legalism, not a back-sliding into the Jewish calculation of works, but, in view of the weakness even of the reborn man,[7] it is the final and crucial question as to what dominates the Christian life: spirit or flesh, the life of faith in Christ or the life of man in the world.

Nowhere did Paul discuss fundamentally whether the punishment of a sinful Christian was an absolute rejection or a relative chastisement. Incidental expressions suggest, however,

[1] 2 Cor. 5: 9; cf. 1 Cor. 11: 32; 1 Cor. 9: 23   [2] Phil. 3: 12; 1 Cor. 3: 1
[3] 1 Cor. 3: 14 f.; 2 Cor. 5: 9 f.   [4] 1 Cor. 1: 8; Phil. 1: 10; 1 Thess. 3: 13
[5] Phil. 3: 9   [6] Rom. 14: 23   [7] Gal. 5: 17

that the latter was his view. Indeed the incestuous man of
Corinth, while still alive, was to be handed over to Satan who
would destroy his flesh—but his Christian spirit would nevertheless be saved at the Last Day.[1] On the other hand, we must
not forget that the Apostle threatened sinful Christians with
death and therefore with final rejection such as faced every
non-Christian.[2] He reckons with the possibility that even a
Christian, who has been baptized and endowed with the spirit,
can turn once more to the flesh and to sinfulness, in such a way
as that God will withdraw His grace and hand him over to
damnation. Paul believed, indeed, that God calls and rejects
how and whom He will. It was only in the future that an
attempt was made to treat the problem of a Christian's sinfulness in a definite and systematic way.

In addition to baptism, Paul speaks of a second sacrament,
the Lord's Supper. He did not regard the Supper as a simple
table-fellowship with the Risen Lord, as in the first church;
rather, it was the fulfilling of an institution founded by the
Lord Himself the last time He was with His disciples. Paul
had received from the Lord—and this can only have taken place
by means of a revelation—and had handed it on to the churches,[3]
that this common meal in particular was celebrated in memory
of Jesus, and that the death of the Lord was proclaimed by it
until He came. Nevertheless, it was more than a mere memorial
feast, such as was customary in many places elsewhere in the
ancient world. Rather it was similar to a sacrificial meal, since
those who took part entered into a mystic fellowship with one
another, and also with the Risen Lord in whose honour it was
celebrated. The fellowship made them one. The one food, the
one bread which they ate, bound them together and made
them into *one* body, the pneumatic body of Christ.[4] The
mystery of the Lord's Supper, thus understood, is similar to the
sacrament of baptism, but the operation is more graphic, for
the wine and bread are not common foods, but heavenly
nourishment. They are the blood and the body of the Risen
Lord, pneumatic substances which enter, with their miraculous
powers, into those who share the meal, transforming them into

[1] I Cor. 3: 15; 5: 5; 11: 32   [2] Rom. 8: 13; Gal. 5: 21; 6: 7 f.
[3] I Cor. 11: 23   [4] I Cor. 10: 16–21

the spiritual body of Christ. Woe to him who takes these essentially supermundane elements dishonourably, and as if they were ordinary food, for they will become poison in his body, and bring illness and death to such a wicked person.[1]

The possession of the spirit is, therefore, the peculiar characteristic of the Christian. How is it shown? The common opinion in the churches was that phenomena of exaltation of all kinds were to be regarded as its signs. There were manifold forms of religious enthusiasm, including the gift of "prophecy", i.e. inspired ecstatic speech that might rise to the level of revelations, and issue in heart-stirring searchings of the soul.[2] Among those who were specially gifted, enthusiasm might develop into that complete ecstasy which was connected with the apocalyptic vision of the heavenly spheres. Paul himself records, in awed humility, that, on one occasion, he had been caught up into the third heaven, had seen Paradise, and there heard inexpressible words.[3]

The gift of speaking with tongues, or glossolalia, was widespread. He who was thus uplifted by the spirit, uttered meaningless sounds, half-aware, or in complete unconsciousness, sounds which were regarded as the language of heavenly spirits and which were interpreted by those who were expert.[4] Paul had had a rich and personal experience of these utterances of the spirit, and esteemed them highly,[5] but he does not measure their value, as the majority did, by their strangeness, but by their significance for edifying the church. Glossolalia, with its excitements, was apparently much practised, but Paul would only tolerate it in the assembly of the church if someone was present who could interpret the "supernatural" language. Otherwise he would restrict its use to the private chamber of the individual concerned.[6] On the other hand, he paid high respect to the spirit-given words of a prophet delivered during Christian public worship. Naturally, he praises miracles and healings of the sick[7] as witnesses of the power of the spirit; but he also sees the spirit at work in the missionary preaching of itinerant apostles, in the Scriptural exegesis of the teachers, indeed even

---

[1] 1 Cor. 11: 27–30   [2] *Ibid.*, 12: 8–11; 14: 1–3, 24 f.   [3] 2 Cor. 12: 1–4
[4] 1 Cor. 14: 2, 9–11, 23   [5] *Ibid.*, 14: 1, 18, 39   [6] *Ibid.*, 14: 28
[7] *Ibid.*, 12: 9, 28

in the administering work of the presidents, and of those in the church who looked after the poor.[1] Moreover in the very connection where Paul instructed the Corinthians in this whole matter, and urged them to strive after ever higher gifts of the spirit, he called them to go beyond this kind of spiritual life, and walk in the way of love.[2] One could find the works of the spirit, in the usual sense, in places where the cymbals of the Great Mother re-echoed. There were many mysteries in which the angels spoke, and all sorts of secret wisdom were proclaimed. But where the spirit of Christ was to be found, love was the most valuable fruit.[3] Love gave meaning to all spiritual action and conduct, penetrated and consecrated the entire Christian life. Glossolalia, prophecy, and esoteric wisdom were only partial, vanishing with this present world. When perfection came, they would disappear; but faith, hope, and love would remain, these three—and the greatest of these was love. In this way, Paul planted his conception of Christianity among the religions of his time, and yet raised it to that mountain-height where Jesus preached of faith and hope, and that love of God which is fulfilled by loving one's neighbour. Elsewhere, Paul called it faith working itself out through love.[4] That is how the canticle of love, in 1 Cor. 13, was meant to be understood. Love was the purest expression of the spirit; in comparison everything else was of minor importance and without content. In the religious cross-currents of the times, this religion could only go under if it lost its soul.

Paul spoke to his contemporaries in their own language and from their own point of view. He made the gospel of salvation graphic by using the same pattern as the oriental, redemption religions, and he presented Christ in the form traditional for a saviour coming from heaven. Mankind was in bondage to a curse, an evil power, the dæmon of sin. Adam had sinned long ago in the garden of Eden, and the act of the primogenitor brought doom upon the whole of mankind. But, with God in heaven, there lived a "second Adam", the original man,[5] who came down on earth to redeem. He gave mankind a vital power which could loose them from their bonds, and bring them back

---

[1] 1 Cor. 12: 4–11, 28–30   [2] Ibid., 13: 1–13   [3] Cf. Gal. 5: 22
[4] Ibid., 5: 6   [5] 1 Cor. 15: 44–46

to God. This power was heavenly pneuma; it took up its abode in man, drove out the lower beings dominating his soul, and made him divine. Exactly so might an oriental mystagogue have spoken to his disciples, and both Gentile and Jewish hearers would find it easier to follow Paul when he spoke like this, than do twentieth-century students for whom it is difficult even to enter the atmosphere of such ways of thought. Yet we see how well adapted was this form of expression for winning men who were searching for redemption—the yearning desire of the age. It is of vital importance for understanding Paul's thought to notice that, no matter what forms of expression he used, they were never allowed to dominate their content, that content remained intact, and in full operation. In this respect, once more, those who came afterwards were not able to keep in step with the great Apostle. Rather they brought Christendom into the many dangers of which the history of dogma is full.

Although Paul laboured more than any other Apostle to free Christianity from Judaism, yet, in the bottom of his heart he remained faithful to his race and clung to it with profound affection. He found a theological basis for both sides of this attitude. Let us first consider the question of Christian freedom from the Law. The problem had been only half-solved at the convention in Jerusalem, and, as a consequence, the issue pursued him wherever he went. The law of Moses was holy, of divine origin[1] and expressed God's will for the whole of mankind, but it was a mistake to hold that it was fitted to point the way to salvation. Centuries of experience showed that no man was in a position to fulfil it, whereas only unconditional and unfailing obedience could endow man with the required righteousness before God. The tragic element in the history of the Jews was that, owing to a false estimate of the meaning of the Law, they pursued the delusive idea of salvation through their own righteousness. God's purpose in giving the Law was really quite other. Its prohibitions were meant to awaken and excite sin which dwelt in the flesh, compel it to show all its power, and thus make man conscious of his own powerlessness. Then, in doubt of his self-sufficiency, man would look towards God for

[1] Rom. 7: 1

rescue.[1] The Law was not a means of salvation, but had value only as a preparation; it was a "tutor bringing us unto Christ".[2] It left the man who understood its secrets in no manner of doubt about the case, for it prophesied its own abolition. With the appearance of Christ, faith replaced the Law as the genuine principle of salvation. Unlike the Law, faith did not require works upon works, but required the entire personality to yield itself up to the grace of God; it was the new life of the spirit.

Given this universal standpoint, the question could never again be raised whether the ceremonial law was to be separated, e.g. from the moral law, and so, perhaps, be regarded as of no effect. By its very nature, the entire Law was antiquated and had lost all its power over the new man. Its promises still held good, although they no longer applied to "Israel after the flesh", the physical descendants of Abraham, but to the true "Israel of God", i.e. the Christians, who, like Abraham, lived by their faith.[3] Jews and Gentiles, without distinction, were "children of Abraham" and heirs of the promises, in as far as they walked in the footsteps of his faith. With this construction, every national limitation of Christendom was set aside, every prerogative of Judaism was denied, and, at the same time, the Old Testament was claimed for the new universal religion as the sacred book of promises and prophecies.

Nevertheless, Paul could not find it in his heart without more ado to deny his people all pre-eminence, even if in the end they possesed only advantages of honour[4] such as the Holy Scriptures, the promises, the cultus, the name of "son", and the physical genealogy of Christ. Over against this, however, stood the dreadful and undeniable fact that the people of Israel, almost in its entirety, had refused the divine message of the gospel. Ought God to have rejected His people?[5] Paul did not think this conclusion could be drawn, and therefore he proposed a theory in the epistle to the Romans[6] which testified to his unmistakably warm love of his race, a love that was prepared to forgo his own salvation if only his race could be saved.[7] Paul proceeded to argue that God had temporarily hardened his race, and permitted only a small selection to

[1] Rom. 7: 7–25   [2] Gal. 3: 23–25   [3] *Ibid.*, 3: 6–9: 6, 16. Rom. 4: 1–25
[4] Rom. 3: 1–2; 9: 4 f.   [5] *Ibid.*, 11: 1   [6] *Ibid.*, 9–11   [7] *Ibid.*, 9: 3

attain salvation, whereas a multitude of Gentiles had come to
Christ. In the end, this would arouse envy in Israel, who would
then throw aside their blindness and become subject to Christ.
Thus, at last, God's mercy would comprehend all men, and
the whole of Israel would be saved. God had concluded all men
in disobedience only in order that He might have mercy upon
all. Hence behind the life-work of the Apostle to the Gentiles,
there lay the undiminished hope of future salvation for his own
race also, although for the present he must deny it.

This position in regard to the Law forms the basis of Paul's
theology, the foundation for his attitude in missionary praxis,
and for his totally refusing any legal requirements from the
Gentiles. From this standpoint, moreover, he could require
Jewish-Christians to forgo their ritual table-customs when
necessary, in order to express the unity of the Christian church,
and could sharply oppose Peter in Antioch when he attempted
to establish requirements to the contrary. If the Law had no
significance as a means of salvation, obedience to it could no
longer be made a duty of conscience. In particular, concessions
in this regard could easily endanger a true estimation of faith
among the Gentiles. Paul's letters show with what stubborn
persistence he opposed the many kinds of legal requirement.
He found it impossible to differentiate between the ceremonial
law which was antiquated and the moral law which still held
good unchanged, although such a differentiation characterized
the church at a later date; for him the Law was antiquated in
its totality just because it was law. The reborn man did not
need to read God's will in the book of the Law, for the spirit
would lead him into everything good and well-pleasing to
God; he need only yield himself to its leading. Naturally, the
intimations of the spirit would agree with the Decalogue, but,
in place of the Jewish legalism with its concern for details, was
the free activity of the Christian character as brought to life by
the spirit—this was the vital difference from Judaism. Therefore, in accordance with a saying of Jesus, the Apostle sum-
marized the Decalogue in the commandment to love one's
neighbour, and described love as the fulfilment of the Law.[1]
He followed the example of the Master in pressing forward

[1] Rom. 13: 9 f.; Gal. 5: 14; cf. Matt. 22: 37-40

from formalism to essence, from the letter to the spirit; for him
casuistry was dead. Understanding him in this way, we are
in a position to gain a true estimate of his meaning when he
occasionally speaks[1] of the "fulfilling of the Law" by those who
are reborn. On the other hand, we can see how those who
came later found here the backdoor through which they
brought the Law into credit again in the churches.

It was no contradiction of his general position that, on
occasion, he undertook a vow according to Jewish rite;[2] or
that, among Jewish Christians, he subjected himself to the prescriptions of the ceremonial law; or even that he was prepared,
on the advice of the original Apostles in Jerusalem, to carry out
a ceremonial vow in order to supply mistrustful brethren with
a proof of his faithfulness to the Law.[3] Here no confusion of
counsel was to be feared, and therefore, in accordance with his
fundamental missionary principle, he became a Jew to the
Jews, just as, in the outside world, he was free from the Law
among those who were free from the Law,[4] in order by one
means or another, to save souls.

[1] Rom. 8, 4, 13: 9; Gal. 5: 14, 6: 2; 1 Cor. 9: 21   [2] Acts 18: 18
[3] *Ibid.*, 21: 20–26   [4] 1 Cor. 9: 20

Chapter Eight

THE CHRISTIAN MISSIONARY CHURCHES

PAUL'S ACTIVITY COVERED A GENERATION BEGINNING FROM the death of the Lord and ending in the sixties, in the reign of Nero. This period has been rightly called the Apostolic Age, for in it the missionary labours of the first generation of disciples laid the foundations which were decisive for all the future. If we assemble the scattered notices which have been preserved in incidental records, we can see the broad outlines of the extent of Christendom.[1] On the other hand we have not the slightest information about the size of the churches or the nature of their constitution.

There were churches in Judea outside Jerusalem,[2] and similarly in Galilee and Samaria. Others were to be found in Lydda, and on the Plain of Sharon to the north, as well as in the coastal towns of Ashdod, Joppa, and Cæsarea. All this region was the missionary sphere of Philip "the Hellenist". We know further that the Hellenists, who had fled on account of the persecution of Stephen, carried on missionary work in Phœnicia, Cyprus, and Antioch, the capital of Syria; and that they developed the last named into a centre of Christianity free from the Mosaic law.[3] Here was the centre of the first mission to the Gentiles. It was here, as a consequence, that Christianity became so plainly distinct from Judaism that it was given its own Greek name. From then onwards, those who believed in Christ were called "Christians",[4]—naturally by those outside the movement, whether Jews or Gentiles. In Palestine the Christians were called "Nazorenes",[5] and this nickname was applied even to Jesus Himself, and this, not only by outsiders,[6] but also in the Christian church.[7] What it meant is still not clear in spite of much research on the subject.

We hear mention of Tyre, Sidon, and Ptolemais[8] as Phœnician cities with Christian churches.[9] We learn nothing more

[1] Harnack, *Mission*, ii, pp. 622–26   [2] Gal. 1: 22; Acts 9: 31; 8: 5; 14: 25; 9: 32–36
[3] *Vide supra*, p. 72   [4] Acts 11: 26   [5] *Ibid.*, 24: 5
[6] *Ibid.*, 6: 14; John 18: 5, 7; 19: 19; Luke 18: 37; Matt. 2: 23; 26: 71
[7] Acts 2: 22; 3: 6; 4: 10; 6: 14; 22: 8; 26: 9; Luke 24: 19
[8] Harnack, *Mission*, 1, 412, n. 1   [9] Acts 27: 3; 21: 3, 4, 7

about the work of the missionaries in Cyprus; and when Paul
at a later date visited the towns of Salamis and Paphos, he
began missionary work afresh.[1] Once more, however, nothing
is recorded about the success of the work. It would be helpful
to know more of Paul's activity in Cilicia and Syria, which he
himself mentions,[2] but neither he nor Acts gives us further information. Instead, exact details are given of numerous places
where Paul founded churches on his later missionary journeys.
They were scattered over a wide area. In the south of Asia
Minor, churches arose in Pisidia and Lycaonia, and, further to
the north, in Galatia. Ephesus constituted a new centre whence
Paul's disciples evangelized the Lycus valley, including the
cities of Laodicea, Colossæ, and Hierapolis. Possibly it is in this
period that we must place the beginnings of the churches of
western Asia Minor known to us from the Apocalypse: Pergamon, Thyatira, Sardis, Philadelphia, and Smyrna. Paul's
missionary journeys in Greece gave birth to churches in Philippi,
Thessalonica, Berœa, and Corinth with its port Cenchreæ. We
hear of no church in Athens before the second century, for the
record in Acts 17: 34 shows that the author was informed of
only the smallest beginning in Paul's time, and it is uncertain
whether this did not die out again. We must take it *cum salis*
when the Apostle says, in Rom. 15: 19, "from Jerusalem and
round about unto Illyricum I have fully preached the gospel",
for he means the western border of the orinet, and there is no
need to suppose that he actually went to Dalmatia.

It is surprising that there should have been quite a large
church in Rome even as early as the time when Paul wrote to
it. We have already expressed the view that it may have owed
its foundation to Antioch.[3] Paul's testimony[4] makes it certain
that it was Gentile Christian, a fact which excludes the possibility of its having been founded by Palestinian missionaries.

It is also a matter for surprise that even yet we should not
have the least information about the beginnings of Christianity
in Egypt. It is true that the Apollos of Acts and 1 Corinthians
came from Alexandria,[5] but we do not learn whether he
became a Christian there, or elsewhere. It is only towards the

[1] Acts 13: 5–12   [2] Gal. 1: 21; Acts 15: 23   [3] *Vide supra*, p. 111
[4] Rom. 1: 6   [5] Acts 18: 24

end of the second century that we hear of Alexandrian Christianity; by that time there was a large and virile church of whose history we know nothing at all. Records of a later date furnish grounds for supposing that the capital of Egypt received its Christianity from Rome. In the second century, the gnostic movement found very fertile soil in Egypt,[1] and left a deep mark even on the church catholic of Alexandria, but there is no record of events previously.

These numerous separate churches doubtless exhibited a host of differences in outer appearance and inner life. These differences derived not only from the personalities and the customs of their founders, but also from the geographical and ethnographical, the social and religious, conditions of their members. In general, the Christian missionaries made use of the methods which the Jews of the diaspora had adopted for their own communities, and for propagating their religion. Even if Acts here and there presents events as if they happened according to a stereotyped scheme, yet on the whole it undoubtedly reflects the actual procedure when it describes Paul and his companions travelling from one town to another, and beginning as a rule by preaching in the synagogues. What then followed must have been equally stereotyped, viz. sooner or later a conflict arose and the intruding teachers were driven out of the synagogues. Meanwhile they had made some converts, of whom a few were Jews, and more were proselytes. The nucleus of a Christian church was formed. Then contacts were made between proselytes and serious-minded Gentiles who in some places entered the church and became the majority; then they stamped their character upon it. The Christian message was understood, formulated, and then applied in practice, differing in each case according to the spiritual heritage which the believers had brought with them into the new fellowship.

We have already discussed the fundamental characteristics of the Jewish Christianity of the Jerusalem church, and of the Jewish communities which stood in closest connection with it. In regard to the Gentile churches of the Pauline type, we learn many details in the Pauline letters, especially in those to the Corinthians, which refer to many of the problems peculiar to

[1] Harnack, *Mission*, ii, 705 ff.

newly-founded churches. Most of the members of the Corinthian church belonged to the lower class, as Paul reminded them pretty plainly.[1] As there were also many poor people in the church at Jerusalem, there is reason to think that this state of affairs obtained generally. But we must not forget that members of a higher class also belonged to the same churches. In Corinth, Crispus had been the leader of the synagogue,[2] and, along with him, Paul mentions a certain Gaius as an eminent member of the church.[3] Later, Paul lived in his house,[4] just as he had enjoyed the hospitality of Titius Justus on his first visit.[5] These three persons were not poor, any more than the married couple, Aquila and Priscilla, who found work for Paul. Later they removed to Ephesus, where they possessed, or rented, a large house, and still later they gathered a "house-church" round themselves in Rome.[6]

The differences between poor and rich occasionally came to light in an unpleasant manner. Paul vigorously censured the custom[7] that, in the common love-feasts, the well-to-do should get together, and eat the good things they had brought with them, before the church was fully assembled; whereas the poor, who could not come punctually, nor bring well-filled baskets, had to go without. But there was no rooted hostility of the poor towards the prosperous, nothing of a "proletarian movement".

The only question raised was whether a Christian ought to liberate a slave of his who had become a Christian. Paul dealt with the question from the side of the slave, and explained to him that there would be no point in striving after the earthly freedom of a citizen if one lived in the freedom of Christ.[8] Even in writing to Philemon, it never crossed Paul's mind to come to final grips with the problem of slavery; he simply begged Philemon to receive back in a friendly way his runaway slave—who carried the letter—and to regard him no longer as a slave but as a brother, since, in between, he had become a Christian. Philemon could have done so by enfranchisement, or he might have interpreted the report in a purely human, and Christian,

[1] 1 Cor. 1: 26–28   [2] Acts 18: 8   [3] 1 Cor. 1: 14   [4] Rom. 16: 23
[5] Acts 18: 7   [6] Ibid., 18: 2–3; 1 Cor. 16: 19; Rom. 16: 3–5
[7] 1 Cor. 11: 21 f.   [8] Ibid., 7: 21–24

and non-juristic manner. In any case, it was Paul's view that adherence to Christ was not necessarily followed by a change of status; on the contrary, each was to remain in the condition in which he was called.[1]

Similarly in regard to the problem of marriage: the married man was not to think of divorce, nor the unmarried of marriage.[2] In Corinth, the marriage problem had disturbed the people's minds, and diametrically opposed answers had obviously been given. Many brought with them into their new Christianity the attitude of indifference to sexual relations which was all too characteristic of ancient times; they regarded intercourse with the opposite sex as the morally indifferent satisfaction of a natural requirement like eating and drinking. The traditional Jewish ethic must have already stood out against this view, but Paul increased the antithesis still further[3] by maintaining that a Christian's body was no longer at his own free disposal, but was the body of the Lord, and was profaned by union with a loose woman: an argument which brings out clearly the realistic character of his Christ-mysticism.

On the other hand, there were some Christians in Corinth who regarded all sexual intercourse as improper—even within marriage. This was an entirely un-Jewish point of view, although it was frequent in later antiquity as a consequence of dualistic philosophy. It was to be met among the Essenes, the Therapeutæ, and also in Hellenistic Judaism. These latter were influenced by various forms of Philonism. The prescriptions of sexual abstinence on grounds of cultus, which were to be found in the native religions, were also in harmony here. In both cases, the fundamental feeling was that sexual intercourse was in itself of lower moral value and unclean. It is significant that Paul completely agreed with this standpoint, and expressed his conviction, as if it were an axiom, that it was better for a man not to touch a woman. He emphasized his desire that all should be like himself, i.e. unmarried.[4] But he perceived that this was not possible, and therefore he recommended—as a concession to human weakness[5]—that existing marriages should be maintained; or, if the parties were unmarried, and if necessary for

[1] 1 Cor. 7: 20; cf. Col. 4: 1; 1 Tim. 6:   [2] 1 Cor. 7: 27   [3] *Ibid.*, 6: 15
[4] *Ibid.*, 7: 1; 7: 26   [5] *Ibid.*, 7: 6

avoiding irregular intercourse, that marriage should be entered into. It was not sin, but it led to sufferings and cares which were better avoided in those crucial days when the world was ageing and the End drawing nigh.[1] This view of marriage, in which Paul was at one with the most earnest sections of his church, gained the victory, and decided the whole attitude of the Church of the future. It was a question of opposition to "this world" to which marriage really belonged: any idea of uplifting marriage into the spiritual sphere, as among Stoic thinkers, was foreign to the Pauline horizon.

The church at Corinth made an experiment of another kind, one frequently imitated in the church universal of a later date. Granting that sexual life was of lower moral value, "spiritual marriages" were contracted, i.e. a man and a woman lived together in a house in spiritual and religious fellowship, but without sexual intercourse, a form of asceticism which probably often broke down under the pressure of outraged nature. Paul did not prohibit this custom, but advised those whose consciences were suffering, to change the common life into a true and full marriage if nature demanded it, and there would be no sin.[2]

Yet another marriage problem occupied the Corinthian church,—that of divorce, particularly in the case of mixed marriages. Divorce in those days was an extremely frequent, and legally quite a simple, matter; but what Jesus had said about the indissolubility of marriage was remembered in the Christian church, and it was therefore felt that a man who put his wife away, made her an adulteress.[3] Jesus' words were meant by Him to lay a serious charge on the conscience, but the Church treated it as a legal ordinance, and modified it to make it of practical application. Matthew inserted adultery by the wife as an exception which justified divorce.[4] Paul obviously interpreted the Lord's pronouncement quite freely, and with regard to the circumstances. The general rule held good, for him, that a man and his wife ought not to divorce their marriage; if, however, they did so, they must at least not marry anyone else, but rather become reconciled to one another. Even mixed marriages,

[1] 1 Cor. 7: 9, 26–31, 36   [2] *Ibid.*, 7: 25–28
[3] Mark 10: 6–12   [4] Matt. 19: 9; cf. also 5: 32 with Luke 16: 18

i.e. where one of the parties had remained a pagan, were not to be dissolved, at any rate not at the instance of the Christian spouse. In Paul's opinion, the "sanctity" of the latter partner passed over in some way to the other, as is certainly and admittedly the case among the children who belong to both. Thus Paul extended the idea of the mystical body of Christ into the conception of a naturalistic fact similarly to what we have already seen in the Apostle's teachings on the seventh Commandment.[1] But supernatural fellowship with Christ does not operate in a magical way, nor necessarily lead to the salvation of the pagan partner. If he should desire divorce then she need have no hesitation either from respect to the Lord's word, or because there was hope of her husband's conversion: let him go, since God has so ordained it for him![2] That was the Apostle's own view, and he distinguished it plainly from the Master's commandment.[3] These discussions plainly betray a distress of conscience in Paul as a man who has passed from the license of the world into the earnestness of the new æon; they also show Paul's realism as a mystical believer who wished to hold fast to the divine element among all the material circumstances.

Paul's way of handling an isolated case of sheer immorality is of similar import. A member of the church "hath his father's wife"—we are not told if it was an irregular marriage with the step-mother after the father's death, or something else. In any case, the apostle was angered that the church had not already excommunicated the evil-doer. The church must now assemble, Paul would be with them in spirit, and they must consign the sinner to Satan with a solemn curse in the power of Jesus' name. Satan would fall upon him as he did upon Job, as if the man had been a sacrifice dedicated to himself; he would torment him with illness and finally kill him. That will be his bodily punishment, but the spirit of Christ dwelling in the wrong-doer would finally be saved on the Day of the Lord.[4] This instance shows how the Church was beginning to develop its right to punish a sinner. In cases like these of serious transgression of the Christian moral code, the church in full assembly had the duty and the right of excommunication. The punishment

---

[1] 1 Cor. 7: 8–17; cf. 6: 15–16, and *supra*, p. 135   [2] 1 Cor. 7: 15–17
[3] *Ibid.*, 7: 10, 12   [4] *Ibid.*, 5: 1–5

however was not simply a formal, juristic exclusion from the fellowship, but was, at the same time, a sacramental cursing with supernatural effects. Expulsion from the circle of the elect "saints" handed the sinner over to dæmonic powers and grievous punishments, but they did not deprive him of that redemptive nucleus of divine substance which still dwelt in him even when profaned by him, for it was indestructible, and would ultimately regain its due honour. Thus ecclesiastical law had come into existence at this early stage.

A further question that troubled the Corinthians was that of civil law. Even in this young community of Christian brothers, legal dispute arose about money and property: that in itself was bad enough, writes the Apostle,[1] among Christians who should rather suffer wrong than do it. But it was altogether unfitting that the contending parties should resort to secular courts—as if they themselves were pagan. Their past, of course, made it seem natural and unexceptionable to them. Paul, however, was a Jew, and his tradition[2] was to bring cases to the courts of his fellow-countrymen and his fellow-believers, and thus it appeared to him only right that the same custom should be unconditionally required also of self-respecting Christians. He gave the reason for this demand, however, not by referring to the Jewish custom, which would have helped little, but by insisting that the Christian had a higher status on which to act as judge than that of the whole world beside, including the very angels. Everything was subject to the judgment of the "saints". This being so, ought they at any time and for any reason to recognize pagans as judges over them? No! only Christians could judge Christians; and people expert in the particular issue would be found in the church. As a matter of fact, they were so found in the course of time, and the claim to exercise intra-ecclesiastical justice was maintained even in civil cases. But it is significant that a *corpus juris civilis christianum* was never developed, whereas the Jews codified, in the Talmud, a complete system of civil law.

The discussions of the seventh Commandment already mentioned[3] must have been occasioned by the requirements of the

---

[1] I Cor. 6: 7–8   [2] *Vide supra*, pp. 77 f.
[3] *Vide supra*, pp. 136 f.

Apostolic Decree,[1] for it prohibited fornication. The assumption becomes very probable when we also notice that the prohibition of eating sacrificial meat, which occupies the premier place in the Decree,[2] had raised ill-feeling in Corinth. Strictly speaking, all meat offered for public sale was sacrificial meat, for pagans, too, slaughtered "ritually", and dealt with all slaughter-animals as if they were sacrificial. One would have had to buy *kosher* meat from a Jewish slaughterer to be sure of avoiding sacrificial meat, and there is no need to say that that appears to have been impracticable. The idea of having their own slaughter-house would only have occurred to a church which felt itself firmer on the earth than did the first Christians. Hence there would be genuine difficulty if the prohibition were interpreted strictly, and the stronger members of the church would not wish to have anything to do with this narrowness, and would regard it as a piece of formality that ought not to be tolerated. They would feel that there were no "gods" but only the one God, and even if the pagan gods were really believed in as dæmons, still to Christians there was only the one God, the Creator of the world, and the one Lord, Jesus Christ. Such a faith meant that the idea of worshipping idols found no place in one's heart, and thus the eating of meat which happened to come from a sacrificial animal was quite an indifferent matter which it was foolish to forbid. Paul agreed, within limits, and gave practical advice for avoiding the difficulty. A Christian might in good conscience eat anything offered for sale in the meat markets, and could unconcernedly accept the invitation of a pagan friend to a meal in his house. But if this obvious course were disturbed, one should be on guard. If a joint be explicitly described as of sacrificial meat, and if one's attitude were thus being put to the test, then it became a matter of conscience and one must refuse to eat. If this were not necessary for the sake of one's own conscience, then it should be done out of regard for the weaker brethren to whom sacrificial meat was still in the nature of an offering to the old gods, and therefore a dangerous matter with noxious qualities for a Christian.

[1] Acts 15: 29; 21: 25   [2] *Vide supra*, pp. 108 f.; and also Rev. 2: 14, 20 mentions only these two prohibitions since "sacrificial meat" includes the remainder

This fear did not appear to Paul to be altogether groundless, for even he still regarded the gods as actually existent beings of a dæmonic kind. He who sat at their table for a sacrificial meal, entered into their magic circle and gave himself to their fellowship, i.e. would be possessed by them. Similarly, *mutatis mutandis*, a Christian sitting at the table of the Lord and partaking of the holy meal, became a partner of his Master, became indeed His body, and a participator in His spirit, for Christ had taken up His abode in him. Thus the one fellowship excluded the other. Therefore, according to the Apostle's view, the eating of sacrificial meat was never a neutral action when done in cult-form, for thereby the dæmons gained their destructive power. Thus a Christian might in no circumstances accept an invitation to a sacrificial banquet. And in both respects, as permission and as prohibition, this instruction of Paul's became normative for the entire early church.[1]

The problem just discussed brings us once more into the sphere of a realistic kind of mysticism, which comprehended both the pagan and the Christian cultus in a single set of principles. The Lord's Supper appeared as the Christian sacrificial meal and effected a mystic fellowship with Jesus analogous to the fellowship which the pagan theologians deduced from table-fellowship with their gods;[2] for the idea of the sacredness of a sacrificial meal, and its power of making the participators into brethren, derives from the prehistoric roots of nature religion. What Paul says on this subject could count on being understood in the churches because it was born of their own way of thinking. His mystical sacramentalism,[3] in regard to both the Lord's Supper and baptism, was in the closest contact with the belief of the church of these "Hellenists", and would be readily accepted by them, and, indeed, easily degraded into a rude realism. Baptism must surely have appeared to many a Corinthian gentile Christian as an infallible means of purging away sin, and as a guarantee of future salvation: we only need to carry through Paul's expressive parallel of the death and resurrection of Christ. The "old man" sinking in the water dies the death of Christ, and the "new man" rising from the water,

---

[1] Just., *Dial.*, 34, 8–35, 1. *Didache*, 6, 3
[2] *Handb. z. N.T.*, Excursus on 1 Cor. 10: 21   [3] *Vide supra*, pp. 121 f.

the Christian, receives the resurrection of Christ, and is thereby delivered from all further moral struggle; once for all he is now saved and assured of salvation. This argument accorded quite logically with the system of thought of the ancient mysticism of redemption—and Paul had to wrestle seriously with such arguments. He cited the example of Israel as a warning; they had enjoyed the benefits of baptism in the Red Sea, a heavenly meal of manna, and a miraculous spring in the wilderness. This was not, as it were, a mere symbol, but a pneumatic reality, for the rock out of which Moses struck the water was Christ Himself! Nevertheless the Israelites perished because they sinned against God and, in particular—let the Corinthians take note—by idol sacrifice, immorality, expressing doubts, and murmuring against God. Their sins wiped out the good effect of the sacraments:[1] and the same could happen again even now to every Christian.

The crudely magical way in which the Corinthians conceived the sacrament was shown by a strange custom which Paul mentioned in passing. If a convert died before receiving baptism, another let himself be baptized "for him". We do not know in what form this took place, but we have evidence from a later period in regard to a similar custom. The corpse was baptized, and another person gave the answers to the liturgical questions instead of the dead. In many places, even the Lord's Supper was administered to the dead man.[2] These ideas prevailed in Corinth, and tended to tone Christianity down to a nature religion. In spite of the fact that all his own ways of thinking were rooted in the same type of ideas, Paul defended himself against them with all his might, and strove in the opposite direction.

Probably derived also from pagan usage[3] in the cultus, was the view that the new initiate stood in particularly close mystic union with the missionary who had administered to him the sacrament of baptism. In this way, little personal communities might have arisen in the Corinthian church, who felt themselves linked to their spiritual father by religious bonds, and not merely by those of sentiment—a feature which, of course,

[1] 1 Cor. 10: 1–12   [2] *Handb. N.T.*, Excursus on 1 Cor. 15: 29
[3] Reitzenstein, *Hell. Myst.*, 3rd edition, 40

was out of accord with the Pauline doctrine that the whole church was the one mystical body of Christ. Paul attacked this forming of cliques or parties on more than one ground. The point of view, which has just been described, he set aside with the sharp words:[1] "I thank God, I baptized none of you except Crispus and Gaius, so that none of you can say you have been baptized in my name." He had both preached and organized in Corinth—for one and a half years. But he had baptized very few people, and even those only in the very first period: Stephen who was the first convert,[2] Crispus who was the leader of the synagogue,[3] and a certain Gaius with whom later on he lodged;[4] "for Christ did not send me to baptize, but to preach the gospel". That is a crucial assertion for our understanding of Paul's inmost being, for this practical attitude of his chimes with all he had expressed in writing. For him, all sacramental mysticisms, like all pneumatic enthusiasms, were secondary. Even if he valued these things as means of raising moral conduct to a high level, and even if he gave a true explanation of them to his readers, he used them only because they served to give a graphic representation of the nature of the "new creature", as firmly united with God. But he dropped them as soon as they began to endanger this objective. The people in the church conceived the matter in the opposite way, and held readily to a formalistic sacramentarianism. This made the person of the baptizer particularly important to them; and Apollos the learned Alexandrian, as well as Peter, gained adherents from this standpoint during their work in Corinth. It followed that they themselves must have frequently baptized. If Paul did not do so, the question arises: Who then baptized the converts made by him? Possibly Timothy or Silas? Or even Corinthian Christians, and if so, on what authority? Unfortunately no answer is forthcoming, important though it might be for the origins of spiritual offices.

Paul's letters are particularly important in reflecting various details in regard to Christian officials; they are often enumerated by him,[5] and at their head stand apostles, prophets, teachers. These were the original officials of the Christian

---

[1] 1 Cor. 1: 14–17   [2] *Ibid.*, 1: 16; 16: 15   [3] *Ibid.*, 1: 14; Acts 18: 8
[4] 1 Cor. 1: 14; Rom. 16: 23   [5] 1 Cor. 12: 28; Rom. 12: 6–9

church, and they were maintained as such until the beginning of the second century; the Church Order of the *Didache*, which belongs to this period, affords us the best commentary on Paul's words.[1] The apostles or evangelists travelled about in the world, and preached to those who were still unbelievers; they had no permanent place, because their task was inconsistent with their remaining settled. The prophets, however, worked continuously in one place; they were filled with the divine spirit, and preached to the church as messengers of a higher revelation. They prayed for and with them, but also saw visions, prophesied, and read what was in one's secret heart. They were the "priests in charge" of the church, and conducted its worship as the spirit prompted them. Similarly the teachers addressed the church as heralds of the Word, the visionary and ecstatic types of enthusiasm being little practised by them. Their special function was the explanation of the Scriptures on a basis of reasoning, and pedagogical instruction of a theological kind, even if for the most part in a very primitive form. All these three offices required the entire devotion of the whole of a man's strength and left no room for a secular calling. Hence the officers had a claim upon the churches for their livelihood. The *Didache* sketches this picture, and it agrees with much other evidence from the earliest period.[2]

The distinctions between the different officials were not sharply made, and Paul's mode of expression shows clearly that he was entirely unacquainted with any definite system. It is clear, however, that the terminology was borrowed from the Jewish diaspora.[3] Apostles was the name given by the Jews to the official emissaries who brought the commissions of one congregation, especially that in Jerusalem, to another; the term was used occasionally by Paul in this way.[4] Then in earliest Christendom, the emissaries of the gospel, and especially those who went out from Jerusalem, were described in this way as "apostles of the original church". Paul's right to this title was energetically contested because he could not boast of a Jerusalem commission. He therefore boldly called himself an apostle of Jesus Christ, and insisted that he was, indeed, not

---

[1] *Didache*, 11–15. *Z.W.T.*, 55, 108 ff.   [2] Harnack, *Mission*, i, 332–79
[3] *Ibid.*, i, 340. *Handb. z. N.T.*, Excursus on Rom. 1: 1   [4] Phil. 2: 25; 2 Cor. 8:

sent by the Jerusalem church, i.e., by human agency, but had received his commission directly from the Lord Himself.[1] He maintained his position; and soon phraseology began to follow the Pauline model, and named as "apostles" only those disciples who had been called by the Lord Himself, including Paul together with the Twelve. Side by side with this usage, for a long time there remained in existence the older custom which continued to designate every missionary as an apostle.

It requires no proof to show that the office of a teacher, with his task of explaining the Scriptures, was taken over from the Jewish synagogue; and that the office inherited from the Jewish community the high honour in which it was held. On the other hand, we know nothing of a Jewish office of prophets[2] in the time of the early empire. To the Jews of those days, the prophets were either the great Biblical figures of the past, or else, at least in the eyes of the people, outstanding men of God in the present. That was how they regarded John the Baptist, or Jesus, or, here and there, someone who proclaimed the future, and knew how to gain the respect of the masses, even if the Scribes took no official notice. Josephus often tells of such prophets, both true and false.[3] They used to arise in a manner which reminds us in every way of those prophets who came from Jerusalem to Antioch, and prophesied to the church there. The most important of them, Agabos, appeared again, years later, in Judea.[4] The connection between the Christian and Jewish prophets of that time is thus quite clear. But there can be no doubt that the character even of the Jewish type of prophets was affected by those whose religion was Hellenistic, and this influence must have extended also among the Christian prophets. Pagan religious societies had prophets as leaders of public worship, a custom which became usual among the Christians. We can see the beginning of the process in the Pauline period. The record of Acts[5] in regard to the church in Antioch is very instructive. At the head we find "prophets and teachers", and these, at the command of the Holy Spirit, chose two men from their number to be "apostles". Thus three kinds

[1] Gal. 1: 1   [2] E. Fascher, *Prophetes*, 161 ff.
[3] Jos., *Ant.*, 15, 373 f., 20, 97; *B.*, 1, 78–80 =*Ant.*, 13, 311–13, *B.*, 2, 259–261 = *Ant.*, 20, 167–170, *B.*, 6, 285 f.
[4] Acts 11: 27–30; 21: 10   [5] Acts 13: 1–3

of officers were known before Paul, but the distinctions between them were still fluid. Moreover, these offices were not instituted by men, but by God; they were "charismatic", i.e. dependent upon a special gift of divine grace. He whom God chose by imparting His own spirit was a teacher, prophet, or apostle; and without this "charisma" no one could exercise the office.

In addition to the spiritual officers who served Christendom as a whole, were others who came into place owing to the needs of daily life, and who, in spite of occasional idealization, really resulted from the sociological circumstances of individual churches. Wherever men unite to form a society a means of conducting business must be devised. Outer organization and financial economy require to be dealt with in a practical manner by appropriate persons. Paul frequently speaks of such persons as "helpers", "leaders", "presidents", "servants", and "those who show mercy". In the opening salutation of Philippians (1: 1), are the characteristic titles of certain offices that became normative for the future: "bishops" and "deacons". Their task was to care for the secular business of the individual church, including the prime concern of looking after those in need. We cannot say with certainty how these titles arose, but it appears to be certain that they were not adapted from Jewish usage. Nor do we gain much light from the analogies which have been adduced from mundane spheres or from the religious organizations of the pagan world. The simplest assumption is that the names were freely given on the model of some leading place—one might readily think of Antioch, and that thence they were adopted by the rest of the Gentile-Christian churches. "Bishop" means "overseer" in all the innumerable applications of the term. The business heads of the church, to whom the finances were confided, might easily be named in this way. "Deacon" means "servant", and in particular, one who serves at table, a waiter. Perhaps this gives a hint of the original significance of the office. The deacons served the church at the Lord's Supper,[1] and carried the bread and wine to the homes of those who were absent. These absent ones were mostly, and as a rule, the sick; and thus the deacons combined their special office with that of looking after the sick. In practice

[1] Ignat., *Trall.*, 2, 3; cf. Just., *Apol.*, 65, 5, 67, 5

therefore, they became the assistants of the bishops in discharging services of love to all the members of the church who were in need. According to the *Didache*[1] both these offices were conferred by election, and it must have been the same in the times of Paul. Naturally, in the way the choice fell, was seen the verdict of the spirit working in the church. Paul ever and again described, and taught his readers to value these offices of Christian works of love as of a charismatic character, for the help of the divine spirit was needed to carry them out. Nevertheless, there was a difference for the simple observer, in so far as the bishops and deacons could be chosen from amongst the known men of the church, and what was required of them did not go beyond the capacities of an ordinary person. The charismatics, on the other hand, were supermen to whom God had granted miraculous powers. They saw what no human eye was in a condition to see, and they spoke what was higher than any reason; in addition—they worked miracles; healing the sick[2] and exorcizing dæmons were for a long time afterwards the signs of a genuine charismatic gift. Only the charismatics were officers of the church of God which embraced the whole world, the one church of Christ. The bishops and deacons were merely assistants in the service of the local church, i.e. of an accidental institution existing under mundane conditions, with no independent life-force in the Christian sense. These men were of lower status and lesser authority.[3]

Work in the service of the church was not confined to men. Paul calls[4] an obviously well-to-do and philanthropic lady, named Phœbe, a "deacon" of the church at Cenchreæ, the port of Corinth. Even at that time, there had long been women deacons in the Christian church[5] who, when their sex made them specially suitable, came forward and gave signal help in caring for the poor and the sick, and at the baptism of women. But women also shared in the higher gifts of the spirit. Philip the evangelist had four daughters who were prophetesses,[6] and obviously in the Montanist movement of the second century, women prophets appeared again. In reality, they had never died out from the church, but, under other names and without the

[1] *Did.*, 15, 1   [2] 1 Cor. 12: 28–30   [3] *Did.*, 15, 2   [4] Rom. 16: 1
[5] Hinschius, *Kirchenrecht.*, i, 8   [6] Acts 21: 9

official character enjoyed in early Christendom, they have continued to the present day. Thus, even in the Corinthian church, there were women who had been seized by the spirit, who prophesied, and led in prayer. Paul did not agree, for although he held in theory that "in Christ, there is neither Jew nor Greek, neither slave nor freeman, neither male nor female",[1] nevertheless, in practice, he held firmly that woman was subject to man by a divine ordinance in creation. He therefore required that a woman prophet should wear a veil as a sign of this condition, and he put forward this requirement as the general custom in the Christian churches.[2] But in another connection, his own view came unreservedly to expression: a woman must maintain complete silence in the assemblies of the church, and if she wished to know anything, she might ask her husband at home; this also was to him the recognized Christian custom.[3] These views agree with each other, for Paul's point was that, in general, a Christian woman in the assemblies for public worship was condemned to an entirely passive rôle, corresponding with the goodly custom among both Gentiles and Jews. But if the prophetic spirit should seize a woman, then no one was empowered to silence her, or rather, the spirit speaking through her. On the other hand, she must at least veil herself in order to satisfy custom.

What then really happened in the assemblies for worship among the missionary churches? Was there a definite liturgical order, and whence did it come? Out of Judaism, or paganism, or was it a complete novelty? Satisfactory answers have not yet been provided for the many questions that have been raised. There is little or no information about the liturgy in the early writers; probably this was because such matters seemed too self-evident to need recording. Nor would Paul have discussed any of these if disorders had not arisen in Corinth causing him to issue exhortations and to give directions. The gifts of the spirit were a prominent feature in this church, and that in their enthusiastic form.[4] Glossolalia was cultivated eagerly and practised without restraint, and this in such a manner that, at times, several persons were simultaneously seized by it. Paul vigorously

---

[1] Gal. 3: 28   [2] 1 Cor. 11: 3–16   [3] Ibid., 14: 33–35
[4] Vide supra, p. 125

attacks this state of affairs;[1] one must take turn after another, and, in one and the same meeting, only two or at most three prophets. The same held good for those who "speak in tongues"; for them there was the further condition that someone must be present who could interpret their utterances. Otherwise glossolalia must not be practised in the church; for the purpose of public worship was to "edify" the church. What did not serve this end, but only furthered private devotions, must now cease. It was from this standpoint that everything was to be judged which an individual might have to offer, whether prophetic speech giving a revelation, didactic instruction, glossolalia with accompanying interpretation, or hymn singing. "And everything should take place in the appropriate form and in order." We are driven to the conclusion that order was not the strong point of the Corinthians, and that their services must have sometimes been quite tumultuous. But we shall do well not to generalize from the circumstances in Corinth. We ought not even to regard the strongly marked over-emphasis on ecstatic enthusiasm as characteristic in this degree of all churches. There must have been very great differences in this respect.

From the hints which Paul lets fall, we may almost gain the impression that there were no fixed orders of public worship, but that prophetic utterance, glossolalia, didactic addresses, prayer, and singing were contributed according as the spirit led individuals. Nothing is said of Scripture-reading in any of the epistles. Thus it is possible that as a matter of fact the actual order of worship by prayers and hymns, in these early churches, was developed independently out of the actual needs of Christian teaching and of general edification. All this would be without fixed forms, but such as were settled each time by the needs of the moment. Attention has been drawn[2] to the fact that the Hebrew synagogues of the period did not sing any of the Psalms, but that, on the other hand, the practices of the synagogues of the Talmud, and the Hellenistic synagogues of the diaspora, differed greatly from each other. In this matter, however, we are in the happy situation of being able to refer to extant writings. There still survive a number of early

[1] 1 Cor. 14: 26–40   [2] W. Bauer, *Wortgottesdienst*, 21, 11

Christian psalms composed on the model of those in the Old Testament, and having direct parallels in the Psalms of Solomon. Three hymns of this character are preserved in Luke's gospel,[1] Mary's hymn of praise, that of Zacharias, and that of Simeon. In the Revelation of John we find a large number of hymns voiced by the heavenly choirs in counterpart to the earthly services of Christian worship. Most of these are not modelled on Jewish exemplars, but genuinely Jewish hymns without any specific Christian characteristics.[2] They cannot be regarded as original Christian compositions; rather, they are apparently hymns used in the Greek synagogue of the diaspora, and taken over by the Christians. Later, following these examples, genuinely Christian hymns were composed such as other passages in Revelation have preserved,[3] the secondary element being readily traceable. Here we can detect contacts with the forms of worship in the Hellenistic synagogue—the one case where texts are at our disposal. If sermons by prophets or teachers had been preserved we should probably have been able to penetrate further into the study of the liturgy.

The Christian churches would seem to have broken new ground, however, when they drew up formulas of a credal nature expressing their beliefs about the Lord and the redemption He had effected. The most impressive are to be found in the great Christological passages in Philippians, 1 Timothy, and 1 Peter.[4] These are only beginnings, followed by important developments finally issuing in the official creeds; and this not only in the "Apostles' Creed", but also in numerous creeds drawn up much more nearly in the form of hymns.[5]

Thus there is at least the possibility of gaining some conception of the "psalms, hymns, and spiritual songs" which were heard in the early churches;[6] they were all very similar to those used in Jewish forms of worship. But where we tread upon gnostic ground, as in the *Acts of Thomas*,[7] the influences of an

---

[1] Luke 1: 46–55, 68–79; 2: 29–32. Gunkel in the *Festgabe für Harnack* (1921), 43–60
[2] Rev. 4: 8, 11; 15: 3–4, and the double choruses in 11: 15, 17–18 and 7: 10, 12 (where only "the Lamb" is interpolated)
[3] Rev. 12: 10–12, 19: 1–2, 5, 6–8
[4] Phil. 2: 5–11; 1 Tim. 3: 16; 1 Pet. 3: 18–32
[5] Lietzmann in the *Festgabe für Harnack* (1921), 226–42
[6] Col. 3: 16; Eph. 5: 19   [7] *Acta Thomæ*, 6–7, 108–13

exotic religion are open to our hand. Christian poetry soon grew to great proportions in this environment, whereas it died away in the normative church catholic.

At any rate, our observation of the further development of the forms of Christian public worship teaches that though the churches were apparently not fettered as to their liturgy, but possessed a freedom conferred by the spirit, yet they did not produce new and peculiarly Christian forms of service; rather they lost all originality. The earliest period was marked by the tempestuous working of the spirit. But, as a rule, the Christian churches soon adopted the forms used by the Hellenistic synagogues, and they constitute the foundation of Christian public worship to the present day. The diets of worship were not only suited for the edification of the church proper, but, similarly to the services of the synagogue, could also be attended by unbelievers who might become converts to the new teaching. Side by side with the diets stood the celebration of the Lord's Supper, as a cultus-act properly so-called, and here, as in the Jewish ceremonial meals, only the members of the church might take part.[1] We have already seen[2] how Paul taught his believers to observe this feast. It was always held in the evening;[3] it was attended as the love-feast of the church; and each one contributed according to his means.

The Lord's Supper commenced with a blessing, followed by the breaking of a loaf, the pieces of which were distributed to be ritually eaten by the participators. All who ate of this bread, which was the body of Christ, became united in one body among themselves, the body of Christ.[4] Then began the meal proper, which ran its course in agreeable fellowship, and due enjoyment of the food and drink. After the meal, the president pronounced a blessing upon a glass of wine, and gave it to them all to drink—they now drank the blood of Christ. From the feast of the Lord's Supper celebrated in this way, many of the greetings must originate that we find in the Pauline letters, or that are preserved in later formularies as their earliest liturgical material; e.g. "Lift up your hearts," cried the liturgist to the church which had sat down to the meal while still burdened by the cares of the day. The exhortation frequently met with in

[1] *Did.*, 9, 5   [2] *Vide supra*, pp. 124 f.   [3] 1 Cor. 11: 20–34   [4] *Ibid.*, 10: 17

the conclusion of the Pauline letters:[1] "Greet one another with the holy kiss", urged the Christians to unite with one another in a conciliatory attitude of mind, as enjoined by Matt. 5: 23 f., and in brotherly love before making the sacrifice.[2] The greeting: "The grace of our Lord, Jesus Christ, and the love of God, and the fellowship of the Holy Spirit be with you all," was well fitted to introduce the sacred ritual proper. The church would then respond: "and with your spirit" as it does to-day. Since we find this formula at the end of 2 Corinthians[3] we may conclude that the letter was intended to be read aloud in a "closed" assembly of the church, and that the celebration of the Lord's Supper was to follow the reading.[4] Presumably, the custom held similarly with regard to the writings addressed to the whole church.

The circumstances reflected in the story of Paul's life, show that there was a marked cleavage in early Christianity. On the one side was the Jewish-Christian church at Jerusalem, conscious of its roots in Judaism, and true to the Law in a way that constantly threatened it with a Pharisaic narrowness. On the other side, was the decided repudiation of Jewish ritual, in accordance with the preaching of the Antiochene Hellenists, and of Paul. We have already shown that the solution reached in the compromise of the Apostolic Decree,[5] was intended to form a basis for bridging the cleavages in the churches of the diaspora. This Decree of the Jerusalem church was known in Corinth about the year A.D. 52. We may well suppose that Peter brought it there, and thus to have occasioned the discussion into which Paul enters in his first epistle. If so, then Peter stood for compromise as far as the Judaizers were concerned.[6] The Decree conceded to the Gentiles freedom from the Law, and burdened them only with a single ritual requirement so as to enable Jewish Christians to enjoy table-fellowship with them. On the other hand, the Pauline requirements went further by demanding full freedom from the Law, and his theory was that Jewish Christians were likewise free. His views were set aside tacitly by the Decree, but, we may suppose,

[1] Rom. 16: 16; 1 Cor. 16: 20; 2 Cor. 13: 12; 1 Thess. 5: 26, cf. 1 Pet. 5: 4
[2] *Didache*, 14, 1–3   [3] 2 Cor. 13: 13   [4] Lietzmann, *Messe u. Herrenmahl*, 229
[5] *Vide supra*, pp. 108 f.   [6] Hirsch, *Z.N.W.*, 29, 67 ff.

definitely and clearly so in the course of the negotiations among the churches. This meant, however, that Paul's apostolic authority was contested. In the young church at Corinth, various parties were formed; each adhered to the person of some leader. Those who were faithful to Paul opposed the adherents of Peter. The third group mentioned is the Apollos party, who may be regarded as those having a turn for philosophy, for Apollos was an Alexandrian, and a learned man. To them, the Pauline theology of the cross was intolerable,[1] because they sought a rational foundation for the new faith, and one that would appeal to the Greek spirit. Finally, Paul mentions a fourth party in Corinth. They named themselves "of Christ", in emphatic distinction from the others, obviously because they would not allow that Paul and the other leaders were sufficient authorities, and because they relied upon alleged revelations given by the Risen Lord. As against this party, Paul remarked with a certain irony that he himself really belonged to Christ as much as certain other people, and that he himself had been blessed in high degree with divine revelations.[2] Thus the most varied tendencies wrestled with each other in this church: ecstatic enthusiasm, Hellenistic "wisdom", the Pauline doctrine of freedom, and the Petrine semi-Judaism. The last was particularly dangerous to Paul's plain requirements, because its aim was to appease Jerusalem, a policy which threatened to ruin the success of his life's work. Paul did not wish merely to keep the Gentiles free from the Law—in Galatians he had passionately struggled for this and against the Jewish emissaries—but also to win the Jews over to the new freedom of the children of God. To him, Christ was nothing else than the end of the Law, for Jews and Gentiles alike, and that was what he laid down before the Roman church in his weightiest epistle.

The Pauline letters afford only incidental glimpses of this contest between old and new, but they make it possible for us to surmise with what passion and earnestness the struggles were being fought everywhere in the numerous churches of the newly-won Gentile Christians, viz. those founded by Paul, the missionary churches of Barnabas and the other Hellenists,

[1] 1 Cor. 2: 1–5   [2] *Ibid.*, 10: 7; 12: 1–4

including the important church of Rome. All of these churches had to settle their attitude to the question of the Law, and did so, as the future was to show, in the sense of freedom from it. Jewish radicalism, in the matter of the Gentile churches, had had an isolated success in Galatia and perhaps also at an earlier date in Antioch; but it had no future, and served only to keep Jewish Christians faithful to the Law. As time went on, it was, in practice, more and more confined to the churches in Palestine and its immediate surroundings. In the empire beyond, the Gentile Christians were free, and they attracted Jewish converts to themselves.

Other and smaller questions continued to disturb consciences —about the worthiness and necessity of asceticism of various forms, including abstinence from wine, and vegetarianism,[1] the latter being frequent and regarded as devout among widely differing kinds of people at that time. With the advent of Apollos, arose the question of the attitude of the young religion to Greek philosophy, and educated Christians were always troubled by the problem. Paul's disciple, Epaphroditus, laboured as a missionary in the Lycus valley, and founded churches in Colossæ and Laodicea. There, in Phrygia, spirits rose up out of the ground, and through the swelling clouds of syncretistic speculation, the phantom of gnosticism already showed its enigmatic face, to the wrath of Paul as he lay in prison.[2] The Apostolic Age, with its simple antitheses and its broad outlines, was drawing to an end, and the omens of a new period were visible on the horizon.

[1] Cf. *Handb. z. N.T.*, Excursus on Rom. 14:1   [2] *Op. cit.*, Excursus on Col. 2:23

Chapter Nine

THE ROMAN EMPIRE AND ITS RELIGIOUS LIFE

THE BATTLE OF ACTIUM HAD BEEN FOUGHT, THE LEUCADIAN
Apollo had pressed the myrtle of victory upon the brow
of Octavian, and Cleopatra had chosen death. There was an
end to the century-old struggle which the Greek world, in conjunction with the orient, had fought against Roman encircle-
ment. Once for all Rome had conquered, and from mud,
destruction, and blood, arose the miracle of the statecraft of
Augustus, the empire of peace which comprised the whole
world, the Imperium Romanum. Its material foundation was
assured by the army, which had been trained in the ancient
Roman tradition and by the magnificently organized system of
administration. Its soul, however, was the "Latin genius"
which was born in these days. The gift of oratory and a turn
for practical philosophy had been put into swaddling clothes by
Cicero. But a simple conception of life, a healthy understanding
of human nature, a flair for politics and law, a sense of form
and value, were its heritage from ancient times. Livy now
endowed it with a glorious history and a mythology of an
origin from heroes. Horace originated a lyric poetry, which
combined a sunny enjoyment of life with meditation and fine
patriotism. Ovid added to this compound the charming
elements of a graceful eroticism, until bitter experiences drove
him into the arms of a more learned Muse. But Virgil, above
all others, understood the deepest nature of his people when he
sang to them the saga of the Æneid, which the Romans were
never tired of reciting as if inspired, and the images of which
stir the hearts of the Latin races to the present day. It is indeed
the case that the reign of Augustus not only saw Jesus born,
but also that Latin genius which for nineteen centuries has
determined the history of Europe.

But Horace was right. The Greeks, who had been conquered
by the soldiers, had long gained a spiritual victory over the
conquerors; for when the world empire arose, the Latin genius
had not only been suckled with Greek milk, and educated at the

Greek school, but had clothed its native religion in a Greek garment. Elements which were not now at home sank into oblivion. But cultured people in Rome had learned from Greek philosophy how to apply rationalistic criticism fully to traditional religion. When, therefore, the dreadful decades of the Civil War had destroyed all the ethical foundations of public and private life, religious feeling and practice had also suffered very severe damage.

It is a highly valuable testimony to the statesmanlike genius of Augustus that he regarded the restoration of a sound religion as one of his most urgent tasks. And it is characteristic of his practical sense that he did not command sermons to be addressed to the people, but that he reinstated, in large degree, the ancestral religion as a state function. He rebuilt the ruined temples and, by means of ceremonial worship, sought to win the masses of spectators to take some part. In this way, the lost religion was to be given from above to the people. It was the right way, but there would have had to be a genuine religion in the upper circles if it was to penetrate below. This was not the case. The æsthetic mythology of Horace, which was instinct with genuine patriotism, well reflected the mind of the best men who surrounded the emperor. That at best was what his newly appointed augurers and pontifices thought; and the children of the aristocracy, of the year 17 B.C., must have had even less religious feelings when they sang Horace's *Carmen Sæculare* than the choir of a large modern city in rendering one of Reger's Psalms. Hence, the emperor's restoration of religion only availed as an act of imperial policy. It was the incarnation of an æsthetic culture conditioned by patriotism. In this last sense it entered into the being of the Latin genius as a permanent quality. But it was not religion.

The autochthonic ideas and powers of the simplest conceptions of a nature religion were still alive among the masses of the people, as also were the religions of the east which were streaming through numerous channels into the west. Of these, the most important were the Egyptian cults which, already for nearly a century, had carried on a vigorous and successful propaganda. The buildings, pictures, and inscriptions of Pompeii give the necessary information in these matters. After

Pompey had imported them as slaves, the Jews were added to the Egyptians and played a significant part in Rome in the period of Augustus. Under Claudius, the first Christians came to Rome; but they spoke Greek, and appeared at first to be adherents of the Jewish communities, who also used Greek as their mother tongue. It was not until the middle of the third century that the Roman Christians made use of Latin in church worship, and thus at last were culturally at home in Rome. It follows that Christianity was not influenced by the west during the times when its foundations were being laid; it grew up in the east, and arrived ready-made in the west. Therefore, if we wish to examine the conditions under which it was first modelled, we must consider the religious circumstances of the orient in the time of the early empire. But even that is an extremely difficult problem, for the literary sources of this period are almost entirely lacking; the surviving religious writings of the eastern people come from either a definitely older, or a distinctly later, period. Scarcely any contemporary literature is extant, witnessing to the faith which lived in the people, and not the mere sacerdotalism of the priests, or a matter of theological speculation. Thus we have to make the attempt to draw a picture by combining the surviving fragments. The correctness of this picture will, at best, be supported only by its own inner probability.

Antioch, the cradle of Hellenistic Christianity, is hidden from us, inaccessible beneath the dwelling-houses and gardens of the present day Antakie. The second important scene of Paul's activity was in western Asia Minor. This region has been largely explored by the systematic excavation of the most significant towns, and answers have been found for many of the questions important for our purpose. Nowhere in the world do the epigraphs speak so clearly and so frequently of the greatness of Alexander, who used the Greek sword, and carried to the east the might of the Greek spirit. The Hellenistic period began when he founded his empire and when the marshals who succeeded him organized the states into which it was subsequently divided.

A new economic civilization, with a new intellectual outlook, sprang from, and prospered in, the old Greek colonies along the

western coasts of Asia Minor. Alexander himself consecrated
the majestic temple of the city goddess Athena in Priene. King
Lysimachus rebuilt the city of Ephesus by the sea, and protected it with mighty walls. Miletus, which had been destroyed,
rose again from its ruins and the royal residence of the Attalids
was built upon the city hill of Pergamon. All these achievements
of the period of the Diadochoi bring the pride of their Greek
nationality visibly to expression. They were conscious of standing under the protection of the Greek gods and they stamped
their images and emblems upon their coinage. Numerous
dedications found among the inscriptions tell us of their public
and private worship. Their temples dominated the city and
spoke to the citizens of their faith in the same way as the
medieval cathedrals of European cities testify to the religion
of the times in which they were built.

Zeus, Athena, and Dionysos lived upon the height of Pergamon. Asklepios had his great temple in the valley below the
city. Half-way up the hill, the sanctuaries of Demeter and Hera
were to be found. Priene felt itself to be the daughter of Athens,
and honoured Athena Polias as its tutelary goddess; her huge
temple excelled any other building in the little town, including
the area dedicated to Asklepios in the market-place, and the
temple of Demeter on the northern declivity. Miletus had
preserved its ancient tradition, and the temple of Apollo
Delphinios constituted the centre of the cult even for the
Hellenistic city. The famous sacred street leading to the shrine
of the oracle of Apollo in Didyma gained a new significance
when, about 300 B.C., two architects, from Ephesus and Miletus,
began to build the marvellous temple whose ruins, even to-day,
fill spectators with astonishment and awe.

Ephesus was entirely dominated by the worship of the
"Great Artemis". Her ancient temple, which was rebuilt in
ever greater dimensions after each destruction, was the most
impressive building in the city, one of the seven wonders of the
world even after being burnt by Herostratos in 355 B.C.
Cheirocrates rebuilt it more magnificently and thus it stood
until it was destroyed by the Goths in A.D. 263.

The Artemis who was worshipped here, however, was not
the Greek huntress, the virgin sister of Apollo, although the city

coinage, throughout the entire Hellenistic period, represents her in this way. Rather she was the mountain mother-goddess native to Asia Minor, the mistress and protectress of wild animals. In the Roman period the coinage no longer shows the bashful figure of the Hellenistic copy, but faithfully reproduces the original temple idol. According to the evidence of numerous replicas, this idol must have been greatly favoured in the time of the Empire, a partiality which can only be explained by the ever increasing influence of oriental religion upon the civilization as a whole. This image was carved in ebony. It represented a woman standing bolt upright. Her body was bound from head to foot by wrappings between which a number of metal bosses can be seen. At a later period sculptors reproduced these bosses as the numerous breasts of the goddess of fertility. A crescent moon was shown behind her head which was decorated by a mural crown; in her hands, which are stretched out from the body towards the right, she holds long sheaves, or even ears of corn. Lions creep fawningly up to her arms, and deer stand on either side of her. This Asiatic mountain goddess was the mistress of the soil of Ephesus when the Greeks took possession in early times. The colonists gave her a Greek name, a Greek temple, and many Greek forms of worship, but she remained Asiatic, and her worship must have kept alive the native religion. But our sources are not sufficient to give us all the details.

From Ephesus, her worship came to penetrate the Archipelago and the Greek motherland. It also spread far and wide in the interior of Asia Minor. In many cities a closely analogous development took place, for it is this very goddess that is meant by Artemis Leucophryene of Magnesia on the Meander, as is seen both in her character and in the form of her image. In the same way, this Asiatic Artemis is to be found in various places, but with a great variety of epithets.[1] In Ephesus itself at the north-east corner of the Panajir-Dagh, about half a mile from the temple of Artemis, the site of a cultus has been found where the "Mother of the Mountain" was worshipped under the open sky.[2] She was also known as the "Phrygian Mother".

[1] *Pauly-W.*, v, 2767. Roscher, *Lex.*, i, 593
[2] J. Keil in *Oesterr. Jahreshefte*, 1926, 256 ff.

On numerous votive tablets she is represented as a woman wearing a mural crown, and standing between two lions, with a shell and a tambourine in her hands, a typical representation of Cybele. Her youthful companion, who is always present, we should call Attis. These Greeks named him Apollo, but this fact shows clearly how all these names were only "echo and smoke". The description of the goddess as the "Mother of the Mountain" is the nearest approach to a definitely religious conception. She was worshipped as Artemis in Ephesus in the great temple, and as the Phrygian goddess on the lower slope of the hill. In both places she was presented in Greek form, but in different ways.

At first the priests of the Ephesian Artemis were eunuchs who had probably emasculated themselves according to Phrygian rite while in ecstasy. The priestesses were virgins. This is what Strabo records on the basis of his sources, but he briefly adds, on the ground of his personal observation about 50 B.C., "Many of the old customs are still followed, many are not".[1] This notice means that the characteristic of the cultus just mentioned may not have been preserved to the time of the apostle Paul. In the days of Alexander, however, this Artemis may have been hymned as the leader of a tumultuous throng of Mænads,[2] and, according to the inscriptions, the mysteries of Artemis must have existed until the third century A.D. In the second century these ceremonies appear to have begun to suffer neglect, for, about A.D. 200,[3] they were newly financed and reinstituted by private subscription. A romantic writer of the third century A.D. describes the great annual festival of Artemis, in which those who took part indulged in the greatest excesses.[4] The *Kuretes* who were connected in some way with the cult of Artemis, brought mystical sacrifices in the grove Ortygia, near the harbour, when they celebrated their feasts.[5] The mysteries of Demeter were regularly celebrated in Ephesus even in the time of the Empire, although in connection with emperor worship: evidences of this have come down to us from the eighties of the first Christian century. A religious society localized outside the city united the mysteries of Demeter with

[1] Strabo, 14, p. 641   [2] Plutarch, *de aud. Poet.*, p. 22*a, de superstit.*, p. 170*a*
[3] *Ephesuswerk*, iii, 144, no. lix, 156, no. lxxii, 29; cf. C.I.G. 3002, Hicks, *Inscr.*, 596
[4] *Achill. Tat.*, 6, 3   [5] Strabo, 14, p. 640

those of Dionysos.[1] Mystics of Dionysos were still to be found in Ephesus in the time of the Antonines,[2] and afford a welcome addition to the large amount of extant evidence in regard to the cult of Dionysos which was observed in the theatre. The Dionysian carnival, celebrated at the principal feast of the god, drew the whole town even in the Roman period.[3] The coinage is especially instructive as to how strongly the mysteries determined the atmospheres and attitudes of the Hellenistic period. In 200–55 B.C., not only in Ephesus, but in all the towns of the entire kingdom of Pergamon and beyond, silver coins known as *kistofori* were struck as common money. On the obverse was the mystical kista of Dionysos with a snake in a garland of ivy; on the reverse, a bow in a carrier—perhaps belonging to Artemis—between two snakes. Thus both sides reproduce the symbols of the mystery cult.[4] The inscriptions fully support the widespread occurrence of the mysteries which we may deduce from the coinage. Thus, e.g., the cult of Dionysos was held in high honour in Pergamon. A college of *bukoloi*, i.e. cattlemen, is often mentioned, and they used to celebrate the mysteries of the god in the period of the early Empire; an imperial rescript dealt specially with them.[5] The mysteries of Mētēr Basileia[6] were still in existence in the early Roman period and the ancient mysteries of the *Kabeiroi* of Pergamon are lauded by the orator Aristides, in the Antonine period.[7] A calendar of the imperial feasts preserved on an inscription, indicates a special feast for the mysteries in the month of June.[8]

In Pergamon we are now in a position to observe one of the ways in which, as early as the Hellenistic period, Asiatic religion penetrated into the Greek world. In the year 189 B.C., King Eumenes II married the Cappadocian princess Stratonice, and she brought her home god, Sabazios, into the royal palace of Pergamon and worshipped him as her special protector. However, he showed himself gracious to the Attalid house as well, and, indeed, often appeared to their help, so that, in the year

[1] Dittenb., *Syll.*, 2, 820. Hicks, *Inscr.*, nos. 506 n, 595
[2] Hicks, *Inscr.*, nos. 600–602   [3] Plut., *Anton.*, 24. Lucian *de saltat.*, 79
[4] Regling, *Antike Münzen*, 58 f. Head, *Historia Nummorum*, 534, 575
[5] *Inscr. Perg.*, no. 482, 485–87; cf. 248   [6] *Inscr.*, no. 334
[7] Pausanias, i, 4, 6, Inscr., no. 252, 26. Aristides, *or.*, 53, 5; 2, p. 469, Keil
[8] *Inscr.*, no. 374

135 B.C., Attalus II assigned him official worship, both in the temple of Athena Nicephoros, and in her celebrated sacred grove in the valley below the city. Sacrifices were to be offered to him, and processions and mysteries celebrated. He appointed a member of the royal house to be a priest of the god.[1] In this way the cult and its mysteries[2] spread among the Greeks of the kingdom of Pergamon in the most vigorous manner.

The cult of Sabazios, which originated in Phrygia and Lydia, introduced many new elements into the mysteries of Dionysos. The kistophoric coinage bears witness, among other matters, to this fact.[3] But its greatest significance is in its connection with the Judaism of Asia Minor which equated Sabazios Dionysos with Yahweh Sabaoth. This identification was known in Rome as early as 139 B.C., and occurs again in the imperial epoch; for Plutarch uses it for explaining to his readers the meaning of the Sabbath.[4] In the period of the earliest empire, a college of the "Sabbatists", with a "President of the Synagogue" is noted on an inscription on a wall of rock in the neighbourhood of Elæussa in Cilicia.[5] We are probably justified in claiming this as a witness of some such compound of Jewish with Sabazic elements. Clearly recognizable threads lead from this city to the communities which were very widespread in Asia Minor and on the northern shore of the Black Sea. These communities worshipped the *Hypsistos*, the anonymous "highest" god. Such facts clearly show the connection between the two religions which, on the surface, appear so different.[6] One of their memorials, belonging to the second century B.C., has been found in the present-day Panderma, the port of the kingdom of Pergamon on the Sea of Marmora. Hence we may probably regard the Judaization of the cult of Sabazios as a new phenomenon occurring alongside the purely pagan form, both in Pergamon and far beyond its borders, even at such an early date. It is probably an accident that the extant inscriptions in regard to the communities in Pergamon and Miletus

[1] *Inscr.*, no. 246, iv; cf. Dittenberger, *or.*, 332   [2] Roscher, *Lex.*, iv, 250
[3] *Ibid.*, *Lex.*, iv., 236
[4] Valer. Max., i, 3, 3. Tacitus, *hist.*, v, 5. Plutarch, *quæst conv.*, p. 671 f.
[5] Dittenberger, *Or. inscr.*, 573
[6] Cumont, *Orient. Rel.* (3rd edit.), 59, 231, n. 60. Roscher, *Lex.*, iv, 238, 263, 266. *Pauly-W.*, ix, 448

date only from the second century A.D.,[1] for the college of Sabbatists of Elæussa, just mentioned, existed very near to Paul's time and was also geographically not far distant from his home town of Tarsus; this fact is important for the study of the history of the Church.

Another form of the penetration of foreign religion into the Greek world is illustrated by an inscription carved about 200 B.C. on the temple of Isis in Priene. The city ordered the regular celebration of the cult of Isis, provided the means for it, regulated the income of the priests, and decreed that only the officially appointed Egyptians could offer the sacrifices exactly according to the rite; and every unofficial person offering a sacrifice was threatened with a fine of a thousand drachmas. This corresponds entirely with the Egyptian conception of the value of the proper forms of the cultus. The Ptolemies zealously spread the cult of Sarapis which they had founded, so that, as early as the third century B.C., it had gained a firm foothold in Greece, a fact which shows an active interest on the side of the Greeks. Obviously, the missionary work of the Egyptian priests met with acceptance, and gained adherents in such numbers and importance that, in the end, the city authorities agreed to support the cultus. Like all the Egyptian temples in Asia Minor, the building dedicated to the cultus was itself of the most modest size, and was probably erected by the private subscriptions of the group concerned.

A similar inscription from the same period has been preserved from the neighbouring town of Magnesia on the Meander,[2] where the priesthood of Sarapis obtained a regular agreement from the city authorities, and salaries were fixed. In this case also the temple is a very small building. It would appear that the Egyptian prophets at first sought and found believers among the lower classes, whence the movement spread to other classes. Only under the Empire did it grow to be the normal thing, to the extent that the Egyptian gods were depicted on the coinage. Specimens have been found in Magnesia and Pergamon. Even in Ephesus in the time of the Empire, evidence is not lacking of the worship of Isis and

[1] *Inscr. Perg.*, nos. 330, 331, Dittenberger, *or.*, nos. 755, 756
[2] *Inscr. Magnesia.*, no. 99

Sarapis;[1] and we may assume with certainty that, in the Hellenistic period, this cultus possessed adherents in the port; but the temples of these gods will have had the same insignificant form as that customary in other places. The mighty temple in the market-place belonging to the middle of the second century A.D., which twentieth century scholars have inclined to regard as a Sarapeum,[2] must be one of the three dedicated to the emperor, which Ephesus proudly regarded as its principal temples beside that of Artemis.[3] Neither Isis nor Sarapis appears on Ephesian coinage.

There is no doubt that, in addition to these religions, of which there is so much evidence, innumerable others pressed their way into western Asia Minor in the period of the early Empire. Of these other religions, the memorials either tell us nothing, or date only from a later period. It is noteworthy that inscriptions never speak about the Jews although, by that time, they had long been very numerous in those cities, and had carried on their missionary work amongst the Greeks with some success. What is known with certainty is sufficient to give us a basis upon which we can carry our inquiries further, for we must assume that the principal views and ideas of these religions were known in the milieu of the growing Christendom of Asia Minor.

We must now go on to take account of a new religion which entered into relation with the manifold complex which we have just described. This new religion can be traced from the days of Alexander in a well-marked line through the centuries. About the beginning of the Christian era, it came forward so definitely that all other expressions of religious life were overshadowed by the various forms of emperor worship.[4] Among the people of the orient, it was traditional to regard the king as an incarnation of the godhead. The conception was also current among the Greeks in such a way that a gifted person, and especially a successful statesman or soldier, was held to be the revelation of a divine being. This belief was frequently expressed in a myth to the effect that he was of divine descent, or

[1] *Ephesus*, i, 70, 97, 173, iii, 97. Hicks, *Inscr.*, no. 503
[2] J. Keil, *Oestr. Jahreshefte*, 1926, 266
[3] Cf., the coins of the four Neokorate in Head, *catal. Ionia*, pl. 14, 6
[4] *Pauly-W.* suppl., iv, 806. Wendland, *Kultur*, 2nd edition, 123, 146

else by canonizing him as a "hero". Alexander's achievements from the Bosphorus to the Indus were so tremendous that other men never hoped to outvie him. Indeed, both in the orient and in Greece, it came to be felt appropriate to pay divine honours to this god in human form. The revelation of actual power is always stronger than dogmatic theories, and therefore, under the impress of this extraordinary personality, even the Greeks went beyond regarding Alexander as a "hero", and worshipped him fully as a god. Political considerations played an additional part in the highest circles, and thus the cult of Alexander was furthered and, indeed, soon obligatory. The Diadochoi had already moved in this direction, to lend additional support to their own power. When they also claimed to be divine kings, they invested the idea in the Greek forms which had been accorded to Alexander.

In that region of Asia Minor over which we have cast our eyes there is a small shrine for Alexander in Priene,[1] an "Attaleion" in Teos,[2] and a temple for Eumenes II in Miletus.[3] Numerous inscriptions record the prevalent practice of emperor worship in the kingdom of Pergamon, the forms of which became ever richer as time went on. The most instructive example comes from an inscription in the little town of Elaia,[4] not far from Pergamon. The last king of the little kingdom, Attalos III (138–133 B.C.), returned from war victoriously into his capital. Thereupon the citizens of Elaia decided to award him the following honours: he should be given a golden garland; a statue five cubits high should be set up in the temple of Dionysos "in order that there he might be a companion of the gods"; and a gilded, equestrian statue should be set up in the market-place near the altar of Zeus, on which "the royal priest" was to burn incense every day. Since he had arrived home on the eighth of the month, the eighth of every month was to be a feast-day, and the anniversary of his return was to be celebrated by an annual procession with appropriate sacrifices. The inscriptions upon the columns of the statues give him the divine predicate "Euergetes", i.e. "the well-doer" or "the beneficent",

[1] Inscr., nos. 205, 206, 108, 75
[2] Cf. Inscr. Perg., no. 240. Dittenberger, or., 326, 20
[3] Sitz. Akad. Berlin, 1904, 86. Miletwerk, i, 9, pp.144 ff.
[4] Inscr. Perg., no. 246. Dittenberger, or., 332

and call him the son of the divine king, Eumenes Soter, i.e. of the "Saviour". Such was the insipid, and hence foolish, excess to which the formerly vital appreciation of the genius of Alexander had descended in the course of two centuries. Only conventional reverence remained when the kingdom passed to the Romans; and it is not surprising that Roman generals and governors were accorded similar fustian.

However, with Roman rule, a somewhat new element entered this Greek world: the cultus of the goddess Roma,[1] i.e. the personified genius of the city which had become a world power. It represented, for the empire as a whole, what the "Tyche" of the Greek towns meant to those towns. It was an abstraction artificially cultivated, and did not spring from the soil of a genuinely religious feeling. It was characteristic of times in which the persons of the ancient gods had become shadows and the indestructible religious feeling of the people endeavoured to conceive the powers of history in new forms.

Cæsar tried to use the state-form of Hellenistic kingship in order to give graphic expression to the essential meaning of Rome's historical development. It was for this reason that the republican ideology, which was already approaching its doom, used its last flickering powers to plunge the dagger into his heart, but that ideology crumbled over his corpse. Octavian Augustus was the heir of Cæsar, of both his power and his conceptions; he became the great monarch who ruled the entire world. Although he still wore the republican toga in the sight of the Romans of the city, yet the world, and especially the east, saw him wearing the purple mantle of Alexander. One does not need to say that the same divine honours were offered to him as had been accorded to the kings of the diadochian dynasties, and which had not been denied to the Roman officials who were their successors. At this stage, however, a new content was given to a form of honour which had sunk into being the mere flattery of the court. The entire Roman world felt it a marvellous experience, when, after a hundred years of distress and bloodshed, there was peace at last; when anarchy gave place to a uniform government, destruction to reconstruction, caprice to law, and confusion to order—and it was

[1] Roscher, *Lex.*, iv., 130. Wissowa, *Relig. u. Kultus d. Römer*, 2nd edition, 341

one man who had brought all this about by his immense power, Augustus. Gigantic upheavals, whether for good or for evil, both in nature and in history, make even the dullest souls feel the shadow of men of higher powers, men who determine the course of world events. Then the imperfect intuitions of the masses proceed to fill the forms of customary religion with new life. This was the case now.

For a long time, the figure of Alexander, glorified with the halo of divinity, had filled the imagination of the peoples. History, mythology, and delight in the fabulous, had created an enchanting picture of his glory and boundless power. In his person, the Hellenistic, divine kingship had come for the first time to a credible actuality. And now the appearance of a kingly god-upon-earth was repeated in still greater dimensions in Augustus; and the world echoed again with his praises. The ancient yearning of the orient was mixed with Greek belief and Etruscan augury when Virgil,[1] at the commencement of the Augustan period, prophesied a saviour who would descend upon earth as a divine child, wipe out the sins of the past, and introduce the golden age; or when, in the years of realization, he depicted the glory of the new epoch with the brilliant colours of the legend of Alexander. His prophetic song found a spirited echo among all the poets of Rome; to them Augustus was a god upon earth, *præsens divus*, the prince of an era similar to paradise.

This was not merely poetic phraseology; it was genuine homage felt by those who could express authentically the feeling of the people; it was an expression of religious feeling in so far as this sceptical upper class was at all capable of religion. At the same time it was the spirit of the east which now celebrated its greatest triumph in Rome. A glance at Asia Minor shows plainly how the Hellenistic form of belief in its kings, which had become outworn, rose again with a power that cast its beams far and wide, owing to the impress of the super-man, Augustus. Even Pompey had been welcomed as the longed-for prince of peace,[2] but in vain. Later, in 48 B.C., the cities of Asia Minor greeted Julius Cæsar as a son of god, a god upon earth, and a universal saviour of human life.[3] Forty years later still,

---

[1] *Eclogues*, 4. *Æneid*, 6, 791 ff.   [2] Dittenberger, *Syll.* (3rd edition), no. 751
[3] *Op. cit.*, no. 760

these hopes were realized, and a well-known calendar, inscribed at Priene,[1] sings ravishing melodies about the good fortune of the Augustan period. "Has the birthday of the divine emperor given us more joy, or more benefit? Is it not rightly to be regarded as equally important with the beginning of the world, if we look, not only at the fact, but also at its meaning? For he has re-established an institution which was crumbling and hurrying to destruction. He has given another outlook to the entire world, a world which otherwise would have much preferred destruction if the universal blessing had not been born for all—the emperor." Hence, in the whole of Asia Minor, his birthday, 23rd September, was in future to be New Year's Day, "For this day was the beginning of the message of peace which was conjoined with his person"—the word used is *euangelia*, at that time lightly spoken, but later to become full of meaning. What the people of Asia Minor meant was really nothing other than what the Church, from the sixth century onward, put in a somewhat different form, viz. the recognition of the fact that the beginning of a new epoch was brought about by the epiphany of God upon earth; it therefore dated a new era from the redemptive birth of the divine child, Jesus. The form of this homage corresponded with a genuine faith felt by people who had been redeemed from misery.

Augustus greeted this attitude with pleasure, and, for all the shrewd reticence which he had to maintain in Rome, he gladly forwarded it in the eastern provinces. He ordered the cult of the emperor there to be combined with the worship of Roma. In Pergamon[2] there quickly arose the first of a large number of temples in Asia Minor to Roma and Augustus. In this religious conception of the Emperor-Saviour, statesmen found the idea which alone was able to unite all parts of the empire into a unity. The outer links were the army and the officials; and the world economy made possible by peace and security. What was it, however, which united the innumerable elements of this highly complex phenomenon? Even the most optimistic person could not speak of an all-embracing national feeling. There was really no civilization in common at this early period among the

[1] *Inscr. Priene*, no. 105. Dittenberger, *or.*, 458
[2] Tac., *Ann.*, 4, 37. Dio. Cass., 51, 20, 7, *Inscr. Perg.*, no. 374

many peoples between the Rhine and the Euphrates. Hence belief in the divine mission of the peace-giving, imperial power was graphically expressed in the cult of the God-Emperor; and this effected a community of feeling which passed over the boundaries of the provinces and the differences of race, and created the vitally necessary ideology of the Roman empire.

The imperial cult immediately pressed into the foreground and remained permanently in this position; in the following centuries it adapted itself to the prevailing religious development. It is easy to understand how it would then come about that Christians, who refused to conform, would have to pay with their blood; and why even the privileged Jews themselves were at last shattered by the ensuing conflict. Even to-day the ruins in western Asia Minor teach us that, after the beginning of the imperial epoch, only imperial temples were built. The ancient gods—the health deities excepted—had to be content with what the faith of earlier centuries accorded them, for the active interest of the worship established by the state had centred on the person of the emperor. It was only natural that the experiences of the Hellenistic period were repeated in the worship of the emperor. Yet the high tone of the Augustan period could not endure. In the capital, where, in spite of everything, a critical attitude lived on, the foolish exaggerations of Caligula and of Nero, in giving themselves divine status, caused the cult to decline rapidly into a servile formality. In the eastern provinces the conception of the emperor remained sacred for a longer period, because the personal deficiencies of its representatives remained for a large part concealed, and because they continued to enjoy the benefits of the institution. Nevertheless, even there, decline was unavoidable.

The religious tone of the early empire was characterized, firstly, by the fact that the religion of the ancient Greek gods, i.e. the religion of the official cult, linked with city, race, and family, died away. It was still officially carried on but it lived no longer in the heart. Its place was taken either by irreligious indifference, or by the philosophers' habit of mind. Secondly, religion took possession of the solitary soul of the individual as a question of practical life and hope. Such persons now united with others of a similar cast of mind and began to form a community far excelling that of the old Greek cult-societies. These latter were *ad hoc* unions of men who did not differ in any way from their fellow-citizens. The new communities were a unity, an actual organization, and a miraculous super-human corpus. He who belonged to one felt himself lifted out of the multitude of his "profane" fellow-citizens, and placed in a secret relationship with the powers of the godhead. He had trodden a road which led out of this common world and its narrow confines, into the sphere of the gods; and which at times brought the reality of that higher world blissfully to consciousness. This kind of religion had spread in the form of the mysteries from the east, and at an early date had found its way into Greece. Mythology had preserved the echoes of the one time triumphant progress of the Dionysian mysticism. Although Dionysos had been incorporated among the gods of the Greeks, and his official cult had been preserved, like that of the other Olympians, yet in the end he sank into being the patron of the theatre, and a symbolic figure. Nevertheless, he still remained the actual god of the Dionysian mysteries in which the soul of an individual enjoyed, in Bacchantic rapture, the ecstasy of divine possession; his soul cleansed from everything that disavowed the godhead, or countenanced the influence of evil demons. At long last he had been made divine and thereby assured of a blessed life after death.

There were solemn rites of initiation with fastings and ascetisms, baptisms and meals, strange ceremonies of a primitive cult, intoxicating dances with wild songs to the sound of the flute and the clang of cymbals and tambourines. A confused variety of records, both inscriptions and documents, have survived, but, as yet, it is impossible to analyse them satisfactorily. They belong to eight different centuries, and to all the lands of the Roman empire, and it is only by combining data of the most different origin that we are able to gain any comprehensible idea of the nature of these mysteries.[1] So far, it is impossible to sketch the evolution of a mystery religion, its different forms in various places, or its active and passive relationships with other mysteries. Hence we must be content

---

[1] Cumont, *Or. Rel.* (3rd edition), 192. J. Leipoldt, *Dionysos* (1931)

with a general outline. What has been said about Dionysos applies to the remaining eastern cults. In the Hellenistic period, the mysteries blossom out and, in the Roman period, adopt still further features from the east. In the second century A.D., the orient flowed in religious triumph towards the west, reaching its culmination in the middle of the third century. Hence we may assume that in the Claudian-Neronian period, the important one for our present purpose, even in Asia Minor these forces flourished and were preparing for the struggle of the next century. If we combine the details of information in extant memorials and documents, with the results of an analysis of the Pauline letters, we are possibly in a position to make deductions as to the presence, and the nature, of certain religious currents in the Pauline period.

Although the world which surrounded early Christianity provided this great variety, it was not characterized by simple joys and undiluted happiness. A burden pressed upon it, and the individual felt, in his deepest soul, that he was miserable and in chains. It might either be the stars, as the Chaldeans taught, which pursued their fateful course in the heavens; or an impersonal fate, which could not be visualized; yet, even if one conceived it pictorially as Ananke, or a heartless and capricious Tyche, it was inescapable, and could not be influenced by the sacrifices or the prayers of a poor mortal. Why so? Because he was of another nature, and could only be the object of the will of a higher power. Had he no soul? Yes, but it lay in the fetters of the body, and could not free itself from all the bonds of this world. Therefore—enjoy the good things of this world as long as you may, for afterwards you will fall into dust and ashes. That was the answer given by many children of this world, and it re-echoes to us from many gravestones.[1] But there was a large number of earnest-minded men who could not easily be satisfied merely by knowing the worthlessness of this world, a worthlessness which, at that time, was universally recognized by all who meditated more profoundly upon the nature of things. In such people was to be found a desire for redemption which the eastern mysteries largely satisfied. The

[1] Examples in Buecheler, *Carm. epigr.*, 185-91, 243-44, 420, 5, 1081, 1082 1495-1500. E. Rohde, *Psyche*, ii, 393-96

soul of man was of divine origin, an ancient wrong having plunged it into what was material, and banished it to the body. But a divine messenger had descended upon earth and shown his disciples the way by which the soul could break the fetters of the body, overcome or outwit the hostile powers, mount up through the seven heavenly spheres, and be reunited with the divine original source. That was wisdom, and, at the same time, knowledge and action, suffering and enjoyment. This was what was meant by gnosis, and its practice was the *mysterium*. To turn toward the godhead set one free from the body, for the body itself belonged to the world which was considered to be of lower value. In the middle of the search for pleasure belonging entirely to the present sensual world, mysticism spread many ascetic customs, abstinence from wine, meat, and sexual intercourse, by those who longed for the other world. They longed to free themselves from the senses and sought to have their lives dominated by the spirit which lived as the divine spark in the soul; the *mysterium* showed them the means. It brought death to them and at the same time a rebirth to a new and true life. It brought the divine to life in their hearts, and let them gaze in ecstasy upon the blessed fields of the divine world; and the man whose lips the god had touched could give heavenly revelations. The community of mystics, when listening to him with devout thoughts in their hearts, regarded such a person as a man no longer, but as the mouthpiece of god, an apotheosized man, a prophet. The religion which he proclaimed, in God's commission, from his own experience was a redemptive religion, and its founder, who brought the *mysterium*, was the saviour of the world. This is the conception whose earthly inflections we have already discussed: the saviour, Augustus, had freed the world which was languishing in distress and fated to shed blood. In the mysteries, however, are laid bare the religious roots of his god-head, and of the prophecy of the birth of a divine child bringing salvation to the world. This explains also what it would sound like in human hearts of the time when Paul wrote to his Galatian churches (4: 4), "But when the fullness of time came, God sent forth His Son, born of a woman, born under the law, that He might redeem them which were under the law, that we might receive the adoption

of sons". This repeated the phraseology of a redemptive
religion, and the doctrine of a saviour of the world.

While there is no doubt that the conceptions of "cleanness",
and the corresponding prescriptions as found in the mysteries,
originally flourished among the purely nature religions, and,
consequently, wore an exclusively ritual character, we can
recognize equally clearly the ethical elements that began to
infiltrate in the course of the later development. As early as in
ancient Orphicism, we find the idea of a last judgment on
sinners[1], and learn that their evil would require expiation.
Fasting and continence were the important means, in numerous cults, whereby the wicked man might win back the grace
of the gods; and, as the religion became ever more inward,
these means were no longer understood in the old sense of ward-
ing off dæmons, but as the education of the soul to inner purity.[2]
For example: a temple law of the first century B.C. has been found
in Lydian Philadelphia,[3] which on the basis of a revelation of
Zeus to Dionysos prescribes a whole moral catechism to the
religious community, which they were called upon to observe
anew on the occasion of each monthly sacrifice. It is expressly
declared that entry into this fellowship was open to men and
women, free-born and slaves, without difference. The advance
is specially striking when we compare the numerous Phrygian
inscriptions[4] with confessions of sins, all in the nature of ritual
transgressions. We can also understand whence the change
came: the philosophy of the open air preachers had made the
people familiar with Stoic ideas of equality as well as Stoic
moral principles; and consciences had been aroused.

We must read Epictetus's lectures in Arrian's notes, which
date from about A.D. 100, to gain a vivid picture of what constituted popular philosophy in the time of the early empire,
and indeed long before. Here the most vivid language, and
graphic, frequently pungent, and sweeping, phraseology are
used to attack the shallowness of living a day at a time, and to

[1] A. Dieterich, *Nekyia*, 126. A. Olivierli, *Lamellae aureae orphicae* (*Kl. Texte*, 133),
p. 9, 4, 11, 4
[2] Cumont, *Or. Relig.* (3rd edition), 219
[3] Dittenberger, *Syll.*, 985, cf. 983. K. Latte, *Arch. Rel. Wiss.*, 20, 291 ff.
[4] Cumont, *Or. Relig.* (3rd edition), 219, n. 40. Reitzenstein, *Hellen. Myst.* (3rd
edition), 139. Steinleither, *Die Beicht im Zusammenhang mit der antiken Rechtspflege*,
1913, gives a collection of the texts

drive the hearers to turn to their inner selves. Questions are proposed in regard to the meaning and value of life, and the common views are subjected to an impressive criticism. One prejudice after another disappears when it is breathed on by a philosophy which usually presents itself as robust and sound common sense. The man himself remains to be taught as man and as "cosmopolitan", as a citizen of the world, and as neither Greek nor barbarian, neither free nor slave, neither male nor female, but only as human,[1] and who, as such, is to practise "philosophy" i.e. to think and act according to sound ethical principles.[2] The only thing necessary was to observe nature with unveiled eyes in order to find the right way of shaping one's life. The innate instinct of self-preservation, and the natural desire for happiness, will make plain to anyone who gives them earnest consideration, what he must do, or leave undone, in respect of both himself and others. Even if men, for the most part, do what is wrong, foolish, or harmful, it is only because they give place in their lives to the feelings, to pain and pleasure, and these exercise a determinative influence upon their actions, and thereby confuse clear thinking. If you wrestle for the peace of your soul, then the pure light of reason will shine upon you unclouded, and point you the way of virtue, exercise of which alone means genuine happiness.[3] Thus true inner freedom arises in the soul,[4] and makes it independent of all the changing circumstances of the outer world.

This philosopher-evangelist penetrates very deeply. He teaches that the foundation of all ethical life is the truth that all of us were created by God, the father of gods and men. We have a body in common with animals, but understanding and reason in common with the gods.[5] The creative germ had been sown in the world by God, and has developed in rational creatures; hence we men are partakers of a fellowship which unites men and God; we are related to God, and man may proudly call himself a son of God. He who has grasped that fact knows that God is his creator and father and protector; and never experiences either suffering or fear. He is not anxious about what he will eat to-morrow, although he must stand in

[1] Epictetus, i, 9; i, 6; ii, 10, 1–3   [2] Chrysippus, *fr.*, 253 f., Arnim
[3] Epictetus, i, 4, 3, 28   [4] *Ibid.*, iv, 1   [5] *Ibid.*, i, 3, 1–3

shame before animals who can be certain of their support.[1]
Even if the prison house of the body may impede the soul conscious of her vital relationship with God, nevertheless she bears
the imprisonment in the serene consciousness of standing in the
service of God, who, as commander, has placed her at a post
which she must defend—until the moment when God sets her
free. It will be only a short while before she will hear the
liberating cry and come to God.[2]

This is no longer the home-made and pedantic pantheism of
the ancient Stoa. Over that dry landscape, the fertilizing rain
of a genuine, religious feeling has fallen, and has caused to
spring, from hidden seeds, a real faith in God which inspired
the Stoic preaching of virtue with new power.

About a century before the birth of Christ, a man on the
island of Rhodes came to exercise a far-reaching influence, a
man who was, above all else, the vehicle of this new tendency
in Stoicism. We refer to Poseidonios[3]—and, since he was born
in the Syrian city of Apamea, oriental religions must have been
prominent and formative in his early years. His works, covering
all fields of knowledge, include, beside treatises dealing with
fate and the art of prophecy, a writing about the gods which
was of the greatest significance for the development of Stoic
theology and which enjoyed a very large circulation. When,
soon after 80 B.C., Cicero was a student in Rhodes, he sat at the
feet of Poseidonios who was held in the greatest respect by the
Roman aristocracy.[4] Cicero began to write on popular philosophy in 44 B.C., the year that Cæsar was assassinated, and
he used Poseidonios's work as the basis of the second book of his
study of the nature of the gods. Two hundred years later,
Poseidonios's book was still held in such high regard that the
sceptic physician, Sextus, felt it to be an authoritative account
of philosophical belief in the gods, and accordingly made
many verbatim quotations from the work.[5]

A century later, in St. Paul's time, another capable writer,
who used the pseudonym of "Aristotle", published a work in-

[1] Epictetus, i, 9, 1–9, 16–19   [2] *Ibid.*, i, 9, 16–17, 24–2
[3] P. Wendland, *Kultur* (2nd edition), 134–6. E. Schwartz *Charakterköpfe* (5th
edition), i, 85–93
[4] Cic., *Tusc.*, 2, 25, 61; cf. *ad. Att.*, 2, i, 2; *Hortensius, fr.*, 44, Müller
[5] Cic., *de nat. deor.*, 2; Sextus Emp., *adv. phys.*, 9, 60–136

tended for the use of the cultured people of his times. It avoided pedantry, and gave an account of the universe,[1] the best passages containing a theology of the cosmos in the style of Poseidonios.

Following the example of the early Stoa, Pseudo-Aristotle discussed the cosmological proof of God with penetrating ardour in these writings. The exalted reason of the creator and governor follows from the order and the teleological construction of the world and all its parts; the many grades of creatures compel the assumption of a highest and perfect being; the fact that the cosmos is an organism proves the existence of a soul, giving life to the material world; i.e. a power which penetrates and activates the whole, and which is recognized by its operations, as the supreme, purposive Reason and guiding Providence. By various transformations of itself, this immanent divine spirit creates the four elements, beginning with the finest, fiery æther, and going on to the grossest, earthly material; and every cosmic event is the consequence of their interaction. In this way the innumerable variety of beings were created, and at their head were those endowed with reason, i.e. men and gods, for whose sake alone this entire world was created as a "state", a community embracing both.[2] Whereas, in the last analysis, we can speak only of *one* god as the prime soul, the evolution of the phenomenal world teaches a plurality of gods, even if only of a secondary nature; these are the shining stars which in abiding peace adorn the highest heaven, or which as planets pursue their heavenly paths in an eternally, unchanging order.[3] But in addition, there are innumerable beings of an æthereal nature between heaven and earth, which are appropriately described as dæmons, and honoured by men as gods.[4] Here we have reminiscences of that early Stoic theology of intermediate beings which was intended to rationalize popular belief.[5]

The most fruitful thought in Poseidonios was his monotheism; it recognized, in the old pantheistic prime-being, the creator and sustainer of the world, and gave to the individual

---

[1] Ps. Aristot., *de mundo*, i, 391–401, ed. Bekker   [2] Cic., *nat. deor.*, 2, 62
[3] *Nat. deor.*, 2, 42, 54. Sext., 9, 86 f.   [4] Cic., *ibid.*, 2, 6. Sext., 9, 87
[5] Cf. (e.g.) Chrysipp., ii, 315–321, Arnim

the certainty of divine providence.[1] This is the source of that
faith in God which Epictetus instilled into the souls of his
disciples to make them proud and strong; here is the origin of
the glowing, poetic inspiration which uses the most varied
language to laud the eternal harmony and beauty of the
cosmos.

The author of the pseudonymous *Concerning the World* boldly
took a further step, and passed from the immanence to the
transcendence of God. It appeared to him to be unworthy to
find the godhead everywhere in the world; not in its midst,
but above in heaven, to which we men lift up our hands in
prayer; beyond the utmost limits, and as a pure being in a pure
place, above all the confusion of the lower regions, the God of
the cosmos sits upon His throne, the Saviour and Creator of all
things. Just as the steersman his ship, the driver his waggon,
the conductor his choir, the law the state, the general the army,
so does He govern the world. Just as the Persian "Great King",
unapproachable and invisible, gives out his commands, which
are then passed on from the great ones about the throne, to the
officials, and so maintains order in his mighty kingdom, so, too,
the divine power which preserves all things, operates upon the
nearest material world, i.e. the constellations of heaven; it is
carried further by them, and brought down to our regions
beneath. Naturally it becomes weaker in its benefactions the
further the distance; nevertheless it binds the whole in a harmony which proceeds from him and returns to him. He gives
the signal. Then the stars and the whole heaven revolve, the
sun pursues his double journey, creating day and night and the
four seasons of the year; rain falls and the winds blow at their
proper time; the streams flow and the sea ebbs and flows; trees
become green and fruits ripen; living creatures are born, they
grow and pass away, each one according to its own nature.[2]
What Goethe's angels sang in praise of the Lord on His heavenly
throne was based on the faith of this ancient time. This faith
resounded in philosophic disquisitions and in popular wisdom
literature, in Jewish and Christian liturgies, throughout the
centuries, as the noblest expression of ancient monotheism.

[1] Cic., *nat. deor.*, 2, 164
[2] Ps. Aristot., *de mundo*, 5–6

Chapter Ten

THE FATE OF JEWISH CHRISTIANITY

THE ORIGINAL CHURCH AT JERUSALEM STOOD APART FROM the development of Christianity into a world religion. The free attitude of the Hellenists of Antioch denied the permanent authority of the Law. In the same way, the freedom preached and, in principle, founded by Paul, appeared to it as entirely heretical and to call for definite repudiation. We have already described the conflict of Paul with Peter and the representatives of James in Antioch, and Galatians tells us of Jewish propaganda in the Galatian churches. The propaganda was intended to bring about a complete observance of Jewish ceremonial, including circumcision, among all Gentile Christians. It disallowed any compromise reached in Jerusalem. This aggressive programme had only a restricted and temporary success, if it could claim any at all. In view of missionary work which was making rapid progress among the Gentiles, it was a practical impossibility to fetter the converted multitudes to the entire ritual law, and even the relatively modest requirements of the Apostolic Decree could not be maintained, because the course of evolution had passed over the heads of the people at Jerusalem. From a distance, they were regarded with the highest respect and were recognized as the supreme "apostolic" authorities, nevertheless their views were quickly and entirely disregarded. The only thing that was definitely kept in mind was that they had recognized the Gentile Christian's freedom from the law. They were not able to influence the development of Christianity any further, because the apostolic age was approaching its end in both the east and the west.

As time went on, the relation of the original church to the Jews became more strained. By the favour of his friend Caligula, Agrippa was made king of a great part of Palestine after an adventurous life as a prince. This Agrippa was the relatively unimpressive grandson of Herod the Great, and his life, in both Rome and the east, had landed him into large debts. On becoming king he made himself acceptable by his Pharisaic scrupulousness and his popular behaviour. One of his popular deeds was to imprison James, the son of Zebedee, and Peter, two leading members of the Christians. Subsequently he killed James with the sword, whereas Peter miraculously escaped from prison.[1] But the king only kept his throne for three years (A.D. 41–44) before he died, when the Roman procurator took control of the entire land once more. The Christian church was still threatened. The High-Priest, Chananiah ben Chananiah,[2] dragged James, the leader of the church, before the high court in the year 62, and had him condemned to death, obviously on account of alleged religious wrong-doing, seeing that he was stoned.[3] Although this was disapproved of severely by eminent members of the Pharisaic party, it brought the church to the definite decision to leave Jerusalem. In addition there was growing unrest in the country, and Jewish nationalists believed that their day had come. The apostles received a revelation in regard to coming terrors and therefore the original church left the city and migrated to Pella.[4] This was a Gentile city in Transjordania opposite Samaria, bitterly hated by the Jews,[5] and ravaged by them at the beginning of the war for freedom. But it offered welcome shelter to the Christians.

And now, the tremendous drama of the Jewish war entered upon its first act, after it had already been announced for many years by beacon flame after beacon flame, in various places throughout Palestine. More than one "Messiah" had called the embittered population to arms, and organized bands of the "Sicarii" had wandered, pillaging and murdering not only Gentiles and Samaritans, but also leaders of their own people whom they disliked. In Cæsarea there was, in the end, a conflict between Jews and Greeks which led to bloodshed. On this account Florus the procurator did not meet the wishes of the Jews, although a large bribe had been offered him to that end. On the contrary, he demanded the payment of almost double the sum from the temple treasury of Jerusalem. This caused an insurrection amongst the people, which at first he managed to put down with barbaric methods, but later the rising spread

[1] Acts 12: 1–19   [2] Schürer, ii, 273
[3] Jos., *Ant.*, 20, 200. The Christian legend is given by Hegesippus in *Eus.* ii, 23, 4–18
[4] *Eus.*, iii, 5, 2–3   [5] Jos., *B.*, 2, 458

rapidly. King Agrippa II, who controlled a little of eastern and northern Palestine, failed in his efforts to mediate; open rebellion broke loose in an attempt to throw off Roman suzerainty. The symbol of liberation would be that sacrifices for the emperor were brought to an end.

It was in vain that the Jerusalem aristocracy uttered warnings. They followed these warnings by begging Florus and Agrippa to intervene quickly. The king alone acted and sent two thousand men to their aid. These men tried to defend themselves, along with the Roman garrison, in the upper city. It was useless; the castle Antonia and the palace of Herod were stormed by the insurgents and burnt. The garrison was destroyed partly in honourable battle and partly by breach of terms after they had capitulated. About the same time, the Roman garrisons in Masada, Machærus, and Jericho were overpowered. Meanwhile in the Gentile cities and especially in Cæsarea, there was a general slaughter of the Jews, which the Jews repaid in blood wherever they had sufficient power. All this happened in the late summer of A.D. 66, and the procurator let it happen. Then the higher military authorities began to move: the legate of Syria, Cestius Gallus, combined the available auxiliaries with his twelfth legion, marched from the coast into the Jewish region, and pressed to the walls of Jerusalem, but he could do no more. Surprise attacks were unsuccessful, and he had not sufficient force for a regular siege. Therefore he faced about, and, in descending from the Jewish highlands to the lowlands, his army was brought to a stand on the coast, and definitely defeated by the Jews. The first act of the drama ended with victory for the insurgent people. The freedom of Israel was then proclaimed and silver shekels were coined with the proud inscription "Israel's shekel. Year 1", and "Holy Jerusalem", and henceforward the years were numbered on the coins from the "Liberation of Zion". The aristocracy of the city, who had hitherto been in the opposition, now placed themselves at the disposal of the victorious movement and provided it with leaders.

It is obvious that Rome could not tolerate this weakening of its authority in the east. Nero entrusted one of his best generals, Vespasian, with the task of suppressing the insurrection. The latter carefully prepared the army, and, round a nucleus of three legions, he collected a force of auxiliaries, so that he could march in the spring of A.D. 67 with sixty thousand men into Galilee. The army gathered by the insurgents was at once routed, and the open country of Galilee was soon in Vespasian's hands. But the stubborn enemy drew back into fortified places and offered fierce and stiff resistance to the besiegers, although they were always overcome sooner or later. Even the Samaritans, strangely enough, at this time gathered an armed force on the holy mountain Gerizim, and seemed to threaten the Romans. Therefore a large division attacked and killed them all, eleven thousand six hundred men according to the notice in Josephus:[1] but it is difficult to see what purpose the slaughter really served.

In the spring of A.D. 68, Vespasian successfully began to bring the southern half of the land, as well as Perea, under his control; but Nero's death, and the subsequent frequent change of emperors, caused him to adopt a waiting attitude which lasted to the end of 69, when he put himself forward as a candidate for the throne, and went to Italy. His son, Titus, took over the command of the Jewish campaign after having already held a command under him. Shortly before Easter A.D. 70 Titus marched against Jerusalem where, meanwhile, the great majority of those had gathered who had resolved to fight to the last. The two years of Roman military inactivity had been wasted in bitter quarrelling between various parties who fought it out among themselves. The aristocracy were deprived of power and killed. The Zealots under the Galilean, John of Gishala, held the temple and fought the volunteers of Simon bar Giora, who held the upper city; but the appearance of the Romans rallied them together for common defence. During five long months they fought heroically against the machines and the weapons of Titus, and against the still more terrible power of famine. In July the castle Antonia fell; on August 10th the temple was destroyed in flames; on September 8th the last bulwark of Jerusalem fell in ruins together with the defences of the upper city. Yet it was not until the spring of A.D. 73 that the last sparks of the rebellion were extinguished by the fall of the southern outpost, Masada.

[1] Jos., *B.*, 3, 315

When victory was decided by the capture of the capital, Rome made the full political consequences felt: Judea became a Roman province separate from Syria and subject to a *legatus pro prætore*. It also received a more powerful military garrison, and a whole legion, the tenth,[1] was transferred to Jerusalem, where it camped among the ruins of the city, which had been rendered uninhabitable.[2] The sacrificial system was deservedly destroyed along with the temple. Soon afterwards fugitive Sicarii tried to initiate disturbances in Egypt, and, as a conseqence, the Jewish temple in Leontopolis, which had been in existence at least two centuries, was closed and sacrifices forbidden,[3] in spite of the loyal attitude of the Alexandrian Jews. The sanhedrin was dismissed and the High-Priest deposed at the same time. The Romans were spiteful enough to continue the temple-tax paid by the diaspora, the proceeds being devoted to the temple treasury of Jupiter Capitolinus in Rome. The Jewish national state, and the central religious organization of all Judaism, were thus destroyed.

When, two generations later, Barkochba once more raised the Messianic banner in a fanatical rebellion (A.D. 132–35) the Emperor Hadrian confirmed Vespasian's judgment in a terrible manner. He built on the site of Jerusalem the Roman colony of Ælia Capitolina, and Jews were forbidden to enter under penalty of death.

The Christians of the original church had separated themselves, some years before this catastrophe, from the Jewish people, and so did not share the tragedy. But, by their flight to Pella, they came into contact with Jewish sects of various kinds which had separated themselves at an earlier date, and had prepared places of refuge in the region east of the Jordan as well as east and south of the Dead Sea. Josephus does not mention them, but Christian authors of the second century[4] enumerate many Jewish groups alongside the Pharisees, Sadducees, and Essenes. They bore all sorts of names, mostly meaningless to us nowadays.

Of course the "Samaritans" are familiar enough, they were not Jews in a racial sense but descendants of foreign colonists

---

[1] Ritterling, *Pauly-W.*, xii, 1,671–77   [2] Jos., *B.*, 7, 3
[3] *Ibid.*, 7, 433–36   [4] Justin, *dial.*, 80. Hegesippus in *Eus.*, iv, 22, 7

whom the Assyrians had settled in mid-Palestine. In the course
of time they had accepted the Mosaic religion, but held themselves aloof from the temple at Jerusalem and possessed one of
their own on Mount Gerizim. They expected the Messiah with
a lively hope, and, when the Romans suppressed a Messianic pretender of theirs, they paid the cost with their blood.[1] The
baptizing sects, of which several appeared under various names,
were undoubtedly genuine Jewish organizations. Their characteristic was the custom, already found amongst the Essenes,[2] of
purifying themselves daily by a ceremonial bath, whereas
official Judaism employed such lustrations only for special cases
of defilement. Only in the fourth century do we find further
particulars in Epiphanius,[3] in regard to other Jewish sects. He
collected together all sorts of pedantic details about seven "pre-
Christian heresies" among the Jews, and examined their effects
subsequently on Christianity. Beside the groups known to us
from Josephus, he mentions also the baptists and says that the
Nasarenes[4] followed them. These lived in Galaaditis and
Basanitis, i.e. in the neighbourhood of Pella up to the mountains
of Hauran. In general, they observed the Jewish rites, but
adopted a somewhat critical attitude towards the Pentateuch;
they ate no meat and rejected animal sacrifices—once more
reminding us of the Essenes.[5] Apparently the Ossæans,[6] or
Sampsæans, who lived in the south in Moab or Nabatea, were
closely similar to the Nasarenes, because they agreed with them
in their attitude towards sacrificial worship and the Mosaic
tradition.

It was into this sphere that the Christians came who had fled
to Pella. They had been expelled by the Jews in Jerusalem
because, in spite of all their adherence to the ancient traditional
basis of their religion and race, they were driven by their
religious peculiarities into irreconcilable antagonism. There
was much in the earliest traditions of the Christian church
which was, perhaps, very similar to the older sects; thus
approximations were prepared for, and confirmed occasionally
in later times.

The original church disappeared with the migration to Pella

---

[1] Jos., *Ant.*, 18, 85–87   [2] *Vide supra*, pp. 36 f.   [3] Epiph., *haer.*, 14–20
[4] *Ibid.*, 18   [5] *Vide supra*, pp. 35 f.   [6] Epiph., *ibid.*, 19; cf. 53, 1

and the destruction of Jerusalem. At the same time it sank below the horizon of Gentile Christianity which was in process of conquering the world and which had thereby become dominant in Christendom. It was felt that the judgment of God had fallen on the Holy City, and, to all eyes, it was plainly His punishment for the crucifixion of the Lord. By the destruction of the temple and its worship and the abolition of the Law, Jewish Christianity lacked not only a racial, but also a religious basis for its former claims, and thus was forgotten in the church catholic. It sank to oblivion in the lonely deserts of East Jordan. In later centuries Christian theologians only occasionally cast curious glances at these remnants of a most honourable past, and spoke to their own contemporaries about them as a strange phenomenon. In theological terms, they set these Jewish Christians down under the rubric of "heretics", but only very few people can ever have bothered about them, if only because they lived in such a remote region. But about A.D. 150 the Apologist, Justin,[1] who had been born in Palestine, discussed the question whether Christian Jews, who observed the Law, could be saved. Obviously he knew of such churches, and was inclined to let them count as Christians if only they did not require that same observance from others; but he was aware that many people would not recognize them even then. However, there is ground for assuming that Justin was not discussing an actual problem, but only a theoretic case. Even the warnings of Ignatius, which had been written a generation earlier against Jewish ways, can scarcely have anything to do with the early Jewish Christians.[2]

Towards the end of the second century, a statement was drawn up by Irenæus of Lyons[3] which is the source of the official records of the Church in regard to the Jewish Christians. He calls them "Ebionites", which is a Biblical Hebrew expression for the "poor", and a term which the Jerusalem church used of itself.[4] The name bears witness to the connection between the later Jewish church of Transjordan and the first church in Jerusalem. Irenæus was aware that Ebionites denied the virgin birth of Jesus, used only Matthew's gospel, and would have

[1] Justin, *dia.*, 47, 1–3   [2] Ign., *Magn.*, 8–10, *Philad.*, 6, 1
[3] Iren., i, 26, 2   [4] *Vide supra*, pp. 62 f.

nothing to do with the apostle Paul. They explained the prophetic writings in their own way, and their manner of life was
quite Jewish, and this to such an extent that they even faced
Jerusalem in prayer as if God dwelt there. Is this statement
based on Irenæus's personal knowledge, or on extraneous information from an older source? It is certain that he himself had
found no Ebionites in Gaul, and it is at least doubtful whether
he had met with them in his home town of Smyrna in Asia
Minor.

Almost throughout the whole of the following two centuries,
we hear nothing more of Jewish Christian churches, except that
the old records are passed on, sometimes with minor additions.
Origen,[1] for example, says that, besides the Ebionites already
mentioned, there were others who accepted the Virgin Birth.
Only isolated and shadowy persons are known to have come
over from that little world into the church catholic. Ariston the
apologist came from Pella and thus perhaps was one of those
Jewish Christians. He tells of the war of Barkochba,[2] but
Barkochba was not a Jewish Christian. Hegesippus, who
laboured in the Antonine period, and who was rightly held by
Eusebius in high esteem, made use of Jewish-Christian sources
in his work and shows himself to be a Christian formerly of the
Jewish faith. Eusebius agrees,[3] but does not say that he belonged
to the sect of Jewish Christians. On the other hand Origen[4]
tells of Symmachus, a translator of the Bible, and says that he
had been an Ebionite. Moreover, Origen knew of writings of his
which criticized Matthew, an item confirmed by a later notice.[5]

Not till the second half of the fourth century are further
details available in regard to the remains of Jewish Christianity, in the writings of two men who had investigated the
problem for themselves. Epiphanius, the historian of the
heretics, is our chief source of information. He came from
Salamis in Cyprus, and about A.D. 370 he collected everything
that had come to him about the "Nazorenes" and the
"Ebionites". He describes the former in the same manner as
the Ebionites of Irenæus, and expressly said that they spoke

[1] Orig., *c. Cels.*, 5, 61, cf. 2, 1; 5, 65. *Hom. in Jerem.*, 19, 12, Klost
[2] In Euseb., *H.E.*, iv, 6, 3   [3] Eus., *H.E.*, iv, 22, 8   [4] Orig. in Eus., *H.E.*, vi, 17
[5] Marius Victorinus, *Com. on Gal.*, 1, 19; 2, 26 (Migne lat., viii, 1155, 1162);
cf. in addition Epiph., *haer.*, lii, 1, 8

Hebrew.[1] The Old Testament was read aloud by them in the original text, and their gospel of Matthew was written in Hebrew with Hebrew characters. They dwelt in Pella, in Kokaba in the Hauran, and in Berœa which lay far to the north and east of Antioch. The impression given is that the Hebrew Jewish-Christians of Antioch may, at an early date, have left the entirely Hellenistic church in the great city, and fled to the east—so that Berœa was related to Antioch as Pella to Jerusalem.

Jerome was living about that time in the wilderness of Chalcis, east of Antioch, and he also had found traces of "Nazarenes". He visited them in Berœa and copied their Hebrew gospel of Matthew,[2] asserting that he translated it afterwards into both Greek and Latin; unfortunately nothing has been preserved of these translations except a very few quotations.[3] According to him there was a copy of this Hebrew Matthew in the library at Cæsarea. But this gospel was not, as Jerome thought, the ancient Aramaic original but a translation of our present canonical text into the west-Syrian dialect; it contained not a few legendary glosses. Apparently there was also a Greek retranslation of it for Greek-speaking Jewish Christians, isolated traces of which survive in the Fathers and in critical, marginal notes of New Testament manuscripts.[4]

Of course, these churches of the east, distinct from the church catholic, did not maintain unchanged the traditions of the early period, but, rather, came largely under the influence of the Jewish sects already described, and shared their spiritual life. In Trajan's third year (A.D. 101), a prophet, called Alexis, arose in East Jordan, who was afterwards known by the Syriac form of his name Elxai—Chel-Ksai, meaning "the secret power".[5] He wrote his prophecies in a book which his churches faithfully preserved. The chief historians of the heretics discuss

[1] Epiph., haer., xxix, 7, 4; 9, 4
[2] Jerome, vir. inl., 2, 3, dial. adv. Pelag., 3, 2. Epist, cxx, 8, 2. Epiph., haer., xxix, 9, 4. Euseb., Theophany, 4, 12, p. 183, 29, Gressmann
[3] A. Schmidtke, jüden-christl. Evang. (T.U. 37, 1), 32–41. E. Klostermann, Apokrypha, ii (Kl. Texte, 8)
[4] Ignat., ad Smyrn., 3, 1–2, =Jer., op. cit., 16; the fragment no. 45 in Schmidtke, op. cit., 39 f. proves retranslation from the Syriac. Do nos. 3–5 (Clemens und Origenes, Klosterm. fr., 5, 27) also originate there?
[5] Lidzbarski, H., d. nord sem. Epigr., p. 217 n. and Ephemeris, 2, 198. Epiph., xix, 2, 10

it and preserve fragments.[1] The Jewish basis of religion, including circumcision, ritual ordinances, and Sabbath observance, as well as facing Jerusalem in prayer, is fully maintained
by Elxai.[2] The prophet shared with the sects east of the Jordan
the non-acceptance of the Prophets and of bloody animal
sacrifices,[3] which meanwhile had become impossible on account
of the destruction of Jerusalem. He set a high value upon
washings, "the baptisms" which he particularly recommends
as therapeutics for illness and dæmon possession.[4] Christ was
the Son of the "Great and Highest God" and was called the
"Great King". He was a pre-existent being of divine power
who already in previous ages had been incarnated in various
persons, e.g. in Adam. Elxai had seen Him as a giant equal in
size to a great mountain whose height could be estimated at
ninety-six miles. At His side, and similarly tall, was His sister,
Rucha, the Holy Spirit.[5]

Thus Christianity was for him the divine religion and his
sacred book was intended for baptized Christians. But he knew
better than the Church, since he preached a second baptism for
forgiveness of sins a second time. Whoever had sexual sins of
any kind upon his conscience, and listened to the words of the
book must at once go and let himself be baptized in the name
of God and of the Great King, and in particular, as is asserted
both here and elsewhere, in his clothes, and not naked as was
customary in the Church. Then forgiveness of sins would be
imparted to him afresh. But during the performance of the
sacred rite, he must call upon the "seven witnesses", heaven,
water, the holy spirits, the angels of prayer, oil, salt, the earth;
these would guarantee that he neither sins, commits adultery,
steals, oppresses, deceives, hates, transgresses, nor finds pleasure
in any evil thing.[6]

It was a genuine baptism of repentance for forgiveness of
sins, and it necessitated conversion. It offered another opportunity for obtaining salvation before the end of all things, just

[1] Hippol., ix, 13–17; x, 29. Epiph., *haer.*, xix, 1–5; xxx, 17 cf. Harnack, *Lit.*, i,
207–29
[2] Hippol., ix, 14, 1; 16, 3. Epiph., xix, 3, 5   [3] Epiph., xix, 3, 6; liii, 1, 7
[4] Hippol., ix, 15, 1; 4–16, 1. Epiph., *haer.*, xxx, 17, 4
[5] Hippol., ix, 13, 1–3. Epiph., xix, 4, 1–2; xxx, 17, 5–7; liii, 1, 8–9
[6] Hippol., ix, 15. Epiph., xix, 1, 6; xxx, 2, 4–5

as had formerly been preached by John, and a conversion quite similar to that preached a generation later by the Shepherd of Hermas to the Roman Christians. He who accepted it, though he were a heretic, would attain "peace and his share with the righteous". Sexual sins are particularly emphasized in this prescription because they appeared to Elxai to press hardest. On this account, he would have nothing to do with sexual asceticism but required early marriage,[1] and in so doing he expressed the popular and universal view of these Judaizing Christians.

The names of the "seven witnesses" testify to the fact that speculations on the elements and their sacramental power, and on the heavenly world of spirits, were not foreign to his sphere of ideas. Fire appeared to him as the element of error and estrangement from God, whereas the sound of water leads along the right road.[2] Moreover astrology supplied him with building material for his system of doctrine. He knew the influence of evil stars and their authority over many days, particularly if the moon entered into conjunction with them. At such times no one might begin any work, baptize either man or woman, but must wait until the moon had left its inauspicious orientation. Of the seven days of the week, the Sabbath was to be kept particularly holy, but also on the third day, i.e. Tuesday, no work might be begun because the number three was the symbol of a universal catastrophe: three years after Trajan's Parthian war (A.D. 114–116), war would break out between the wicked angels of the north.[3] But nothing further is recorded about this unfulfilled prophecy,[4] and we cannot say whether Elxai developed an apocalyptic of his own.

It is not easy to get a clear picture of the essential nature of this prophet from the scattered remarks of his opponents. The Jewish elements of his preaching are clearly recognizable, and are full of a rank imagery with which both the apocalyptic, and the specifically Christian, ideas are decked out. His baptismal ceremonies, and his negation of animal sacrifices and false prophecy, show that he belonged to one of the sects east of Jordan. In addition, his ideas about astronomy and elementary spirits remind us of the polemical discussions in Paul's

---

[1] Epiph., xix, 1, 7   [2] Epiph., xix, 3, 7; liii, 1, 7
[3] Hippol., ix, 16, 2–4   [4] E. Schwartz., *Z.N.W.*, 31, 195

epistle to the Colossians (2: 9, 16–18). Such ideas had probably already become naturalized in dissenting sects of Judaism. Nothing of this is syncretistic in the proper sense; but we are standing at the cradle of a Judaistic gnosis, and the succeeding ages found in Elxai the "secret power", i.e. the incarnation of the godhead in a superman. This idea occurs elsewhere[1] about A.D. 100. The characterization of fire as an evil element was meant to express antithesis to Persian views.

The *Book of Elxai* seems to have been kept a close secret in accordance with the wish of its author,[2] and would never have been known had not a certain Alcibiades brought it about A.D. 200 from Apamea in Syria to Rome. He claimed to be a prophet of Elxai's, though without much success.[3] His preaching about the forgiveness of sins made Bishop Hippolytus suspicious, for Hippolytus was a rigorous defender of penance. He examined the new apostle and his old book very closely, and wrote a detailed account in his work on heretics, and this work is the source of our knowledge. Elxai had little significance for church history, or for the evolution of Jewish Christianity. His teaching is only a welcome testimony to the strength, and fantastic variety, of the gnosis which was then beginning to appear in Syria or round about.

About A.D. 380 Epiphanius, the zealous bishop of Cyprus, not only read the record of Hippolytus, but apparently also the *Book of Elxai*. He mentions two sisters of the prophet's family who were still alive and who were honoured as saints because they possessed miraculous power.[4] But he then asserts that the book had exercised great influence and had been made much use of in the Clementine writings, which Epiphanius regarded as documents coming from the early Jewish-Christian church. For a long time this misled students; and only quite recently have penetrating researches[5] made it possible to recognize the Clementine writings as fictions without historical basis, and valueless for the study of the early Christian and Judaistic period, and without any connection with Elxai and his church.

Unfortunately, Epiphanius commits many sins of confusion also in the details of his account of the "Nazorenes". In

<hr/>

[1] Acts 8: 10   [2] Hippol., ix, 17, 1   [3] *Ibid.*, ix, 13, 1
[4] Epiph., *haer.*, xix, 2, 1 2 ;liii, 1, 5   [5] E. Schwartz, *Z.N.W.*, 31, 151–199

particular he naïvely introduces here facts which really refer to the Ebionites. This makes it most difficult to discover the truth. Perhaps this much can be said: that some "Ebionites" were living on the island of Cyprus, and therefore in his own diocese;[1] he owes his more reliable information to them. He was aware that various apocryphal Acts of the Apostles were in use amongst them, and he specially emphasizes a "Jacob's Ladder" which expressed their aversion to sacrificial rites and burnt offerings, and which calumniated Paul bitterly.[2] He had had in his hands the gospel which was in use amongst them, and he quotes numerous passages from it that make their gospel appear to have been a fantastic redaction of the canonical Matthew, but making use also of Luke. Vegetarianism seems to have been favoured in it, and, clearly, it was hostile to sacrifices.[3] It said that John the Baptist lived on oil-cakes instead of animal locusts; that Jesus expressly repudiated the roasted Passover lamb, and that it was His work to abolish ceremonial sacrifices. Whether this apocryphal gospel had anything to do with the Gospel to the Hebrews, already mentioned,[4] cannot be determined, because the passages quoted are not such as to allow any comparisons, and what Epiphanius himself says[5] is no guarantee of accurate knowledge.

Hence we find in Cyprus the last remains of the separate Jewish church. It was still living a vegetative sort of life toward the end of the fourth century, and apparently it was not much different from the strange church in Berœa and other survivals in the east. It has been suggested recently[6] that Asia Minor also had offered a home to fugitive Jewish Christians. True, Philip the evangelist, who had settled in Cæsarea with his four prophetic daughters, was claimed towards the end of the second century by Hierapolis as a local saint. They averred that he and two of his daughters were buried there, and that a third daughter's grave was in Ephesus the capital.[7] The Easter-praxis in Asia Minor, of which we shall have to speak later

---

[1] Epiph., haer., xxx, 18, 1 [2] Op. cit., xxx, 16, 6–9
[3] Op. cit., xxx, 13–14. Extant passages given in E. Klostermann, Apokrypha, ii (2nd edition) (Kl. Texte, 8), p. 9–12; fr. 2, 6, 5
[4] Vide supra, p. 185. [5] Epiph., haer., xxx, 3, 7
[6] K. Holl, Ges. Aufs., ii, 66 f. E. Schwartz, Z.N.W., 31, 190 f.
[7] Acts 21: 8, 9. Polycrates' epistle to Victor of Rome in Eus., H.E., iii, 31,3; cf. Gaius in Eus., H.E., iii, 31, 4

remained closely attached to the Jewish mode as distinct from the custom which obtained in the rest of the church which had departed therefrom. The Apocalypse of John, which was based on Jewish sources, and which was rooted in Jewish feeling, was undoubtedly written in Asia Minor. Its author presupposes that the Apostolic Decree[1] held good in the church at Pergamon, and that it was endangered by the Nicolaitans. Even the polemic of the Fourth Gospel, against the Jews, seems to become more comprehensible if regarded as essentially a reaction against a Jewish Christianity which remained faithful to tradition. It is better to set aside the tradition that John, the son of Zebedee, lived in his old age in Ephesus, and was buried there, because that tradition was unknown to Ignatius about A.D. 117, and probably rests on a false identification. In any case the arguments are not cogent enough for more than a possibility. The Jewish-Christian church died out quietly, and in isolation. The church of the conquering, universal form of Christianity, which was now waxing mightily, took no notice of the decease of her elder sister.

[1] Rev. 2: 14

Chapter Eleven

THE SUB-APOSTOLIC PERIOD

THE APOSTOLIC AGE CLOSED WITH THE DEATH OF THE LAST apostle of whose decease trustworthy information has been preserved, viz. Peter. The blood-red glow of the Neronian persecution lit up the end of the period during which the young religion had gained a firm foundation in history. The Roman church wrote no chronicle, and the fearful event left no trace behind in the memory of Christians elsewhere. As a consequence we learn no exact details from church sources about this first great attack upon the church. Even Eusebius[1] only touches it in a few words which tell very little. But Tacitus found material here which he could use for his sketch of Nero's savagery and he affords us a record which is of immeasurable value and which shows how the few hints in the epistle of Clement of Rome are to be understood.[2] In July, A.D. 64, a tremendous fire, lasting for more than six days, laid the greater part of the city of Rome in ashes. Nero immediately began to rebuild energetically, prescribed the style and reconstructed with the greatest beauty. Then came a rumour that the fire had been instigated by high authority. In order to root out this suspicion, the Emperor accused the Christians of responsibility, and punished them severely. A few confessed themselves Christians, and were arrested: others began to make the same confession, and in the end a great number were gathered together. It is true that examination brought out nothing which implicated them in the fire, but it was decided that they were "enemies of the human race". They must therefore die, not by simple execution, but in various forms of a hideous game: they were sewed up in animal skins and mauled by bloodhounds; they were bound on oxen; torn to pieces in the arena; crucified. Swathed in bindings dipped in pitch, they were burned as torches in the imperial gardens at the Vatican. It is highly probable that Peter was crucified in this persecution, as is

[1] Eus., *H.E.*, ii, 25, 1–8
[2] Tac., *Ann.*, 15, 44; cf. Suetonius, *Nero*, 16. 1 *Clem.*, 6, 1–2

testified by a very early witness.[1] His body was buried near to
the Neronian circus on the Via Cornelia. It is probable that
Paul had been executed with the sword some time before and
had been buried on the road to Ostia. Both graves were shown
to sightseers about A.D. 200 in the same places where they are
revered to-day. They lie in sites apart from those of all other
cults of early Christian Rome, so that there can be scarcely any
doubt of their genuineness.[2]

But the glare of this outburst only lights for a brief moment
the darkness which shrouds the early history of the Roman
church. That church disappears from our knowledge, and only
becomes visible again a generation later, and this time in clear
light. It happened in the following manner. A quarrel had
broken out in the church at Corinth. The younger generation
had set itself against the authority of the older, and had deprived of office the bishops and deacons chosen by them,
although no material accusation of any kind could be made.
The motive which caused the whole disturbance must therefore
have been simply the desire for a new distribution of the posi-
tions of authority. The formal basis must be sought in parallel
phenomena in ancient confraternities. It was everywhere
customary—for that matter among the Jews also—for the
authorities of religious organizations to be chosen only for a
term, and after the end of their period of office to be replaced
by fresh persons if they were not re-elected. Many members
must have felt that the same custom ought to obtain with the
Church. Action was taken accordingly, and those who had
formerly been chosen[3] by the church were deposed by a new
decision of the church. Of course this did not take place without
opposition, and the noise of the conflict resounded across the
sea as far as Rome.

Then the Roman community, in full consciousness of the
unity of the Church as a whole, felt itself obliged to discharge
a service of love, and so intervened. One of its bishops, Clement
by name,[4] carried out the commission, and wrote a letter to

---

[1] John 21: 18, 19
[2] Gaius in Eus., *H.E.*, ii, 25, 7; cf. Lietzmann, *Petrus und Paulus in Rom.*, 2nd
edition, 1927
[3] 1 *Clem.*, 44, 3; cf. *Didache*, 15, 1
[4] Dionys. of Corinth in Eus., *H.E.*, iv, 23, 11

Corinth. Feeling himself to be the heir of Paul, he shows clearly both in his words of greeting, and in the whole style of his introduction, that he intended to write a letter in the way that the Apostle was accustomed to write to his churches when in need of earnest exhortation. It feels almost like this: if Clement had not been commissioned by the Roman church, but had written on his own initiative, he would probably have written the author's name as "Paul, the apostle of Jesus Christ", and we should have possessed another pseudo-Pauline letter.

The Roman church had to deplore difficulties of her own: sudden blows of fate had followed one another swiftly and had prevented her intervention in Corinthian affairs until this late date. But she intervened now in full force; the leaders of the rebellion were severely chided, jealousy and envy described as the instigating causes, and then in the style of a sermon the author passes on to deliver to the Corinthians a lengthy address which offers us a good example of contemporary religious oratory, and which concludes at last with an extended liturgical prayer. We gain highly important details in regard to the case itself.[1] We know[2] that the early churches were inclined to hold their bishops and deacons in low esteem as compared with the charismatics who were led by the spirit of God; but we are informed also that these officials, who had been entrusted with their office by election, gradually and to an increasing extent, took over the spiritual duties and liturgical functions properly so called—probably *pari passu* with the growing infrequency of prophets with the charisma. In practice therefore they gradually came to be the normal leaders of public worship without abandoning their technical obligations and competence. This meant, however, that they united spiritual and secular power in their own persons.

As long as they were only the business and financial officials of individual churches they could be regarded as analogous to Jewish or pagan leaders in a similar community, and a temporal limit to their office could be required and applied. By the nature of the case, a charismatic could not be deposed, because he had been appointed by God through the gift of the spirit; and he could only lose office by God's intervention, and

[1] *Clem.*, 40–44   [2] *Vide supra*, p. 146. *Didache*, 15, 2

this at the same time as he lost the gift of the spirit. If now the elected *episcopos* took the place of such a prophet, the next thing was to grant that the former could no more be set aside than the latter—and it is this very point that the epistle of Clement explains to the Corinthians. Of course he does not do so by historical evidence like us, but by arguments which were to become of the greatest importance to the entire church catholic. Time, place, and personnel of the cultus, so he explains, were already prescribed by God in the Old Testament and exact regulations established for all spiritual functions; and to transgress these regulations was a deadly sin. In the same way, the divine revelation that had come to the Church followed a definite order: God sent Christ, Christ the Apostles, and these, on their missionary journeys, installed bishops and deacons, just as had already been explicitly prophesied in Isa. 60: 17. Since the Apostles foresaw future disputes, they prescribed that the offices should be taken over by other approved men only after the death of their first holders. Thus those bishops who stood in the traditional succession, who had been appointed "with the assent of the whole church", and who had exercised their office blamelessly, were not to be deposed on any account, for their status had been legitimized by apostolic authority. Their status differed fundamentally, and by divine will, from that of the laity.[1]

Here is the germ of the doctrine of the divine ordination of the clergy, and of its indelible character. Not unjustly has the writing of this chapter been described as the moment in which Roman Catholic canon law was born. As yet the theory was not formulated quite clearly, for it does not say expressly that a bishop could only be installed in his office by another bishop. The author only speaks of "other respected men" who install bishops, and, in so doing, act in the place of Apostles.[2] But since Clement traces the traditional succession in the other direction emphatically to God, his ideal is undoubtedly the future lengthening of this chain through a whole series of bishops; and from this point of view we have to regard the "respected men" as bishops. Then the doctrine follows logically, viz. that apostolic succession, i.e. the unbroken transference of office from the Apostles, and

[1] 1 *Clem.*, 44, 1–3; 40, 5   [2] 1 *Clem.*, 44, 3

from one bishop to another, legitimizes the present holder of spiritual power and makes him independent of the local church. Once on a day the church chose its bishops as technical functionaries, but now the bishops chose their successors and the church only possessed the "right of assent". She possesses it, and exercises it, in Rome to the present day, when a newly elected pope shows himself on the loggia of St. Peter's and receives the joyous acclamation of the crowd assembled on the campus.

It is also significant that Clement founded his doctrine on Scripture, i.e. the Old Testament. He regarded it as very obvious that the prescriptions for the cultus in the Holy Book were types of the new Christian ordinations for worship, and he said nothing more about carrying them out in their original sense. From the fact that, in the Old Testament, the forms of public worship were exactly regulated in every respect, and that departure from them was on pain of death, Clement deduced, without more ado, that the same must be the case in the Christian church. And, since he plainly regarded his argument as obvious to the readers of his document, we may draw the conclusion that it was a method of theological thought common to Christians of the day. The Old Testament had, therefore, already been wrested from the Jews and had become the special property of Christians to such an extent that its commandments could be regarded as "types", and used to regulate church life.

But there was more. The entire epistle is dominated in the highest degree by the language of the Greek Bible; moreover, it cites, ever and again, shorter or longer Biblical passages. Its theological proof relies throughout on the Old Testament side by side with two quite isolated passages,[1] where words of Jesus are cited as authoritative bases. God Himself spoke in this Holy Book, as also did Christ[2] through the Holy Spirit, and revealed everything necessary for salvation. Every truth of the knowledge of God, every record of God's commands, of His strictness as a judge, and of His forgiving bounty, were to be found in the Old Testament. This book had led the generations of the past into a better condition of heart, just as it led Christians in the

1 *Clem.*, 13. 2; 46, 8   2 *Ibid.*, 22, 1

present in the right way. Thus the teachings of Biblical history, and the experiences of Old Testament men and women, could offer exhortation to, and example for, a right way of life.[1] We must add that the value, which could be placed directly upon the literal word, was extended significantly by discovering allegorical meanings, and concealed prophecies, about Christ;[2] this will enable us fully to understand the central place of the Holy Scriptures in the Christianity of the church at Rome. It was the foundation book of divine revelations, fitted to teach the "chosen people", and to point them the way to salvation. This meant, however, that this people belonged to the host of those who were denoted by the allegorical name of "Israel", and whom God had chosen through Christ out of all the peoples of the world,[3] i.e. the Christians. The literal reference to the Jewish people was no more taken into account than the ritual observance of the ceremonial law.

The content of the divine law consists, above all else, of moral prescriptions formulated in commandments, or illustrated by historical examples; indeed God's joy in His works of creation is put forward as an example for human conduct.[4] It also teaches that God is no pitiless judge, but forgives the repentant sinner who contritely confesses his transgressions, and does not harden his heart. God is gracious to such a man, and brings him back to the way of truth.[5] This way itself, however, consists, first of all and above all, in observing the Jewish-Hellenistic moral doctrines which we have already discussed in connection with the literature of the diaspora described on an earlier page.[6] Dependence upon this Jewish moral theology is so strong that long passages in 1 *Clement* could have been just as well prescribed, or read aloud to the Roman synagogue. If on occasion it speaks of "immortal gnosis", or "deeps of divine gnosis",[7] no conceptions proper to Hellenistic mysticism are implied by these words, in spite of their esoteric sound; but rather a clear knowledge of the divine commands and a right interpretation of God's word in the Old Testament. If we ask about the specifically Christian element of Clement's religion,

[1] 1 *Clem.*, 7, 5–7, 9–18; 19, 1, 43; 45, 2; 50, 3; 53, 1–5   [2] *Ibid.*, 12, 7, 16
[3] 1 *Ibid.*, 29, 1–3; 50, 7; 2, 4   [4] *Ibid.*, 33, 1–8
[5] *Ibid.*, 51, 3–52, 4; 7, 5–7; 48, 1; 35, 5   [6] *Vide supra* pp. 81 ff.
[7] 1 *Clem.*, 36, 2; 40, 1

we receive a very wordy answer with frequent mention of the name of Jesus Christ, on many pages of the letter. If, however, we inquire about the contents, it is Christ who, as the very vehicle of the divine revelation, preaches and completes the teachings just depicted. The commandments of God are indeed His commandments, and in their fulfilment is found the essence of Christian love. Clement, like Paul, sang an exalted hymn of the love which brought all the virtues to perfection and lifted men up to God; or Christ showed what that love was. He sacrificed His blood by His love[1] and lighted our way as the pattern of humility.[2] Moses possessed this love in a similar fashion, and portrayed it in perfection. God's elect were[3] also perfected in this love, so that Christ's own loving work excelled that of the earlier age only in the height of its accomplishment, and not in its innate quality.

Christ, and, in particular, the blood of Christ, are then spoken of in another way and in passages which reveal a deep sense of their value: "It was shed for our salvation, and it brought the grace of repentance to the whole world," and "through the blood of the Lord, redemption comes to all those who believe and hope in God";[4]—otherwise, however, Clement says nothing about "redemption", and, according to his explicit teaching, repentance was possible even in the days of the Old Testament. But was not the resurrection of Christ the point of departure of Christianity and thereby an essentially new element as contrasted with Judaism? Assuredly, for it gave a conclusive sense of certainty to the Apostles, and was now the guarantee of the future hope that the Creator of the world, who had raised so much in nature from death to life, would also justify the faithful confidence of His devout servants, and raise them up, just as He had raised Christ, who was the first fruits.[5] The echo of Pauline teachings is clear, but we notice also that Clement is a long way from grasping their proper sense, and does not base the Resurrection on a doctrine of the pneuma.

Hence Clement, indeed, speaks of man's redemption, not by his own wisdom, piety, or works, but through faith. But when

[1] 1 *Clem.*, 49–50   [2] *Ibid.*, 16   [3] *Ibid.*, 53, 5; 49, 5, 6; cf. 21, 6
[4] *Ibid.*, 7, 4; 12, 7; 21, 6   [5] 1 *Ibid.*, 42, 3; 24, 1; 26, 1

we hear, further, that from the beginning, God had justified all by faith, we find that the formula as far as the wording goes is Paul's, but it is now filled with a strange meaning; Clement's real view is expressed where he closes his exhortations to holiness and the practice of virtue with the sentence that we "are justified by works and not by words".[1] It is true that, even with him, faith is a comprehensive word for the spiritual quality of the Christian status, but, for the most part, it is only one of the Christian virtues and is put on the same plane as the others. He illustrates its nature by the examples of Noah and Abraham, of Rahab and Esther, as consisting of an unconditional confidence in God.[2] Thus it comes about, in one passage where he inserts a long quotation from Paul's epistle to the Romans, that, in clear contradiction to the Apostle's meaning, Clement actually sums up the Christian life as a ceaseless struggle for God's gifts promised in the future on the basis of gifts which we already possess, viz., life in immortality, joy in righteousness, truth in freedom of mind, faith in trust, and restraint in sanctification.[3]

This is not the only passage in which Paul is cited. Shortly afterwards the readers are expressly urged to take the first Epistle of the Corinthians into their hands, and to notice the warnings against schism in the church; still further on in the exhortation, Clement sings a panegyric of love, clearly dependent on Paul's. The Apostle's parable of the body and its members, as a symbol of the unity of the church, appears also in Clement in a shortened form[4]—only as a figure of speech. The mystical conception of the church as the body of Christ is remote from Clement's way of thought. Equally remote are the meaning of the doctrine of justification, and the cosmic drama of the antithesis of flesh and spirit, sin and grace, Adam and Christ. The only one of all these matters that is alive in him is the conception of the spirit as the most precious possession of Christians, "abundantly poured out upon them"; but the spirit stands in the forefront of his teachings rather as an organ of

[1] 1 *Clem.*, 30, 3; 32, 4
[2] *Ibid.*, 1, 2; 3, 4; 5, 6; 6, 2. Examples are 9, 4; 10, 7; 12, 1; 55, 6; cf. 26, 1; 35, 2
[3] 1 *Clem.*, 35, 1–6 of which 5–6 comes from Rom. 1: 29–32; cf. 62, 2, 64
[4] *Ibid.*, 47, 1–3; 49, 5 from 1 Cor., 13: 4–7; the parable of the body, 37, 5–38 1; cf. 1 Cor. 12: 12–31, 46, 7; cf. also 1 Cor. 1: 13

revelation in the Old Testament and in the apostolic period. We hear nothing more of the pneumatic enthusiasm of the early church, although the incorporation of the spirit into the Trinity is proclaimed in the confessional formula:[1] "We have one God, and one Christ, and one Spirit of Grace poured upon us, and one calling through Christ."

Apart from the Old Testament, a few sayings of the Lord, and the Pauline epistles, a final source is cited which leads to an unexpected disclosure, the Roman liturgy. Not only at the end of the letter where Clement turns to prayer, but in three places earlier, phrases, which are unmistakably formed in a liturgical manner, strike the ear, and must have come from the formula used in public worship by the church at Rome.[2] They show that this church had borrowed its liturgy from the synagogue; that is the origin of the "Holy, holy, holy"; the song of praise at the orderly creation of the world and the benevolent purpose of the Creator of man; and the prayer of praise, petition, and intercession, which concludes the whole. The Christian changes and interpolations are recognizable, but the Jewish character of all the rest of the text is just as certain. And since this congregational prayer fits perfectly into the rest of the letter, it follows that a conclusion based on this letter is valid for the Roman church. It reproduces, not some special liturgy, perhaps drawn up by Clement, but the practice of Roman Christians at the end of the first century, and therefore leads to an important inference.

This church was not born of the Pauline tradition, but had only a remote and outer contact with it. It grew directly out of the Greek-speaking synagogue, and represented a conception of Christianity such as we must assume was held in those circles of proselytes who were converted by the Christian preachers, and who accepted the new gospel. In other words: just as the external considerations, with which we have already dealt, made it probable that the Roman church was founded by missionaries from Antioch, so this, the earliest document of its inner life, confirms that hypothesis in every way. Christianity to this church was the religion of the moral code commanded

[1] 1 *Clem.*, 2, 2; 46, 6; for the Trinity 46, 6; 58, 2
[2] 1 *Clem.*, 33, 2–6; 34, 5–8; 38, 3–4; 59, 2–61, 3

by God, written down in the Old Testament, and finally revealed by the last and the greatest of the prophets, Jesus, who was the personal vehicle of the Holy Spirit. To be a Christian meant to follow these ethical commands, and, if in spite of honest desire, it was not possible to fulfil them completely, the sincere confession of sin, together with a genuine desire to do better would gain the forgiveness of a merciful God. Nevertheless the fundamental proposition stood firmly, viz. that works were all important. That had been the case from the beginning of the world, and would remain so until the Day of Judgment.

The specific kind of Christianity found in the church at Rome did not recognize the authority of the ceremonial law of the Old Testament, and can never have done so. Its religion was that of the Hellenistic proselytes, who, on their Jewish side, had adopted the specific ethic of Judaism, while spiritualizing its ritual by allegory. In churches where freedom from the Law was really maintained, as can be proved of even the earliest pre-Pauline church at Antioch, Christianity must have been conceived as the direct continuation, the fulfilment, of the religion of Jewish ideals such as had already been preached to proselytes everywhere. This conception did not hinder their taking over cult-forms and liturgical prayers from the synagogue. That is what had happened, too, in the Roman church.

We know too little of Peter to be able to say what influence he exercised on the Roman church's way of thinking. But Paul had been known personally to some of Clement's generation; to these he was the celebrated world-apostle and, like Peter, the model of a martyr. Over and above that, he was the author of letters which were held in the highest honour, and were, even then, known far and wide in Christendom; copies were current throughout the world, but had already suffered the first sign of literary corruptions on being transcribed, even in Rome.[1] They were fine examples of a Christian epistolary style, their well-defined formulas, exhortations, and teachings, influenced the church's manner of speaking, but the Roman Christian had not felt the least breath of the Pauline spirit. It is not an eviscerated Paulinism, but a purely Hellenistic proselyte

[1] 1 *Clem.*, 35, 6, cites according to the Western text Rom. 1: 32

Christianity, that we meet with here in Rome, an independent growth from a root in the first church, and of importance for the future. The Roman church could trace its descent back to the Hellenistic circle of Stephen.

The next document of the church at Rome may date from a generation later. It is known to us by the name of the second Epistle of Clement, but it faithfully preserves the same spirit. This pseudepigraphic writing is a sermon which a presbyter had delivered to the church,[1] and which we may place in Rome on account of its relations with 1 *Clement*. The Christian life is depicted as a continual struggle with the world and its wiles, a struggle to maintain the purity gained in baptism.[2] To live according to Christ, according to God's commandments, is the genuine confession of the Lord;[3] and the attitude required of the Christian is that of repentance, of hatred toward this world and its brief but destructive pleasures.[4] "Let us do righteously in order that we may be saved at the end; and even if we must suffer pains for a short while in this world, we shall reap the immortal fruit of the resurrection." This struggle, however, is not easy, and even the preacher knows himself to be altogether a sinner;[5] but, although all cannot win the crown, all must strive to come as near to it as possible. God rewards honest striving, the active repentance that is shown in prayer, fasting, and especially alms-giving. He rewards the "righteous" with the glory of the coming kingdom, and He casts sinners into hell.[6] Reward and punishment are the motives of the Christian life.

In this writing also, the Old Testament is the inexhaustible source of revelation, and, side by side with it, the words of Jesus appear as the words of God;[7] but, just as in 1 *Clement*, a certain carelessness in citing the words of the Lord is unmistakable, so also we find, in 2 *Clement*, such a rank growth of fantastic extensions and confabrications of sayings[8] that we see, quite clearly, the freedom with which men of this generation handled the most worthy traditions of the original church. A

[1] 2 *Clem.*, 19, 1; cf. 17, 3   [2] *Ibid.*, 6, 9; 7, 1–6; 8, 4–6   [3] *Ibid.*, 3, 4; 4, 2
[4] *Ibid.*, 5, 1–7; 6, 3; 8, 2; 19, 3   [5] *Ibid.*, 18, 2
[6] *Ibid.*, 16, 4; for the Kingdom: 5, 5; 9, 6; 11, 7; 12, 1; for Hell: 6, 7; 17, 7; 18, 2
[7] *Ibid.*, 13, 4   [8] *Ibid.*, 4, 5; 5, 1–4; 12, 2; 13, 2

generation later, gnostic caprice, which outgrew everything else in this sphere, had made the Church ripe for a careful sifting of tradition, a fact which was of importance for its own welfare, and for ours.

The letter which bears the name of James breathes the same spirit, viz., a Christian faith which has been nurtured in the Greek synagogue. On account of the pseudonym which its author uses, this letter was included in the New Testament canon. It appears to have been known at an early date in Rome, but the place in which it was written cannot even be guessed, although such information would be valuable. Like 1 *Clement*, it stands in literary dependence upon Paul, but it goes beyond him in so far as it is not intended for a single church, but presents its greetings to the whole of Christendom in the entire Roman empire, for that alone is what is meant by the "twelve tribes of the diaspora". This term, which for many centuries had no longer corresponded to any racial entity, was now the symbol of the "true Israel" of the Biblical promises, and thus of the Christian people. In this form, which finally denied all Jewish claims, it could have been coined only in the Gentile church. This Gentile church, however, was not Pauline; on the contrary, it regarded James as the leader of the first, Jerusalem, church. Taking him as the supreme authority, it now issued the epistle of James to exhort the entire Church, and to utter warnings against the characteristic language of Paul. It was not true, e.g., that a man was justified by faith apart from works; rather we must say that a man was justified by works, and not by faith alone. Even the examples of Abraham and of Rahab, adduced in Romans and in Hebrews as a proof, spoke, on closer examination, against the Pauline theory of faith.[1] This is a definite and conscious polemic against the teaching of Paul.

But when the author carries the discussion further, and understands by "works" the exercise of all the Christian virtues; and when faith is for him the rational acceptance of a proposition,[2] it becomes clear that he had not the least understanding of Paul. The reason was that the opposition to the

---

[1] Jas. 2: 14–26; for verse 23, cf. Rom. 4: 3; for verses 21 and 25, cf. Heb. 11: 17, 31
[2] Jas. 2: 19

Pauline thesis had no longer any reality. The Jewish legal righteousness and its "works" had disappeared and been forgotten, together with all the obligatory rites. The vital thing, the perfect, royal law of freedom, was expressed in the commandment to love one's neighbour,[1] and this, when applied, issued in a number of ethical commandments corresponding to the Jewish catechism for proselytes. What is adduced by James as Christian exhortation is so entirely Jewish that many of its details show how possible it is that the epistle was, originally, a product of the Greek synagogue, made Christian by a few additions where necessary. The name of Jesus Christ is, in fact, only mentioned twice,[2] and in purely formal phrases. Nothing is said that distinguishes Christian feeling—so near had this non-Pauline Gentile Christianity of the succeeding age returned to missionary Judaism.

It was from a church of this kind that the oldest Church Order arose. By a fortunate discovery, this Order became known, in the year 1883, to the world of scholars, and since then it has enriched and established our knowledge of the growth of the ancient church in an unforeseen manner. It bears the title: *Teaching of the Twelve Apostles*, and is usually cited, by its Greek name, as the *Didache*. It combines in the shortest form all the principal prescriptions for the regulation of church life. It begins with directions for giving instruction to catechumens. There follow prescriptions for baptism, fasting, prayer, and the Lord's Supper. Then it deals with the officials who were the vehicles of the spirit, i.e. apostles, prophets, and teachers; and a short discussion is added about observing Sunday. Then it goes on to deal with bishops and deacons; and the little book concludes with an urgent admonition to shape the Christian life with reference to the imminent parousia of the Lord, the omens and accompanying phenomena being described. Everything is in the briefest form and the most sober language.

It is particularly significant that the teaching given to the candidates for baptism should be built upon the Jewish plan of the "Two Ways" as used in the Hellenistic synagogue for instructing proselytes, and of which the roots were buried deep

---

[1] Jas. 2: 8; cf. Matt. 22: 40   [2] Jas. 1: 1–2: 1

in the past. It begins with the Jewish confession of faith
(Deut. 6: 4–5) and the Decalogue, and then develops, in
several variations, the principle of a pure ethic, free from all
ritual elements. The Christians of the *Didache* now added the
commandment of love of one's neighbour as prescribed by
Jesus,[1] and as found, similarly, in the Old Testament, followed
by the rule: "Nothing that you do not desire to happen to yourself, must you do to any other." It is significant that the Golden
Rule is given in the negative form, otherwise usual, and not in
the positive redaction in which Jesus laid it down.[2] Then a
series of sayings of the Lord are placed before the next section
of the Jewish text, sayings which demand love of one's enemy,
self-sacrifice, and generosity. We see clearly that the question of
the giving, and the right acceptance, of alms caused the writer
anxiety. That is understandable, because earthly possessions
were to be employed by a Christian as a means of redemption
from his sins.[3] The way of life was an ethical struggle for an
exalted goal, and flagellation of one's self was a valuable means of
attaining it, but which, of course, not everyone could employ.
Thus, near the end, we read the comforting words:[4] "If thou
art able to take the whole yoke of the Lord upon thyself, thou
shalt be perfect. But if thou canst not do it, then thou shalt do
as much as thou canst."

Its asceticism extended to food, and we are reminded of the
vegetarians, who had already been mentioned by Paul,[5] when
the exhortation proceeds: "In regard to food be as abstemious
as you are able. But withhold unconditionally from meat
offered to idols, for that is worship of dead gods." Hence, in
this church, the prescriptions of the Apostolic Decree were
binding upon everyone. But already a differential ethic had
been developed: the "perfect" take upon themselves the entire
yoke, including obligatory asceticism; the great majority do as
much as they are able, according to their ability. Sins appeared
scarcely avoidable, but they could be annulled by the consistent giving of alms, and by public confession before the
assembled church.[6] Fasting was practised in the Jewish mode
but, as distinct from the "hypocrites", i.e. the Jews, it is to be

---

[1] Mark 12: 28–31   [2] Matt. 7: 12; Luke 6: 31   [3] *Did.*, 4, 6; cf. *Barn.*, 19, 10
[4] *Did.*, 6, 2–3; cf. 11, 11   [5] Rom. 14: 2   [6] *Did.*, 4, 6; 14, 1

on two other week-days; it was also prescribed as an express preparation for receiving baptism. The Lord's Supper is accompanied by prayers based on Jewish models. In these prayers, the church gives thanks for the divine gifts of life and knowledge brought to them through Jesus, and for spiritual food and drink; and it prays that Christians scattered throughout the entire world should be united in the Messianic Kingdom for which it earnestly longs. Neither here nor elsewhere in the *Didache* is anything said about the death and resurrection of Jesus, about His Cross and the meaning of His sacrificial death, about sin and the redemption of mankind, nor even about the divinity, pre-existence, and ascension, of Jesus.

The *Didache* gives the clearest possible outline of a type of Christianity entirely free from the Mosaic law. It has grown out of the earliest Christian mission as sent out by the Hellenistic, proselyte church. The document lauds Jesus as the teacher of a higher ethic and as victor over Judaism. Its Christian life depends on the operation of the spirit in the Church, and it looks forward to the coming of the Lord and His glorious kingdom. All the efforts of the Christian, all striving for steadfastness and perfection, are dedicated to this goal. The entire period of faith will have no value if, at the last moment, the Christian does not bravely withstand the threatening dangers, and reach perfection.[1] The Christian way of life does not consist in a consecrated endurance, but in straining all powers to full stretch, in the midst of a world which is tottering to ruin more markedly every day. The Christian is always on pilgrimage and he must hasten to meet a bright future, which comes down from heaven as a gift of God, but which must be striven for in a hard, self-denying struggle against one's self, and against the distractions and allurements of the present age.

An entirely different atmosphere blows over the fields into which the life-work of Paul had struck root and borne vigorous fruit. Of course, we find the characteristics of epigonism here too. This is not surprising, for in comparison with such an exceedingly creative person, all who come after him must necessarily appear less forceful. But in contradistinction from the dilute, ethical religion of the theologians and their churches,

[1] *Did.*, 16, 2

which we have already considered, the Christianity of the
disciples of Paul was of far greater power.

As an addendum to the series of the Pauline epistles, a
writing has been preserved which was provided by the libra-
rians of the church with the title, "To the Hebrews", in
accordance with the content. It is a religious tract intended to
edify and instruct Christians. Using general phraseology it
combines a retrospect on the most recent past with hints about
the anxieties of the present.[1] At the end and quite intentionally,
it makes use of one of Paul's own concluding formulas.[2] This
fact shows that, even although the author belonged to the
sub-apostolic period,[3] he meant to write in the spirit of the
great Apostle, and to be heard with corresponding respect.
Hebrews is remarkable from the literary standpoint: it begins
as a theological tractate, is continued as such, although inter-
spersed with digressions in the manner of a sermon, but ends
as a pseudo-Pauline letter. This has not diminished its value to
its readers in either ancient or modern times; only to scholars
has it been the cause of much useless and fruitless speculation.

Hebrews has *one* great theme: Christ. Everything revolves
round Him from the first word to the last; yet not round the
Jesus of gospel tradition, but the Son of God preached by Paul.
He was before all time, and had created the world, including
everything of both higher or lower nature; He became man,
died on the Cross for us, ascended to the right hand of God, and
would soon appear again to those Christians who steadfastly
yearned for Him.[4] But the author was not a mere imitator or
expounder of Paul; rather he had an independent mind able to
carry Paul's ideas further and enrich them from his own
thought.

In place of the brief, almost reticent, phraseology with which
Paul[5] speaks of the pre-existent Christ, we find here[6] the
method of statement which became basic for future theological
developments, viz. that the Son is the reflection of the divine
glory and the impress of His being (His "hypostasis"). These
expressions come from the language employed by Hellenistic

[1] Heb. 10: 32–34   [2] *Ibid.*, 13: 18–25   [3] *Ibid.*, 2, 3
[4] *Ibid.*, 9: 28, 10: 25   [5] Phil. 2: 6; *vide supra*, pp. 117 f.
[6] Heb. 1: 3; cf. Windisch, *ad loc.*

Jews in their theology; the terminology has a philosophic sound and points the way to future dogma. Since the Son was higher than all angels, higher also than Moses, so also His word, preached by the apostles, confirmed by signs and wonders, and testified by the outpouring of the Holy Spirit, was more powerful than the Law proclaimed by angels and served by Moses.[1] Just as John at a later date, so also now, Hebrews expanded Paul's thought, and stressed the "cosmic" significance of the incarnation of the Son of God:[2] God sends Him "into the world", and He "comes into the world". Then Hebrews comes to the cosmic drama, to which Paul had devoted very few words, and describes it fully in his own way, whilst owing almost every trait to Paul himself. Christ became our brother, similar to us in every respect, clothed in flesh and blood. He experienced human weakness, was tempted like us; this had taught Him sympathy with us, and enabled Him to help us in the danger of temptation.[3] To the Pauline phrase about the Redeemer who was obedient unto death,[4] he adds the gospel picture of the Jesus who struggled in Gethsemane,[5] "who in the days of His flesh, having offered up prayers and supplications with strong crying and tears unto Him that was able to save Him from death, and not having been heard for His godly fear, yet learned He obedience by the things which He suffered; and having been made perfect, He became unto all them that obey Him the author of eternal salvation."

While such passages show a psychological deepening of the Pauline *motif* of obedience, their elaboration of the contemplation of the Passion should be regarded as the principal theme of the entire tractate. The author describes the objective soteriological significance of the death of Jesus, in so far as he conceives it, not only as a sacrificial death as such, but as the ideal celebration of the high priestly sacrifice; and he supports this view by the kind of Biblical exegesis used by Hellenistic Jews. The king and priest Melchisedek, who mysteriously enters history without father and without mother, is the allegorical anti-type of the Son of God; and when he takes tithes

---

[1] Heb. 1: 4, 2: 1–4, 3: 1–5   [2] *Ibid.*, 1: 6, 10: 5   [3] *Ibid.*, 2: 11–18; 4: 15
[4] Phil. 2: 8
[5] Heb. 5: 7–9: the "not" has fallen out of our text; cf. Harnack, *Studien*, i, 249

from Abraham, the tribal father of the Israelite people, and blesses him, he shows thereby his higher worth. This in turn proves that the high-priesthood of Christ is higher than the Old Testament priesthood that goes back to Aaron, Levi, and Abraham.[1] It proves also that the new covenant (the new "testament"), whose mediator was Christ, was superior to the earlier covenant concluded with Abraham which is regarded as "antiquated" according to definite expressions of the epistle.[2] But no testament is valid apart from a death, no priestly, expiatory sacrifice is effective without blood.[3] This is exemplified in the Old Testament ritual, and expressed through the annual sacrifice of blood by the High-Priest in the Holy of Holies; but the full reality was brought about only by Christ when He, the sinless One, offered His body as an expiatory sacrifice for our sins and, once for all, made with His own blood an eternal expiation of the guilt of sin. Thus He became the true High-Priest after the order of Melchisedek, and His work made an end of every earlier priesthood. He preceded us into the Holy of Holies of heaven, where He sits on the throne at the right hand of God.[4]

To a man of this standpoint, Judaism is no longer a problem for the Church itself as it was in Paul's day. Rather it is the antiquated forerunner of the true, new religion; a subject to be discussed theologically, not because it represents a threatening danger, but because a full examination of the essential difference makes it possible to gain a deep understanding of the Christian position. Judaism and Christianity are fitted by Hebrews into an old antithetic scheme, which Jewish thinkers had previously used to contrast the heavenly world of perfection and the earthly world of weakness and sin. Thus, by contrast, the Levitical worship of sacrifices now appears as shadow and imitation as distinct from the heavenly truth of Christianity, the law given from Mount Sinai as distinct from the heavenly Jerusalem and its church of the first-born. But towards the end of the epistle,[5] the eschatological attitude of a Christian, who is a stranger upon this earth, is nevertheless expressed in a similar metaphor: "We have here no abiding city, but we seek

[1] Heb. 7: 1–19   [2] Ibid., 7: 22; 8: 6–13; 9: 15; 12: 24   [3] Ibid., 9: 7, 16–18, 22
[4] Ibid., 8: 5; 9: 23; 11: 10; 12: 18–23; 6: 20; 8: 1, 2   [5] Ibid., 13: 14

one to come." That is the heavenly Jerusalem as the goal of Christian hope.

In this way, the scriptural testimony to the sacrificial death of Christ becomes at the same time for the author a means for proving that Judaism had served its day. His purpose is not apologetic; rather he seeks to deal with the problems actually facing the Church; and how strongly his thoughts are conditioned by the needs and distresses of the Church is shown by the numerous digressions of his speculations and exhortations which he keeps introducing. For him also the Christian life is a warfare, a voluntary denial of happiness, and a bearing of suffering after the example of Christ: it is a wrestling even unto death against sin in the knowledge that God's fatherly love is revealed even in painful chastisement.[1] Patience is paired with faith in the reality of the things hoped for, and hope lightens the burden of the struggling Christian so that he can hold out to the end.[2] Paul had expressed himself similarly, but our author has his own answer to the question of a Christian's sinfulness, and this shows clearly how far he was removed from the pneumatic enthusiasm of the first period, and how largely he was influenced by the experience of the Church. That a Christian does not live an entirely sinless life was known to him as well as it was to Paul, and hence he too encourages his readers to fight against sin. In this way the sins which are actually committed appear as manifestations of human weakness and as involuntary transgressions. But if we sin deliberately after we know the truth, then no further expiatory sacrifice is available for us. Judgment waits for us because we have trodden the Son of God under foot and despised His blood, and—it is a terrible thing to fall into the hands of the living God. In another passage he declares it impossible that a baptized Christian who has fallen into sin could repent again because he has crucified the Son of God by his deed and brought Him into contempt.[3]

It is clear that under this "fall" a genuine denial of Christ and His teaching was understood, and that "deliberate" sin must have consisted in a gross transgression of the Christian

[1] Heb. 12: 1–11   [2] *Ibid.*, 12: 2; 10: 36–11: 1; 3: 6, 14; 6: 11
[3] *Ibid.*, 10: 26–31; 6: 4–6

moral law. In the same way, the immoral and the adulterers
were expressly consigned to the divine judgment, and the
possibility of repentance was refused to "immoral" Esau.[1] Thus
even at this early date a distinction was made between "venial"
and "mortal" sins. It dominated the entire practice of the
Church from this time forward,[2] as it attempted to realize the
Pauline ideal of a Christianity free from sin, but in this modified
sense. Moreover in place of the cautious reticence of Paul[3] we
have a clear pronouncement as to the lot of those who commit
mortal sin. This whole doctrine, however, had only become
possible because the absoluteness of the Pauline conception of
sin had been surrendered and a relative toleration had taken
its place. This was of course a step backward to a Judaizing
moralism which however we must regard as an attempt to
translate the genuine paradox of the Pauline teaching of
justification and sanctification into something rational, and so
make practicable what had been found impossible. This turning
aside from the definiteness of genuine Paulinism is to be found
elsewhere in our author—or rather in the whole trend of the
succeeding period. He praises faith frankly, and also cites the
saying about the righteous man who lives by his faith: but for
Hebrews, faith means the firm conviction that the Christian
hopes had already been realized, i.e. the inherent expectation
of the heavenly Jerusalem which was founded upon the
certainty that God is, and that He had created the world and
would reward His own.[4] When we compare the deductions of
Hebrews with the very similar words of Clement of Rome[5] it is
obvious that the former possess a greater reality and a more
specifically Christian quality; measured by Paul, however, they
still sound weak. With the narrowing down of the Pauline conception of faith, the doctrine of justification retreated into the
background because the presuppositions necessary for its understanding, which were difficult enough to grasp in themselves,
completely disappeared when Jewish Christianity became a
separate entity. The extent to which this separation had taken
place is shown by the comfort which the author offers to his
readers[6]: he says that God would not be so unjust as to forget

---

[1] Heb. 13: 4; 12: 16–17   [2] 1 John 5: 16   [3] *Vide supra*, p. 124
[4] Heb. 10: 38; 11: 1, 6, 10, 16   [5] 1 *Clem.*, 9, 4–12, 8   [6] Heb. 6: 10

their work and their loving deeds which they had done to His honour at an earlier date, and were now doing in ministering to the "saints".

We do not know where Hebrews was written, and no attempts to guess the author have reached a convincing conclusion. Not even the assertion made about A.D. 200 in the west[1] to the effect that the letter was written by Barnabas, can be regarded as an ancient tradition. It is a pure guess and, when examined critically, it seems far from probable. Since the concluding phrases are consciously modelled on Paul's lines, they might have been written by someone outside his circle altogether,—if only on account of their literary pseudonymity. Otherwise the Italians, who sent their greetings (13: 24), could quite well be conceived as members of the church at Rome, and this might be taken to mean that the epistle was written there. It was certainly known at an early date in that city, for 1 *Clement*[2] unmistakably quoted and imitated it. But it gives us no reflection of the religious and theological position of the Roman church, such as we gain from anything which we have discussed so far. If the author had written in Rome, he must have been a newly-arrived, or an itinerant teacher, who had received his education in Jewish, Hellenistic circles, and his Christian faith from Paul. The question may be raised whether after Paul's activity in Rome there were disciples of his who preserved his ideas, and on occasion expressed them forcefully in contradistinction from other views. Further, one may ask whether the warning against various strange teachings, with special emphasis on food restrictions,[3] had reference to the prohibitions in regard to meat, as contained in the Apostolic Decree, or to after-effects of Roman vegetarianism with which Paul had himself already dealt. Such questions may be raised, but there is no hope of a satisfying answer.

The writing which bears the name of Peter and which was taken up into the New Testament canon as 1 Peter breathes the same Pauline atmosphere. It deals comprehensively with the subject of a Christian's rebirth, by the word of God and by faith, and leading to a hope of salvation. It may well have been

---

[1] Tertullian ,*de pudic.*, 20   [2] 1 *Clem.*, 36; cf. 17, 1; 9, 3–12, 8
[3] Heb. 13: 9; cf. Rom. 14: 2

a sermon addressed to newly baptized persons, and adapted to form a circular letter. At least this would account for the fact that it attempts to discuss all the principal heads of the Christian doctrine of salvation. Redemption had been planned by God before the foundations of the world were laid, but had been revealed now when the present age declines towards its end. In previous ages the prophets had already foreseen it, but now the evangelists carried the eternal word of God throughout the world, viz. that Christ had redeemed us from a vain life and had died for our sins.[1] A sacrificial lamb, He had accepted suffering and death, and had borne our sins upon the cross in order to set us free from them.[2] Then He had descended into hell in order to preach there to the spirits in prison and to offer them the opportunity of hearing the gospel.[3] After that, He rose from the dead, ascended to heaven, where He now sat at the right hand of God as ruler over all spiritual powers, whence we await His coming as the judge of the living and the dead.[4]

The theme is not developed systematically, but, formulated in various ways; it passes to and fro through many homiletic discussions and digressions, the Pauline evangel being the foundation of the Christian faith, both in the author and of his hearers and readers. This evangel is expanded somewhat further, as in the teaching of Christ's descent into hell, and, to some extent, handed on in a formal fashion, as in its theory of sacrifice and propitiation (a theory which Hebrews had developed in its own way): the principle of salvation "through faith" is maintained, but it is no longer conceived vitally. Nothing is said about justification or the righteousness of God. Christians are just "the believers" and faith is either faith in God, or else the confident expectation of the future revelation of the Christ who is still invisible.[5] The hope of the parousia is still alive, and the conviction of the near approach of the End is a motive for the exhortation to be sober and constant in prayer.[6]

The profound, mystical idea of a Christian's fellowship with the sufferings of his Lord,[7] a fellowship which had been brought

[1] I Pet. I: 18–20, 10–12, 23–25; 3: 18   [2] Ibid., I: 19; 2: 24
[3] Ibid., 3: 19, 20; 4: 6   [4] Ibid., I: 3; 3: 21–22; 4: 5–7
[5] Ibid., I: 5, 9, 21; 2: 7; I: 8   [6] Ibid., 4: 7, 8   [7] Vide supra, pp. 119 f.

about by the spirit, was by this time no longer comprehensible; but suffering for Christ's sake had become a terrible reality for Christians throughout the world. It was felt as a temptation, a testing of the genuineness of faith; and the Pauline phrase about "sharing the sufferings of Christ" was understood in the sense of following His example. Thus there arose the conception that the very suffering of a Christian had propitiatory power in itself; it set him free from sin and led him along the path of fulfilling the will of God.[1] The presupposition of this conception was that a man was "reborn" through Christ, and "like a new-born child" began his life afresh with a longing for purer, spiritual milk.[2] Here we have a metaphor drawn from Hellenistic mysticism, and, at an early date, it may have been employed at baptismal services in the Christian churches, after being taken over from the initiatory ceremony of some mystery or another. When Paul speaks of a new life effected by baptism,[3] he presupposes this conception, in the last analysis. But what followed for our author was, not mystical excesses or dreams of a sacramental certainty of salvation, but a conception of Christians as the temple of God, a temple built on Christ as the foundation stone and governed by the spirit; a "holy people" who feel themselves strange in this world, and contend with the devil and the lusts of the flesh in order to do the will of God.[4]

References to the Christian life, exhortations to persons of different status in the form of family regulations, warnings against the snares of the world and the wiles of the devil, constitute the practical kernel of this writing, and indicate the way of "purifying the soul in obedience to the truth".[5] The author's ethic, like his dogmatic, bears a Pauline stamp; but it is a diluted Paulinism, because it has lost the final and, for religion, the deepest motives of the genuine Paul.

This writing is another that can be conceived as originating in Rome, for the city "of Babylon", whose church sends greetings at the end, can only be the capital "of this world" described by its apocalyptic name, i.e. Rome; and the companions of the writer, Silvanus and Mark, belong to the Pauline circle, the

[1] 1 Pet. 5: 9, 4, 12–13; 1: 6–7; 2: 21; 4: 1–2   [2] *Ibid.*, 1: 3, 23; 2: 2; 3: 14
[3] Rom. 6: 4   [4] 1 Pet. 2: 5–15; 5: 8   [5] *Ibid.*, 1: 22

latter in particular during the Roman imprisonment.[1] The pseudonymous author in this case is not Paul, but Peter; and that he could be put forward as the author of such an entirely Pauline document was only conceivable at a time, and probably also in a place, which were at a considerable distance from the scene of the last historical activity of both Apostles. Once the author settled on Peter as the patron of his epistle, he had decided the place from which it should be written, and the circle from which a few secondary figures should be chosen. But what acceptance could a Roman writer expect in addressing persons in the missionary regions of northern and western Asia Minor? Hence, the hypothesis at once arises that the letter was really intended for these churches, and, consequently that it was written in one of the original Pauline churches in the province of Asia. Here no one would dream of anything else than that Peter, while in Rome, had been converted by Paul to his teaching.

A few pages earlier, we showed that Paul's mystical ways of thought, together with his metaphors familiar in Hellenistic religion, had not led to some sort of nature religion, but were expanded in the opposite direction into an ethic which the Church could apply—a feature which entirely corresponded to the Apostle's own leaning. The same holds good to an even greater extent in Ephesians, which, at a considerably earlier date, was modelled on Paul's letter to the Colossians. In the latter, Paul defines his attitude towards an incipient gnosticism —we shall have to deal with this later—and in so doing develops ideas which can only be understood as intentionally contrasted with the doctrines he is refuting; in fact, Paul outlined a kind of cosmic mysticism. Ephesians, however, uses the same words, but without reference to views current in the Christian church. Like other Pauline conceptions they have many ethical implications.[2]

The expression *pleroma* ("the fullness" of God), used without explanation in Colossians is used frequently in Ephesians, although not to characterize the cosmic significance of Christ. Rather, it refers to the Church[3] which is filled by the spirit of

---

[1] Col. 4: 10. Philem. 24; cf. also 2 Tim. 4: 11
[2] Dibelius, *Handb.* on Eph. 4: 16   [3] Eph. 1: 23; 3: 19; 4: 13

Christ. It is true that Paul often[1] named the Church as the "body of Christ", and in Colossians he extended this metaphor to the whole of the spiritual beings, whether above or beneath the world, who serve Christ, or whose head is Christ. In Ephesians[2] the same passage is stripped of its higher meaning and used to describe the Church. Occasionally, Paul employed[3] the metaphor that a Christian was a temple of God in which the spirit had its dwelling; we now meet the same metaphor, but with the express meaning that the Church as a whole, "is built on the foundation of the apostles and the prophets, Christ being the corner stone"—just as 1 Peter also employed it.[4] The relation of Christ to the Church is exemplified for the author[5] by marriage, as in the Old Testament figure; and he characterizes this relationship with the word "mystery", a term which had been of great importance in Paul, but in another sense. The conversion of the Gentiles to Christ appears to him[6] as a revelation of a long-hidden, divine mystery confided to "His holy apostles and prophets", whereas what was said in the passage from Colossians, copied here, meant the gospel in its full extent, the gospel that was proclaimed to "His Saints" as such, i.e. to the Christians. It is therefore plain that Ephesians is the work of a writer of the sub-apostolic period.

The Church with its numerous individual congregations constituted the object of the author's spiritual care in the so-called Pastoral Epistles, i.e. the two letters to Timothy and the one to Titus. Here the Church found itself under a necessity of adopting a definite constitution because it must reckon with the possibility of an extended existence. The second coming of the Lord was still expected, but that expectation no longer furnished a criterion for testing the value of one's work and life: the Lord would indeed come but[7] "only at His own time". The world lived now in its last period and the apocalyptic "final times" were here. Thus prophecy was fulfilled, as the Church was finding to its cost, the prophecy[8] of the appearance of heretical persons and Satanic seducers who confuse doctrine

[1] *Vide supra*, p. 119   [2] Col. 2: 19; Eph. 4: 16; 5: 30
[3] 1 Cor. 3: 16–17; 6: 19; 2 Cor. 6: 16
[4] Eph. 2: 20–22; 1 Pet. 2: 5; cf. *Hermas, Vis.*, iii, 3, 3. *Sim.*, ix, 13, 1
[5] Eph. 5: 31–32   [6] Eph. 3: 4–6; cf. Col. 1: 24–26   [7] 1 Tim. 6: 15
[8] *Ibid.*, 4: 1

and morals. The Pastoral Epistles were meant to deal with this case inasmuch as they insist on the apostolic ordination of the church officers (including the presbyters, as well as the bishops and deacons), who had been commanded to care for "sound teaching" and the moral life of the Church. Hence in these writings we find a large number of ethical exhortations, some of which are introduced as detached injunctions, quite in the Pauline manner. Others are fitted into the favourite category of the family regulations, and extended, by the addition of relevant sections, into genuine regulations for the Church.

Numberless efforts have been made to gain a clear and un-broken picture of the opponents who were attacked, but the effort fails ever and again on account of the shadowy character of the records. "The heretics" were concerned with myths and endless genealogies, and these myths were "old wives' tales", and of Jewish origin; both they and the genealogies were bound up with foolish questions, with disputes and discussions "about the law":[1] they were concerned with "clean" and "unclean", with abstaining from certain foods, and also the prohibition of marriage; and finally the assertion was made that the Resur-rection had already taken place[2]—this could only mean that, when a Christian received the gift of the spirit, he was *ipso facto* granted victory over death.[3] Whether they deduced therefrom that the true Christian did not die, or that bodily death was an indifferent matter, whether they, like the Corinthians whom Paul attacked,[4] denied the Jewish idea of the resurrection, cannot be determined more exactly. But since their teaching is expressly described[5] as "gnosis falsely so-called", we have every right to say that it was Jewish gnostics that were attacked in the Pastoral Epistles in the references to the office and the doctrine of the Church; only we are unfortunately not in the happy position of being able to complete their picture from other sources, or to connect them with gnostic schools otherwise known.

The Pastoral Epistles are the earliest documents in which we may see how the Church had to contend with heretics. The

[1] 1 Tim. 1: 4; 4: 7; 2 Tim. 4: 4; Tit. 1: 14; 3: 9; *re* Jewish, 1 Tim. 1: 7; Tit. 1: 10, 14; 3: 9
[2] *Ibid.*, 1: 15; 1 Tim. 4: 3; 2 Tim. 2: 18   [3] *Vide infra*, p. 231
[4] 1 Cor. 15: 12   [5] 1 Tim. 6: 20

first traces of gnosticism were to be found in Paul's time in the Lycus valley,[1] and by the time of these letters, it had adopted a Jewish dress, crept into the churches, and brought about confusion. It was then attacked in accordance with the literary models which the Apostle himself had formerly employed in Colossians, and the Pauline style of letter was of service to our author for making his writings effective in developing the authority of tradition. The very language of the author is modelled on the Pauline letters, and his theological formulas, which occur from time to time, have been derived from the same sources. The letters appear to have originated in Asia Minor, a region which is expressly[2] mentioned as the home of the heresies that they attacked; they undoubtedly arose in a church of Pauline tradition, and the praise given to Onesiphorus of Ephesus[3] makes it likely that this city was the author's home.

We must take notice in this connection of another writing current under the name of Barnabas. A greeting by way of preface endows it with the epistolary form which by now had become customary. Apart from this there is no literary artifice, for it is a straightforward, theological tractate. The author frequently says with emphasis that he does not speak "like a teacher", but rather that he desires to be regarded as a member of the church.[4] Apparently he had really been a "teacher", of a kind known to us as Christian officers in the *Didache*. He was a learned manikin, more than a little proud of his dexterity, and, on account of this, he wishes to make the results of his inquiries available to Christian people in general in the form of a pamphlet. Apparently he had made the acquaintance of Christianity in the shape depicted in the *Didache*: he regarded the catechism, contained in the Teaching of the Two Ways as of fundamental significance; and he pressed home the necessity for standing firm in the stress of the final woes, by suggesting that otherwise the entire period of one's life and faith would be of no value.[5] However, he knew of the Pauline teaching in the form, and with the kind of understanding, which it enjoyed in the sub-apostolic period—a kind of superstructure on a foundation of Jewish ethic. Thus we find in him a similar attitude to

---

[1] *Vide supra*, pp. 195 f.   [2] 2 Tim. 1: 15   [3] *Ibid.*, 1: 16, 18
[4] *Barn.*, 1, 8; 4, 6–9; 6, 5   [5] *Barn.*, 18–20; 4, 9; cf. *Did.*, 16, 2

that which we saw in Clement of Rome, except that now Paulinism is emphasized much more markedly; it is felt to be an essential element in Christian theology, and is presented as such. Faith, love, hope, are the characteristics of a Christian, and righteousness is now added.[1] Christ is the pre-existent Son of God, and the Father, at the creation of the world, spoke to Him the word:[2] "Let us make man." Hence Christ co-operated at creation. Although He was Lord of the entire world, He nevertheless decided to appear on earth in the flesh, to preach to Israel's deaf ears, and so complete the heinousness of the sins of this people who killed the prophets. The Pauline *motif* of stiff-neckedness is thus presented without any reconciliation at the conclusion.[3] Therefore He accepted death upon the cross for our sakes, in order that He might bring us forgiveness of sins through His blood, and that we might thus be created anew.[4] He had vanquished death, and revealed resurrection from the dead; and, at the last day, He would come to judge both the living and the dead.[5]

Those are the principal heads of his theology;[6] they re-echo throughout the epistle and they provide him with the most important individual points of his argument. The purpose of his work is everywhere to prove that the whole of Christianity had been prophesied beforehand by the prophets in the Old Testament.[7] Strings of quotations, apparently derived from the tradition of some catechumen school, serve this purpose. Over and above this, however, he strains his exegetical ingenuity to the utmost, in order to buttress his proofs down into the smallest details, using allegorical artificialities, and tracking out unsuspected relations. He is still following the customary paths, however, when he interprets the food-laws of the Old Testament spiritually, e.g. the prohibition to eat pork was, according to him, not intended to be carried out literally but only to warn against intercourse with men who are similar to pigs; and, from this standpoint, he finds it possible to draw comparisons between other forbidden animals and certain types of human sins.[8] His symbolism of the cross cannot have been un-

---

[1] *Barn.*, 1, 4, 6   [2] *Ibid.*, 5, 5; 6, 12; 14, 5   [3] *Vide supra*, p. 128
[4] *Barn.*, 5, 1; 6, 11   [5] *Ibid.*, 5, 6; 7, 2, 9   [6] Cf. especially *Barn.*, 5, 1–14
[7] *Barn.*, 1, 7   [8] *Ibid.*, 10, 1–8

known to the Church: he finds the cross foreshadowed by the outstretched hands of Moses in prayer, and by the brazen serpent which Moses lifted up in the wilderness.[1]

It is not surprising that, in Old Testament passages which speak of living water and the like, he sees evidence of baptismal water. It is more forced when he explains the "tree (wood), planted on the water-brooks" by Paul's doctrine of baptismal death:[2] "In confidence in the wood of the cross do the baptismal candidates go down into the water." The scapegoat, which is sent away into the wilderness, in acordance with Lev. 16: 7–10, is for him, of course, Jesus; but in this connection he also explains the later rite, which had come to him through some Jewish source. According to this rite, the animal was spat upon, and stabbed; a strip of red woollen cloth was then bound on its horns and afterwards laid upon a thorn-bush in the wilderness. Barnabas regarded the lot of the scapegoat as reflecting the sufferings of Christ even in detail, and the strip of red cloth reappears at the Parousia as the purple mantle of the Lord when He returns to act as judge.[3] Naturally circumcision was not to be regarded as a bodily operation but to be understood as circumcision of the ears and heart. When we are told that Abraham circumcised his three hundred and eighteen servants, this is to be regarded as a particularly subtle reference to the death of Jesus on the cross: for the number eighteen is written in Greek with the letters I and H (=a long Greek "e"), i.e. the first two letters of the name Jesus, and the letter representing the number three hundred is the Greek T, i.e. the cross.[4]

By this method, he seeks to prove everything that appears to him worth proving, including chiliasm: a thousand years are like a day in the eyes of God. Hence the six days of creation mean a period of six thousand years after which the present evil time will be destroyed, and the Son of God will come again and judge the world. Then will dawn the Sabbath of the millennial kingdom in a world which has been transformed into a thing of beauty. Then will follow a new world, which will apparently be reckoned as an eighth millennium, since its symbol was Sunday the eighth day as solemnized by Christians.[5]

[1] *Barn.*, 12, 1–7; cf. John 3: 14   [2] *Barn.*, 11, 1–8, following Ps. 1: 3
[3] *Barn.*, 7, 6–10   [4] *Ibid.*, 9, 1–9   [5] *Ibid.*, 15, 1–9

The author describes this extraordinary learning with the exalted name of "gnosis". He intended his readers to gain from his book "perfect knowledge" as well as faith,[1] the final result being that the relevance of the Old Testament is altogether denied to the Jewish people. He declares, in spite of the fact that many teachers assert the contrary, that we must deny outright that God had concluded a covenant with Israel which now applies to the Christians. The covenant which God offered Moses, was never accepted by Israel, for Israel had immediately taken to idol-worship and thus refused it. Therefore God had suspended the covenant for the sake of us Christians and revealed it through Jesus in order that we might be loosed from darkness, and, as a holy people, receive the heritage promised to the patriarchs.[2] Similar propositions in Hebrews were not based on genuine discussions with Jews or Jewish Christians,[3] and that is equally the case with Barnabas. But the recent erection of the temple of Capitoline Jupiter on the ancient holy site of the temple in Jerusalem (A.D. 123), an event which brought about the war of Barkochba, is regarded by him as the fulfilment of the prophetic saying Isa. 49: 17, and referred to the second destruction of the city, the people, and the temple.[4] This affords us at the same time a hint that the writing originated shortly after this insurrection which ended (A.D. 135) in the last years of Hadrian's reign. We can say nothing with any probability of accuracy as to the place in which it was written.

Our survey of the writings of the sub-apostolic period shows that, after the early separation of Jewish Christianity, two streams began to flow in the church mixing in varying ways and degrees. The first was the mission of the Hellenists, who were free from the Law. These worked in large areas round about themselves, especially among the proselytes of the Greek synagogues, to whom they offered the gospel as a teaching of purified morality on a monotheistic basis, as it had been preached and deepened by Jesus. They took over from Judaism not only the Old Testament, but also, to a large extent, its liturgy and mode of worship; and they successfully used its

[1] *Barn.*, 1, 5; 5, 4; 6, 9 (9, 8; 10, 10), 13, 7; 18, 1   [2] *Ibid.*, 4, 6–8; 14, 1–9
[3] *Vide supra*, p. 208   [4] *Barn.*, 16, 3–4

Hellenized learning and its propaganda writings for their own purposes. Side by side with this stream, was that of the Pauline churches with their proud heritage of the letters of the great Apostle. Thus its theology was rejuvenated ever afresh, a theology which comprehended heaven and earth, and probed the profundities of the Godhead. The Pauline churches stressed his doctrine of redemption through Christ and His death, as well as the pneumatic, and personal character of Paul's Christ-mysticism. For the practical purposes of everyday life there resulted, here again, a refined, ethical doctrine built and Christianized on a Jewish basis, and corresponding, in essence, to the views of the other group. Concurrently with the decay of understanding of the original power of the Pauline thoughts, and with the rise of the necessity for the moral education of the churches, the differences gradually smoothed themselves out. In the days of Trajan and Hadrian, early Catholicism began to show its face. It had taken over from Judaism its moralism and its liturgy; from Hellenism its popular sacramental theology and various forms of pneumatic mysticism; from the Pauline world of thought his theology as a doctrine of God and Christ, of redemption through the blood of Christ, and of sanctification through the spirit.

Chapter Twelve

JOHN

AT THE BEGINNING OF THE SECOND CENTURY THERE WAS
in Asia Minor a group of five writings, which were inter-
related in many respects, and which were regarded as the work
of a single author. His name was John, and, in the tradition of
the church in the succeeding age, he was looked upon as the
son of Zebedee and the disciple of Jesus. The first part of the
book of Revelation includes seven letters to churches in Asia
Minor. The letters had been dictated to John by divine revelation, and he had received them on the island of Patmos in the
open sea off the bay of Miletus;[1] but there is no hint in the book
whether this John was the apostle or not. Nevertheless, it is
clear that the author was familiar with a number of ideas and
phrases characteristic of the other writings in the Johannine
corpus. This is more markedly the case in the two short letters,
2 John, addressed to an unnamed church, and 3 John, to a
certain Gaius. The language is restricted to Johannine phraseology,[2] viz. knowledge of the truth, walking in the truth, the
commandment of brotherly love that is not new but old, the
perfect joy, to be from God, to see God, the testimony. Indeed
one phrase at the end of the third epistle recurs word for word
at the end of the gospel,[3] and the beginning of the first epistle
is unmistakably related to the commencement and the conclusion of the gospel.[4] Even should the Apocalypse be set in a
place apart, if only on account of its linguistic peculiarities,
the identity in authorship of the letters and the gospel is
obvious, both in theological ideas and in idiom. This assumption, however, does not immediately settle the Johannine
problem, but rather makes it more urgent; the main difficulty
lies in the gospel.

The paradoxical character of many of its expressions has
always been a puzzle to expositors. In attempting an exact

---

[1] Rev. 1: 9   [2] 2 John 1: 4, 5, 12; 3 John 3: 4, 6, 11, 12
[3] *Ibid.*, 12; John 21: 24   [4] 1 John 1: 1–2; cf. John 1: 1–4; 20: 25–27

exegesis, commentators become involved in intolerable contradictions, which cannot be understood nowadays as due to
literary style, or to the absent-minded unconcern of a capricious
or careless writer. They are only comprehensible by assuming
far-reaching interpolations of an editor, or, perhaps, that the
original form has been re-arranged in several places. But it
would be useless to attempt to separate old sources and later
additions completely from one another: everything is so firmly
interconnected that, although we may be able to point out the
different elements here and there, yet we cannot unravel the
threads. And since it was the author of the letters who was
responsible for the definitive redaction, then, in spite of all
contradictions in detail, nothing will ever affect the final
result. There will always be a single, harmonious, religious
and theological attitude throughout the entire "Johannine"
literature, of which the gospel constitutes the main part. And
the gospel has the appearance of belonging to an epoch, and of
trying to present a message, which are very remote from the
traditions and purposes of the synoptists. Of course, even the
latter plainly and abundantly show that the churches influenced
the form into which the gospel-material was cast; but, in their
case, the re-casting of the tradition, or the transformation of
legendary elements, took place in a naïve and obvious manner,
and indeed, to some extent, entirely unconsciously. The Fourth
Gospel, however, is the free and bold, creative work of a man
who, starting from his knowledge of Christ, depicts the earthly
forms of revelation of the incarnate logos, and only employs
tradition to add detail and graphic quality. On the whole, however, in the free exercise of his fantasy, he goes far beyond the
old limitations in presenting, and in meaning to present, not
history but theology.

The synoptic tradition relates miracles of the Saviour with
great restraint; He performed them owing to His sympathy
with suffering and need; but for our author, the miracles are
cogent proofs of a god-like power; they are not done for the
sake of the person concerned, but to reveal the glory of God
and His only-begotten Son.[1] For these reasons, they go beyond
all human power to grasp: Lazarus's body had already begun

[1] John 11: 4, 15; 9: 3; 2: 11

to decompose when he was raised again to life; and, instead of the healing of the blind beggar told simply by the synoptists, John records the healing of a man born blind, "since the world began it was never heard that anyone opened the eyes of a man born blind" (9: 32). At the marriage in Cana, the needs of the guests were not serious, but as a proof of His glory, Jesus worked a Dionysian miracle and changed the water in six large vessels into wine of the finest flavour. Thus He did sign after sign for men to see and believe that the Father had sent Him. But alongside the mere performance of these miracles stands their spiritual value: they are miracles in themselves, and also symbols of final truth. When Jesus had fed the five thousand with five loaves and two fishes, He proceeded to speak on the theme: "I am the bread of life" and drew to a conclusion with a doctrine of the Lord's Supper:[1] "Except ye eat the flesh of the Son of man and drink his blood, ye have no life in yourselves. He that eateth My flesh and drinketh My blood hath eternal life; and I will raise him up at the last day." He introduced the healing of the man born blind with the words:[2] "When I am in the world, I am the light of the world"; and before the raising of Lazarus He said to Martha:[3] "I am the resurrection and the life: he that believeth on Me, though he die, yet shall he live: and whosoever liveth and believeth on Me shall never die."

The Christ of this gospel is free from all the burdens of earth from the outset. The world may take offence at Him because, after all, He is the son of Joseph and Mary, and has come from Nazareth whence no good thing can come[4]—the evangelist never thinks of speaking about the virginity of Mary nor of saying that Jesus was born in Bethlehem, as prophesied. He is in a position to give a higher message: "In the beginning was the word, and the word was with God, and the word was God. All things were made by him; and without him was not anything made that hath been made. And the word became flesh and dwelt among us and we beheld his glory, as of the only-begotten from the Father, full of grace and truth." Christ is the earthly epiphany of the divine logos in human form: he had been in heaven with God before time began, and now He had

[1] John 6: 53, 54   [2] Ibid., 9: 5   [3] Ibid., 11: 25, 26   [4] Ibid., 1: 45; 6: 42

returned to the Father, where He abides in glory.[1] The hypostatization of the divine functions is boldly taken from the Jewish
sphere of ideas,[2] and used as the key to the secret of Jesus. In
the book of Proverbs, the word for wisdom, *sophia*, is of the
feminine gender. John rejected both the Hebrew and the Greek
form, in favour of a term of fairly similar meaning, but mascu-
line gender, viz. the logos. This was a term that Philo, too, had
used instead of *sophia* as the subject of his speculations,[3] because
it could be linked with the logos of the Greek philosophers. And
since the author uses these ideas, not only in the formal expressions of the prologue, but really also throughout the whole
gospel, he is in a position to separate the life of Jesus from
history, and, in a way, to free Him from temporal conditions.

What Jesus says in this gospel is not derived from tradition—
there are only rare echoes of synoptic sayings of Jesus. Rather,
he gives a supra-temporal, eternal revelation of God to His
own, i.e. to the world, in as far as it accepts the word of God.
Only in appearance does Christ speak to the persons whom the
evangelist has ranged around Him; in reality, His words, un-
conditioned by time, sound in the ears of the Church and bring
it to the knowledge of the truth, bring light and life to it.
Nicodemus comes to the Master by night desiring to learn
from Him. Jesus takes up the conversation, and soon begins to
speak of re-birth in baptism, His ascension, His death on the
cross, the soteriological meaning of His incarnation, and the
division between believers and unbelievers. Nothing further is
recorded about Nicodemus; he has disappeared.[4] He would not
have been able to understand a word of what Jesus said—he
had served the evangelist only as the voice uttering the key-
word which starts the address to the Church of the succeeding
age. Similarly in the case of the Greeks who desired to see
Jesus, and therefore applied to Philip: he and Andrew go to
Jesus, and announce the inquirers, but Jesus responds with a
prophecy of His death, into which are interwoven certain
strands from the synoptic account of Gethsemane. A voice from
heaven announces the coming, glorious transfiguration. "And
the people, who stood nearby and heard it, said: it thundered;

---

[1] John 8: 38, 58; 3: 13; 6: 62; 12: 16   [2] *Vide supra*, pp. 99 f.
[3] *Vide supra*, pp. 95 f.   [4] John 3: 1–22

others opined: an angel spoke with Him." Jesus continued His
speech[1]—but we do not learn whether the Greeks ever did get
to see Jesus; they vanish, like Nicodemus, as soon as they have
served the technique of the narrator.

In regard to another matter, we grant that the evangelist
takes great pains to give the impression that he is keeping close
to his facts. He gives not only many notes about the time,[2] and
indeed the hour, of an event, but also numerous data about
place.[3] He goes far beyond all the synoptic traditions and
phraseology, and produces the impression of a most exact
acquaintance with the locality. The details are not always clear,
and cannot always be checked; but if they turn out to be
geographically correct, they prove the author's knowledge of
the Holy Land. There is something to be said for the supposi-
tion that he had travelled in Palestine, and become acquainted
with the local legends alive in the churches there.[4] In any case,
he was familiar with Jewish customs and points of view,[5] naturally of his own times, however. He knows so little of the period
before the destruction of Jerusalem that he assumes, quite
naïvely, that the Jewish high-priest was changed and installed
each year, just like a provincial high-priest among the Hellenists.[6] All these matters are employed to give colour to the
record, colour and life which could only be attained by concrete
touches. For John's subject matter is really always the same, and
the speeches deal with only a few, main, ever-recurring ideas.

The use of another literary device of the same character
makes the hearers appear constantly to misunderstand. The
device is used to introduce another and opposite consideration
into the course of the speech, and give a new starting point for
its continuation. At the same time, it offers the opportunity for
using language with two meanings, concealing ultimate truths
in the most trivial guises. Thus, the Jews misunderstand the
saying about rebuilding the temple in three days;[7] Nicodemus
is perplexed by the new birth;[8] the disciples by the secret food;[9]

[1] John 12: 20–36 [2] Ibid., 1: 39; 4: 6; 6:4; 13: 30; 19: 14
[3] Ibid., 1: 28; 3: 23; 4: 5; 5: 2; 6: 59; 8: 20; 9: 7; 10: 23; 11: 18, 54; 18: 1, 2; 19: 13; cf. 6: 19; 21: 8; also 2: 20
[4] K. Kundsin, Topologische Ueberlieferungsstoffe im Johannesevangelium, 1925
[5] John 7: 22, 27, 37, 41, 52; 10: 22; 18: 28; 19: 40
[6] Ibid., 11: 49, 51; 18: 13 [7] Ibid., 2: 20 [8] Ibid., 3: 4 [9] Ibid., 4: 33

the Jews by the bread from heaven, and the saying about freedom.[1] Thus the saying that Lazarus was sleeping deceived the
disciples just as that about his resurrection deceived Martha.[2]
The fearsome command to Judas, "What thou doest, do
quickly", appears quite harmless to the other disciples;[3] and,
in the parting speeches, neither Thomas nor Philip understand
simple words of the Lord, any more than the Jews earlier on had
grasped similar phraseology.[4] But the Christian who read the
gospel seized the meaning, and perceived clearly throughout
that, in the revelation which was being made to him, were included the solution of all enigmas, and the eternal truth; and
that was the aim of the evangelist's literary devices.

Therefore, just as the figure of the Master reflects not past
history but present faith, so also His surroundings are depicted
out of the experience of the evangelist. The strong emphasis
upon the subordinate rank of the forerunner, John the Baptist,[5]
may of course be a purely literary modification of the synoptic
presentation. But the possibility cannot be excluded that our
author was acquainted with churches of John's followers, to
which churches he tried to assign the true place. On the other
hand, it is quite obvious that the struggles of the Apostle Paul
lay behind him, and what he had won was by now held without
question by the church. Judaism and its issues had vanished,
and if the unbelief of Israel had offered a painful problem to
Paul it was an uncontested dogma for our evangelist.

"The Jews" stand as a compact group hostile to the Lord, to
whom of a truth He preaches, but who never once believe, will
not believe, and cannot believe.[6] Jesus never accommodates
Himself to their company as a fellow-countryman, but stresses
His distance from them. Moses gave "you" the Law, "you"
circumcision; in "your" law it is written—that is how He speaks
to them,[7] and Moses is set in opposition to the Lord not only
in the mouth of the Jews,[8] but also in the language Jesus Himself uses.[9] In the prologue is the epigrammatic saying:[10] The
law was given by Moses; grace and truth came by Jesus Christ.
For Christians the Old Testament had been set aside as Law;

[1] John 6, 34; 8, 33   [2] Ibid., 11: 12, 24   [3] Ibid., 13: 29   [4] Ibid., 14: 5, 8; 8: 22
[5] Ibid., 1: 6–8, 15, 19–34; 3: 22–36; 5: 33   [6] Ibid., 12, 37–40
[7] Ibid., 7: 19, 22; 8: 17   [8] Ibid., 9: 28   [9] Ibid., 6: 32   [10] Ibid., 1: 17

it had meaning and abiding significance only as a book of prophecy pointing to Christ.[1] Jesus had as little to do with the Law as with the Jews; He did not appear in order to be "under the Law", but to be free from, and above it. To the Samaritan woman at the well, He spoke of the coming time when men would pray to the Father, neither on Gerizim nor in Jerusalem, i.e., when the old cult, together with its holy places, would have passed away, and the Christian churches, grown out of Judaism, would pray in spirit and in truth;[2] blind Judaism had died in its sins.[3] That is how a Christian saw the course of history after A.D. 70.

Of course the only implication was that, for the religion of the church of Christ, Judaism had been completely overcome in principle. In the life of the outside world, hatred towards the infant church was constantly and spitefully expressed by the Jewish people, who were still powerful even after their collapse as a nation; there are various echoes of this fact in the words of the gospel. But it was not only the Jews that adopted a hostile attitude to Christ and His church: "the world" outside the Church took up arms against the Christians, with hate and persecution.[4] The world had not recognized the logos, nor had His own people accepted Him,[5] for their nature was contrary to God and their prince was the devil.[6] The kingdom of Christ[7] was not of "this world"—that is the harsh formula which the persecuted church employed to express its sense of hostility to the surrounding world, its aims, and its entire civilization. Elsewhere the tension between the new and the old was expressed by speaking of the antithesis of the new æon to the old; but the Johannine writings contrasts "this world" and the kingdom of God, the sphere of Christ and the Father. The former is "below" on earth, the latter is "above" in heaven, whence the logos had descended and whither he had returned.[8]

Like Paul, our evangelist speaks of a divinely ordained obstinacy, and predestination. He who belongs to this world, i.e. who, like the Jews, has the devil for his father, *cannot* accept

---

[1] John 2: 17, 22; 5: 39, 46; 12: 16; 19: 34, 36, 37, and frequently
[2] *Ibid.*, 4: 21–23   [3] *Ibid.*, 8: 24; 9: 41
[4] *Ibid.*, 7: 7; 14: 17; 15: 18–19; 16: 2, 33; 17: 14
[5] *Ibid.*, 1: 10–11   [6] *Ibid.*, 12: 31; 14: 30; 16: 11. 1 John 2: 16; 4: 4–5; 5: 19
[7] John 18: 36   [8] *Ibid.*, 8: 23; 3: 31; 13: 3; 16: 28

Jesus' word for no one can come to the Father unless permitted by the Father.[1] Christians are not of this world, but chosen from it, and given by God to their Lord as His own.[2] They are "born of God", not "of the flesh" but "of the spirit", as it is expressed in a Paul-like antithesis;[3] and are thereby true children of God.[4] The speech to Nicodemus teaches that this divine birth is effected through baptism as a rebirth by water and spirit.[5] He who has received it is endowed with the Holy Spirit, and sends out its effects like streams of living water. Such a child of God has faith in Christ, and believes, not only on account of the signs and miracles that he sees, but also on account of the message of the gospel that he hears.[6]

What then is the meaning of "faith"? Firstly, the grasping of a religious truth—viz. that "Christ is the Son of God", who comes into the world as "the saviour of the world"; he who makes that confession, believes on Him, on "His name", and thereby, at the same time, on God who has sent Him; he who sees Him has seen the Father.[7] God is invisible and no one can see Him;[8] thus the Son is His phenomenal form, and in Him are revealed to mankind God's being, power, and glory. "I and the Father are one" says the Lord, and "you shall know that the Father is in Me and I in the Father."[9] A further development of the Pauline mysticism of Christ and the church is added to this series of ideas, which have been woven out of the logos theology of Jewish Hellenism, when it is said that: "the glory, which Thou hast given Me I have given unto them; that they may be one, even as we are one; I in them, and Thou in Me, that they may be perfected into one. Abide ye in Me as I in you.[10] As the Father hath loved Me, so I love you, abide in My love. If ye keep My commandments, ye shall abide in My love, as I have kept the Father's commandments and abide in His love." Since God is love, the truth can be stated thus: "God is love, and who abides in love, abides in God and God

[1] John 8: 43, 47; 6: 37, 65. 1 John 3: 8, 10   [2] John 15: 16, 19; 17: 6
[3] *Ibid.*, 3: 6; cf. 6: 63
[4] *Ibid.*, 1: 12, 13. 1 John 2: 29; 3: 1, 2, 9, 10; 4: 4, 6, 7; 5: 1, 4, 18
[5] John 3: 3–8   [6] *Ibid.*, 20: 29
[7] *Ibid.*, 11: 27; 20: 31; 4: 42. 1 John 4: 15; 5: 5; 2: 23. John 12: 44–45; 14: 9–11
[8] *Ibid.*, 1: 18; 5: 37   [9] *Ibid.*, 10: 30, 38
[10] *Ibid.*, 17: 22–23, 26; 15: 3–7

in him."[1] Thus, through the commandment of love, Christ-mysticism leads to God-mysticism. But the love of God and of Christ is not fanatical feeling nor ecstatic rapture; rather, as in Paul's hymn in 1 Cor. 13, it is the active power of God, and is seen in the Christian as practical work in the church. This love is due to a Christian brother as a member of a supra-mundane community; it is not neighbourly love *per se*, such as the Samaritan exercised in the Synoptic parable. Rather, it is the sum of all the commandments: to love Christ means to keep His commandments, and to love the brethren. It is a "new commandment" because it came into the world only with Christianity, but it is an "old commandment" because it derives from God's being and is eternal.[2]

Like love, so also other great forces flow out from God; they determine Christ's nature,[3] and are conveyed by Him into the church: truth, glory, light, life, spirit. But only one of them is described as of God's nature: the Lord says to the Samaritan woman:[4] "God is a spirit." Even the formula "God is love" occurs only once, in the first epistle.[4] It is more frequently said of Christ that He is "the light" or "the life"; once He also calls Himself "the truth", a term which elsewhere is applied particularly to the spirit.[5] Thus these predicates are not far removed from a genuine personification, and the author might even have begun his gospel with the words: "In the beginning was the truth", or "the light". He did not do so because these terms lacked the history which gave force to the term logos. All the other concepts arose at a later stage. They were current in Paul's world of thought, and occasionally we can observe how, in the post-Pauline literature and the language of the liturgies, they approximate[6] to the usage of the Johannine writings.

In discussing the miracles, we have already remarked that two opposite tendencies are combined in the gospel record: the crude realism of miraculous acts in a most exaggerated form

[1] John 15: 9–10. 1 John 4: 16
[2] John 14: 15, 21, 23; 15: 10; 13: 34–35; 15: 26. 1 John 2: 7–10, and oft
[3] John 5: 26   [4] *Ibid.*, 4: 24. 1 John 4: 16
[5] Light: John 1: 4, 9; 8: 12; 9: 5; 12: 46. Life: John 11: 25; 14: 6; 1 John 5: 20. Truth: John 14: 6. Spirit and truth: 1 John 5: 6; cf. John 14: 17; 15: 26; 16: 13
[6] Life: Col. 3: 4; *Didache*, 9, 3. Light: 1 Thes. 5: 5; Eph. 5: 8; Jas. 1: 11; 1 *Clem.*, 59, 2

and, on the other hand, their symbolical interpretation. Similar contrasts recur in the way in which expectation of the End is formulated. The hope of the near return of Christ seems much emphasized both in the Fourth Gospel and 1 John; indeed the latter holds that now is the "last hour", and 2 John characterizes doubt about the coming of the Lord "in the flesh" as a heresy of the Antichrist, and, in so doing, the epistle stands on common Christian ground.[1] The fact that the Apocalypse undoubtedly belongs to the Johannine circle illustrates most clearly the liveliness of the expectation of the parousia, and the way in which it was painted by religious fantasy.

This idea was fully neutralized in the gospel when it declared that, after the Ascension, the "spirit of truth" would be given to comfort the Church, to supply the place of the Christ who had gone from earth and to complete His revelation. It would be sent from the Father as a second "paraclete"—the first was Jesus Himself[2]—in order to abide with Christians, and to be in them for ever.[3] Here the Pauline doctrine of the pneuma is raised to a higher theological stage, and enriched by the Church's experience of further pneumatic revelations. Even the characterization of the spirit as "paraclete"—which always means "advocate" and never "comforter"—must have been customary in the Church, and may well be explained from the Pauline conception of the spirit who intercedes for us in prayer with God.[4] And if this indwelling of the spirit in Christians is equated with the one-ness of the Church with Christ, the presupposition for so doing is in Paul's doctrine of the pneuma which on occasion is brought to its climax by saying that the Lord is the spirit.[5]

In addition to the parousia, other scenes of the final drama shimmer with a double light in the Fourth Gospel. There was, in the Church, a current teaching taken over from Judaism, to the effect that, at the last day, all the dead would be awakened, judged and awarded either damnation or salvation; and the resurrection to eternal life is, in one passage, connected with partaking in the Lord's supper as elsewhere in the New

[1] 1 John 2: 18, 28; John 14: 3; 2 John 7 like *Barn.*, 6, 9
[2] 1 John 2: 1; cf. John 16: 26   [3] John 14: 15–17; 16: 7–15
[4] Rom. 8: 26; similarly Mark 13: 11
[5] John 14: 16–17, 18–20; cf. 2 Cor. 3: 17

Testament.[1] But, on the whole, the gospel teaches that death and judgment have no relevance to those who believe in Christ. Already, i.e. with the preaching of the incarnate logos, judgment has come on the world: he who decides for Jesus, is risen from the dead; he has passed through death to life, and does not come to judgment; but he who denies faith in the Lord, is already judged, because he has not believed on the only-begotten Son of God. He who keeps the word of Jesus will never see death.[2]

While it is undoubtedly part of the literary art of the evangelist to employ certain metaphors and ideas in a double sense, it is nevertheless improbable that, on this basis alone, we can explain these sharply opposed antitheses. Rather there must have been various strata of theological conception which were neither reconciled, nor reconcilable, as the writings of different authors succeeded one another, and this fact complicates still further the problem of authorship, which is already complicated enough.

The opinion of the Church, from the end of the second century,[3] tended to regard the Apostle John, the son of Zebedee, as the author of the whole body of writings: he was held to have lived in Ephesus until Trajan's time, and to have composed the gospel when a very old man. Possibly this legend of the John of Ephesus is hinted at in the appendix to the Gospel, 21: 22. It was not yet known to Ignatius,[4] since he revered the Ephesians only as "members of Paul's church", and the legend of John is proved unhistorical by the additional fact of an ancient record,[5] according to which the two sons of Zebedee were killed by the Jews. This record is confirmed by the extremely ancient prophecy of martyrdom preserved in the gospel tradition,[6] and is in harmony with a fast day of the martyrdom of the sons of Zebedee observed in the Eastern Church; the one difficulty is that the memorial day itself, 27th December, was settled on theoretic grounds only towards the end of the fourth century.[7] The martyrdom of James is recorded

[1] John 5: 28; 6: 39, 40, 44; 12: 48; Lord's Supper: John 6: 54
[2] John 3: 18, 19; 5: 22–27; 9: 39; 12: 31; 8: 51
[3] *Iren.*, iii, 1, 2; 3, 4; cf. Polycrates of Ephesus in Euseb., *H.E.*, v, 24, 3
[4] Ign., *Eph.*, 12, 2
[5] Papias in *Philippus Sidetes*; de Boor, *Texte u. Unters.*, vol. 5, 2, p. 170
[6] Mark 10: 39   [7] Lietzmann, *Petrus und Paulus* (2nd edition), pp. 134 f.

in Acts,[1] but we are not told when, or where, his brother John met his end. There is probably no room for doubt about the fact itself. The Fourth Gospel, like the others, does not mention its author by name; it is true that a "disciple that Jesus loved" plays an important part, but his name is not given. From general considerations, it is usual to assume that the author intended this mysterious figure to be John the son of Zebedee, whom he places explicitly and definitely at the side of, and indeed above, Peter.[2] That view is possible, but cannot be regarded as certain, since it is remarkable that the sons of Zebedee are nowhere mentioned as such in the gospel proper. Only the appendix, chapter 21, names the sons of Zebedee,[3] and appears to be drawing on the legend of the very aged John. Quite at the end of the appendix, yet another writer[4] describes him, too, as the author of the gospel. But here again the text and its applications are a subject of dispute; thus it is still impossible to arrive at assured conclusions. The only things that come to light from the gospel itself are (i) that the Beloved Disciple is not a historical figure, and is not so intended. Rather he is the ideal bearer of the apostolic testimony that flows from the heart of Jesus to those of the hearers; and (ii) that the author was not an eyewitness of an historical event, but the God-inspired interpreter of a supra-historical process.

The part this group of writings played in the history of religion, however, offers a problem that attracts present-day scholars to a still greater extent than that of authorship. We can see clearly enough how Pauline thought has been adopted to a large degree, and then extended and developed in a completely independent manner; and this in a direction of which there are also occasional traces in other writings belonging to the sub-apostolic period. But it is not less significant that this was no mere private evolution of thought within Christian circles, but that a large rôle has been played by influences from the world surrounding this youthful movement. Paul had gathered together all the elements that seemed of service to him from Hellenistic Judaism and the religious currents of the

[1] Acts 12: 2   [2] John 13: 24; 18: 15; 19: 26 f.; 20: 4; 21: 20–22
[3] Ibid., 21: 2; scarcely 1: 41, where the reading should be "as the first"
[4] Ibid., 21: 24

awakening east, constraining them to illumine his experience of
Christ; in the same way, his disciples and successors lived in
continual contact with the world that they wished to convert,
and learned from it how to shape their own ideas in ever new
forms: and the greatest among these successors was "John".

Although, in Paul's old-age, gnosis had appeared in the
distance and as an incongruous factor, and although the
Pastoral Epistles had disowned it as a purely foreign element,
it was operative in full force in Asia Minor when the Johannine
writings were produced in that region. It was not repelled now
in an unreasoning fashion, but greeted as a new form of the
affirmation of God, and valued for purposes of rounding out
and re-shaping the inherited tradition of Christianity. This is
the source of many changes in the traditional presentation of
the gospel story: the heightened glory of the figure of Jesus, the
increase of the miraculous element,[1] the evolution of Pauline
Christ-mysticism into God-mysticism, the tendency to advance
conceptions like truth, love, light, life to the point of personification, and especially the introduction of the formula "to see
God" and "to know God"; including also the ceremonial,
"hieratic" style of the gospel with the striking monotony of its
speeches, the "meandering" turns of its course of thought, and
the "I am" pronouncements of the Son of God.[2]

However, as soon as we attempt to pass from these general
observations to questions of detail, strong doubts arise about the
results of much recent research. For the gnostic material which
can be used for comparison, either dates almost throughout
from a considerably later time, or has been influenced by, and
to some extent makes use of, the Fourth Gospel; or else it lives
in a world having a totally different point of view. On the
other hand, we can understand the Johannine theology, as a
whole and in detail, simply from the tradition of the Church,
from Paul, and from Hellenistic Judaism. Gnosis operated as a
condition and as a formative power, but never beyond a certain
limit, a limit that was set up very early. The epistles of John tell
of gnostics, and characterize and attack them as anti-Christ,
but do not enable us to recognize their teachings clearly: "They

---

[1] E. Norden, *Agnostos Theos.*, 177–239
[2] P. Wendland, *Kultur* (2nd edition), 310 f.

deny that Jesus is the Christ", i.e. perhaps, they repudiated the Jewish idea of the Messiah, as of inferior value, because they would have nothing to do with a second coming of the Lord in the flesh. Moreover, "they do not confess Jesus", or they "annul him" (R.V. Marg.). They certainly asserted that they possessed knowledge of Christ, and yet at the same time set themselves above His commandments.[1] However, the author of the letters preaches that knowledge of Christ was proved by keeping His commandments. The love of God was perfected by observing the words of the Lord: "Thereby we know that we are in Him; he who says he abides in Him must live as He lived."[2] The antithesis to gnostic mysticism, thus expressed, has a gnostic sound, but in content it consists of a re-assertion of a pure Christian ethic.

Johannine Christianity stands firmly within the tradition of a Church whose lines had been settled by Paul. It had meanwhile received powerful impulses from a gnosis whose tide was flowing strongly. But an eminent thinker, "John", gathered the elements into a unity, and that unity sheds its light in the Fourth Gospel. Although there was no one in the succeeding age who rightly understood the master mind of Paul, yet here was a man who comprehended the Pauline thought authoritatively, both in its cosmic breadth, and equally in its religious depth; and clarified its stormy passion into a deep-souled, godly religion of the spirit. He saw in the gospel story the incarnation of the divine logos; for him Christianity was, in very truth, heaven upon earth.

[1] 1 John 2: 22; 2 John 7; 1 John 4: 2–3; 1 John 2: 4; 3 John 11
[2] 1 John 2: 3–6

Chapter Thirteen

IGNATIUS

AFTER ALL THE SHADOWY FIGURES OF UNKNOWN WRITERS belonging to the sub-apostolic period, we meet at last, at the beginning of the second century, a personality who is plainly described: Ignatius. The ancient list of bishops[1] enters him as the second bishop of Antioch and the successor of Euodius. Eusebius informs us, in his *Chronicle*,[2] that he was martyred under Trajan. Unfortunately we are not in a position to make sure whether this dating rests on an old tradition, or whether it owes its origin to a schematic reconstruction of Eusebius himself. But we have seven letters from Ignatius's own hand which afford most valuable information, not only of his death and theology, but also of his own church and of the churches of Asia Minor. These letters were written consciously in imitation of the Pauline epistles, and they were soon taken to heart by eastern Christendom. Polycarp, the bishop of Smyrna, collected them—possibly soon after the author's death —and we still possess the letter with which he forwarded the small corpus to the church at Philippi.[3] It was much read in the following period, and was also translated into other languages. In the fourth century Polycarp's text was extended in Antioch by considerable interpolations, and by the addition of spurious epistles. Elsewhere, the text contains only three letters, much abbreviated. About the middle of the nineteenth century there was much discussion as to the relationship of the three variants of text to one another, and as to the authenticity of any of the letters. This discussion may now be regarded as ended: the seven letters in the redaction which stands midway between extension and abbreviation may be regarded as the genuine work of Ignatius. He wrote them when on his way to meet his death. They are real letters, intended for the churches and are on the Pauline model: the first four were written from Smyrna,

---

[1] Eus., *H.E.*, iii, 22; cf. Ign., *Rom.*, 2, 2
[2] Eus., *Chron. Ol.*, 221, 3 f., p. 194, Helm, cf. *H.E.*, iii, 36, 2–3
[3] Pol., *ad Phil.*, 13, 2; cf. 3, 2; P. N. Harrison, *Polycarp's Two Letters*

the rest directed to Philadelphia and Smyrna; a typical pastoral letter sent from Troas to Bishop Polycarp, concludes the whole.

Ignatius had been arrested as the head of the church, and condemned to death by the Roman authorities, just as happened a generation later to his younger friend Polycarp. But he was not executed in Antioch because the governor expected to gain prestige by putting the bishop of the Syrian Christians on show in the capital. Hence he consigned him to the wild beasts in the arena at Rome, and sent him with a squad of ten soldiers across Asia Minor, where they made halts in Smyrna and Troas, and then brought him to Naples. From there he must have been transferred to Rome and put to death, although we have no exact information. The different *martyria* of Ignatius, contained in the collections, are documents of a later time, and without value as sources. Since he stayed in Smyrna on August 25 of that year,[1] it is not improbable that the liturgical tradition[2] of Antioch, where his memory was celebrated in the fourth century on October 17, has preserved rightly on that day the memory of his death in Rome. Unfortunately the liturgy had no interest in giving the year in which it occurred.

A very special interest attaches to these letters because they are the earliest original documents of the church which, above all others, must be regarded as the cradle of Gentile Christianity, in which also Paul had laboured for a long time, and which we have reason for calling the mother church of Rome. It is here that that proselyte Christianity which was free from the law must have blossomed, and was very clearly represented in the west, in the capital of the empire; here also Hellenistic influences of all kinds may have found entry into Christianity, influences which, either apart from the great Pauline stream, alongside of it, or perhaps even before it, made themselves felt in the churches, and are still recognizable in occasional traces.

Ignatius was much too impulsive a person to be regarded as merely an echo of the average opinion of the church. Very much in contrast to the epistle of Clement of Rome, his letters

[1] Ign., *Rom.*, 10, 3
[2] *Martyr. Syriac.*, of A.D. 411 on October 17; confirmed by J. Chrys., *Homil. in St. Ign.*, i, 2, 592a (Montfaucon); J. H. Lightfoot, *Apostolic Fathers*, Vol. II (2nd edit.), p. 419; H. Lietzmann, *Die drei aeltesten Martyriolgien* (K.T.), p. 14

bear everywhere the stamp of his own spiritual quality. He was very strongly influenced by Paul, and to some extent also by John, and his letters express his dependence, even in face of all the other signs of originality which continually appear, in the way he forms his ideas, as well as in the numerous re-echoes of passages which he almost quotes. But we should always be right in assuming that he is expressing the views of the church in passages where the mystical inclination of the author to spiritualize everything, causes him to make use of metaphors which apparently owe their origin to the cruder realism of the religious thought of the time.

The services for public worship are described by the term "assembly", which was already current and even customary in Paul,[1] although we must note that occasionally he uses the Jewish term "synagogue."[2] Moreover it is obvious that a typological valuation of the Old Testament cultus had become customary: the place of assembly was described as the "place of sacrifice" (*thysiasterion*),[3] and the allusions of Ignatius make it very probable that the conception of the Lord's Supper as "Eucharist", i.e. as the thankoffering of the church, had caused this name to be applied to the hall where it was celebrated.

In this sacred ceremony, the Christian partook of the flesh and blood of Christ or, as it is sometimes called, the bread of God, and as a consequence received a pledge of resurrection, a "medicine of immortality", an antidote against death guaranteeing to him eternal life.[4] His body became interpenetrated with the eternal substance of Christ's body, could withstand dissolution, and so experience a resurrection like the Lord's. Already on earth the Christian bears the "flesh of the Lord" in his body. In the Pauline period, this implied that continence was a duty in the sense of avoiding every kind of immorality,[5] but in Ignatius, complete sexual abstinence is the worthy way of honouring the flesh of the Lord, even if that way were not possible for every Christian.[6] However, it was an unconditional

---

[1] 1 Cor. 11: 20; 14: 23; cf. Acts 1: 15; 2: 1, 44; 3: 1; 4: 26. Ign., *Eph.*, 5, 3; cf. 13: 1. *Magn.*, 7, 1
[2] Ign., *ad Pol.*, 4, 2; cf. *James*, 2, 2. *Hermas. Mand.*, 11, 9, 13, 14.
[3] Ign., *Eph.*, 5, 2. *Trall.*, 7, 2. *Magn.*, 7, 2. *Philad.*, 4; cf. *Rom.* 4: 2
[4] Ign., *Eph.*, 20, 2. *Trall.*, 2, 1; 8, 1. *Rom.* 7: 3. *Philad., tit. Smyrna*, 1, 1; 6, 1; 7, 1; 12, 2
[5] *Vide supra*, pp. 135 f.   [6] Ign., *ad Pol.*, 5, 2

duty for everyone in all circumstances to maintain his flesh as the "temple of God", pure from all the sexual vices of the pagan world.[1] Christianity was the doctrine of immortality, the gospel its realization, and the life of a Christian a struggle for the proffered reward of immortality and of eternal life.[2]

All these sequences of thought existed in germ in the Pauline churches of the early period. They had grown up on soil where religion had a Hellenistic cast, and they had attracted the pagan world in a high degree. Such teachings were grasped even by simple people, and were accepted and passed on by them with a naïve realism. A theology was developing in the local church which was soon to become a great force in the church universal. It led the pagan critic,[3] Lucian, to say scornfully that these contemptible Christian f aternities imagine that they have become immortal and live for ever. They despised death itself and frequently surrendered themselves to execution voluntarily. We have also seen how Paul erected a structure of thought on this foundation, which rose to the heights of an entirely spiritual Christ-mysticism. We can observe a similar effort in Ignatius, except that in him all the lines are extended further, all the motives more strongly emphasized, and all the Pauline limits, which are of classic elegance, are exceeded.

The Christians' confidence, which overcame death and at which Lucian scoffed, comes to expression most attractively in Paul's epistle to the Philippians:[4] he is weary, and desires to depart and be with Christ, for that is far better; but he must still abide in the flesh because he must still labour for the Church. Thus he quietly awaits the day of martyrdom. As distinct from this, the soul of Ignatius burns in flaming desire for a martyr's death. He is obsessed only by fear that the Roman church will procure his freedom and so prevent his death. He desires to be torn by the teeth of the beasts, to be entirely eaten up by them; and he expresses the horrid event in religious metaphors. The teeth of the animals must grind him like corn in a mill, for then he will be "the pure bread of Christ"; by this means he will be offered as a sacrifice to God—the altar is prepared for

[1] Ign., *Philad.*, 7, 2; cf. 2 *Clem.*, 14, 3; also Rev. 14: 4, but without this basis
[2] Ign., *Magnes.*, 6, 2. Eph. 17: 1. *Philad.*, 9, 2. *ad Pol.*, 2, 3
[3] Lucian, *de morte peregrini*, 13   [4] Phil. 1: 23

him, and this death is his liberation effected through Christ; in Him he will attain the resurrection, and the bonds which now fetter his hands and feet will then adorn him as with a spiritual link of pearls.[1] These are not expressions which a great man would use calmly, as, e.g., Paul, but the temperamental voice of one whose "enthusiasm" has grown beyond human measure, a man who felt he would become a man in the highest sense only by martyrdom, and thus a genuine disciple of Christ. He believes himself filled with the Holy Spirit, which cannot err, and which places words of divine truth upon his lips. Now that he is in bonds and awaiting martyrdom, he feels himself blessed with a higher knowledge: he knows of heavenly things, including the different orders of angels, and the groups of spiritual beings. He knows of things visible and invisible,[2] but he expects perfection only with death.

Fellowship with Christ is for him the essence of Christianity: he desires "to be found in Jesus Christ" in order that he might truly live, and he often uses the Pauline formula, "in Christ". But he also puts the matter the other way round, and says that believers have Jesus Christ in themselves. Further, since Christ is God, he calls them not only vehicles of Christ (*christophoroi*), but also vehicles of God (*theophoroi*), just as he had given himself the eponym Theophorus. Really this was only another application of the metaphor of the temple of God which is also to be found in his writings, and which the Christian exemplifies.[3] In the same way, he exhorts his readers to be imitators of the Lord, imitators of God, and, accordingly, he himself strives to imitate in martyrdom the sufferings of Christ.[4] Further, just like Paul, he deduces from this union with the Lord the necessity of following His commandments, "Those who are in the flesh cannot perform what is spiritual, and those who are spiritual cannot perform what is carnal; but what you do even in the flesh, i.e. in the life of the body, is spiritual, for you do everything in fellowship with Jesus Christ." He who has once confessed the faith, does not sin, and he who possesseth love, hateth not.[5]

[1] Ign., *Rom.*, 1, 2; 2, 1–2; 4, 1–3. *Eph.*, 11, 2
[2] Ign., *Philad.*, 7, 1; *Rom.*, 6, 2; 5, 3. *Trall.*, 5, 2
[3] Ign., *Eph.*, 11, 1. *Magn.*, 12. *Eph.*, 9, 2; 15, 3
[4] *Ibid.*, 10, 3. *Trall.*, 1, 2. *Rom.*, 6, 3　　　　　[5] Ign., *Eph.*, 8, 2; 9, 2; 14, 2

Faith and love—here is a second formula summarizing the Christian life: "Faith the beginning, love the end or perfection, and these two are a unity, i.e. God"—which is as much as to say: whoever unites these perfectly in himself, lives in full communion with God.[1] Starting from the idea of mystical unity, he equates the flesh of the Lord partaken at the Lord's Supper with faith, the blood of Jesus Christ with love, and he greets the church at Philadelphia with the words, "in the communion of the blood of Jesus Christ", i.e., in the communion of the love of the Lord.[2] For the Lord's Supper unites one with the Lord who is divine love. John says: "God is love, and he that abideth in love abideth in God, and God abideth in him"; and the high-priestly prayer concludes with the words: "I made known unto them Thy Name and will make it known; that the love wherewith Thou lovest Me may be in them and I in them." The two passages give the foundation of the Ignatian thought although the simile of the Lord's Supper is new. Here again, however, John offers the exemplar: "He that eateth My flesh and drinketh My blood abideth in Me and I in him."[3] Add the three quotations together, and Ignatius' formula is the result.

The Christology of Ignatius became of the utmost significance for the theology of the future. He was not content with the Pauline allusions, nor with the solemn sound of the Johannine phraseology, but proceeded to express his thought in theological formulas. The Church was already busy with drawing up a confession, partly in short sentences, and partly in hymnlike periods; a creed frequently varied by Ignatius.[4] Even in the early stages of the tradition, all sorts of more or less definite formularies kept crystallizing out. Ignatius's own Christology rests upon a Pauline foundation enriched from John, and he boldly proceeds further upon the road they indicated. Before all the æons, Jesus Christ was with the Father, and had appeared at the end of the times upon earth.[5] He was the vehicle of divine revelation, the mouthpiece which did not deceive, the one through whom the Father had truly spoken,

---

[1] Ign., *Eph.*, 14, 1; 9, 1; 20, 1; *Smyrn.*, 6, 1
[2] Ign. *Trall.*, 8, 1. *Rom.*, 7, 3. *Philad., tit. Smyrn.*, 1, 1
[3] 1 John 4: 16. John 17: 26; 6: 56
[4] Ign., *Eph.*, 7, 2; 18, 2; 20, 2. *Magn.*, 11. *Trall.*, 9, 1–2. *Smyrn.*, 1, 1–2
[5] Ign., *Magn.*, 6, 1

the expression of the will of the Father or—making forceful and clearer use of the Johannine formula—the word, the logos of God, who broke through the silence.[1] Thus in Ignatius, more clearly than in John, the roots of the logos conception are plain. In the Wisdom of Solomon, the Hellenistic author had sung:

> For while all things were in calm silence,
> And night in the midst of her swift course:
> Thine Almighty Word leaped from heaven, Thy royal throne,
> As a fierce man of war into a doomed land.

His intention was to describe how Yahweh walked in Egypt on the night of the Passover in order to destroy the firstborn; but in place of the name of God he personified His activity in revelation, and, to the active "Word" of God, he appropriately opposes His meditative silence, out of which action was born. That is how Ignatius understood the passage, and he is not likely to have been the first to say that the active "Word" sprang from Silence. That idea must have been familiar to every Hellenistic rabbi: and Ignatius could have got it from Greek Judaism even if he had not hit upon it independently. In any case he employs the idea freely, in his own way, and without secondary, gnostic pedantry when, in another passage, he equates the Godhead with "Silence".[2] It is true, however, that he carries further the idea, which had been suggested tentatively by Paul, and formulated by John in the prologue of the Gospel, that the logos was God by nature. At last, he characterizes[3] Jesus Christ as "our God", or simply "God"; this he does frequently and by preference. John preached that the logos had become flesh, but Ignatius goes further and says without hesitation that God had come in the flesh or had appeared as man, and this characterization of Christ as divine, leads him, in the end, actually to speak of the sufferings of God, and the blood of God.

Nevertheless the person of the Son is clearly distinguished from that of the Father, and this not only in the numerous

[1] Ign., *Rom.*, 8, 2; *Eph.*, 3, 3. (17, 2); *Magn.*, 8, 2; cf. Wisd. Sol., 18: 14–15
[2] Ign., *Eph.*, 19, 1; cf. Paul's Rom. 16: 25. Schlier, *Religionsgesch. Unters.*, 38 f.
[3] Paul's Phil. 2: 6. John 1: 1. Ign., *Eph. tit.*, 18, 2, *Romans tit.*, 3, 3; 6, 3. *ad Pol.*, 8, 3; *Trall.*, 7, 1. *Smyrna*, 1, 1; 10, 1

passages where Pauline formulas and turns of speech, or creed-like expressions of the church, are reproduced or varied, but also in new and well-considered judgments. Thus, for example, he restates a frequent Johannine thought, and says that Jesus Christ proceeded from *one* Father, was one with Him, and returned to Him; or, further, he describes the Risen Lord as spiritually united with the Father in spite of the fact that He had a real, physical body.[1] The difference between the Father and the Son becomes still more evident when the subordination and the exemplary obedience of the Son are emphasized;[2] the idea is of course Pauline, but the application and, in particular, the parallel relationship of God to Christ, on the one hand, and the bishop to the Church, on the other, or the bishop to the deacons, carries the characteristic signs of the genuine Ignatian mode of thought. The fact that, although the unity is maintained, yet the distinction persists, even after the earthly life of the Lord, is seen in the parallel found in the words: "The Church is united with Jesus Christ as Jesus Christ with the Father, in order that everything might harmonize in a unity." Both in the abstractions of theology, and in the concrete religion of Ignatius, the Risen Lord is a person clearly separated from the Father, the one God of his monotheism.[3] The difficulties which arise, on further consideration, from the juxtaposition of the two antithetic spheres of thought, never rose to consciousness in Ignatius with his rich spiritual resources. Theologians of the succeeding centuries felt the difficulties most strongly, and groaned not a little over the saintly man who had to be respected as an authority from a revered past, and nevertheless explained in an orthodox manner.

With all his naïvety, he deals with Christology speculatively. At the side of this trait is another which is rooted in the religion of the Church, but which borrows its ideas really from mythological schemes. At the end of his letter to the Ephesians, Ignatius proceeds to develop, with obvious earnestness, a theology of redemption which mixes new ingredients with the Pauline and Johannine elements already discussed, and which

[1] Ign., *Magn.*, 7, 2. *Smyrna*, 3, 3
[2] Ign., *Magn.*, 7, 1; 8, 2; *Smyr.*, 8, 1. *Trall.*, 3, 1. *Magn.*, 6, 1. *Eph.*, 5, 1
[3] Ign., *Magn.*, 8, 2

appears to be so important to the writer that he proposes to send to the Ephesians a second letter dealing with this theme. Unfortunately this letter was never written. He first of all teaches that by God's ordinance, "our God", Jesus Christ, was born of Mary through the agency of the Holy Ghost; in passing, he remarks that His baptism implied that the water was "purified" for the future baptism of Christians. Thus he seems to be presenting the conceptions of a Jewish Hellenism which were active in the Church, and which had been written down by Matthew and Luke.[1] The work of redemption began with the birth of Christ; the devil never suspected what was happening; he knew nothing of Mary's virginity, nothing of the birth, nothing of the meaning of the death of the Lord. Yet these were three great secrets which God had prepared in secret and silence, and had brought into effect; they were now patent to all. But how was the secret made known to the æons?

A star lighted up in the sky with a new and unheard of light, and outshone all the stars as well as the sun and moon. These heavenly bodies all crowded round it, wondering and fearful, and then followed in its train. Magic now lost its power to bind, every fetter of wickedness fell away, ignorance was vanquished, and the old kingdom of evil destroyed; God had appeared as man, and introduced a new and eternal life. Then was begun what had already been perfected in the councils of God: the universe shuddered, for now death had been destroyed.[2]

Here we have mythological ideas in poetic language. Lately attempts have often been made to reconstruct the "mythology which lies at its basis". The effort could only be successful if we were able to introduce into the text elements which it does not contain. At the beginning of the chapter, Ignatius is working with a thought which is also to be found in Paul.[3] It is that God had kept a plan of salvation secret, and this enabled Him successfully to deceive the devil and his dæmons. Then follows a new conception which, however, leaves it very much of an open question whether Ignatius means an event in heaven

---

[1] Cf. M. Dibelius, *Jungfrauensohn und Krippenkind*, 1932
[2] Ign., *Eph.*, 18–20, quoted in *Exc. ex Theod.*, 74, 2
[3] Paul's 1 Cor. 2: 6–8. Col. 1: 26. Eph. 3: 9–10. Rom. 16: 25

following the birth of Christ; or a mythological event in the cosmic empire of the spirits, which is accessible only to one who has been blessed by God, although no human eye has seen it; or whether he is giving a parable in a mythological form. In all probability the last assumption is correct, for the radiant star is not the same as that which, in the tradition of the Church, stood over the inn in Bethlehem on the night when Jesus was born. Rather it is a similar legend. For Ignatius, the shining host of sun, moon, and stars is the sum-total of the powers which had hitherto ruled the world. The stars determine the lot of everyone with a necessity which cannot be avoided, and only the wicked art of magic is able to interweave their cosmic powers with human desires. Paganism is regarded as an astral religion and as the servitude of mankind to dæmonic rulers. At length, a certain star grew in brilliance, outshone all the other starry powers, and made them subject to its own will as its obedient satellites: i.e. the power of paganism and its dæmonic gods was broken; God himself had appeared as man, had overcome the doom of death and set in its place an ascent to a new and eternal life; a new æon under the lordship of Christ had begun. The stars and their cosmic power, magic, and the pagan belief in dæmons, were real to Ignatius, and not merely metaphors: and their conquest by the power of God in Christ was for him another real thing. But he consciously describes it in a metaphorical analogy which he only chose because it expressed graphically the victory of the Lord over the evil spirits. The entire work of redemption, at the end of which was Christ's journey to hell to visit the prophets who were expecting Him,[1] was now described by Ignatius as a divine "plan of salvation (*œconomia*) based upon the new man, Jesus Christ". This plan was to be carried out in the Passion and the Resurrection in faith and love, because in Jesus as the incarnate God a new man had appeared and presented mankind with new life. The idea of a rejuvenescence of man, and of a new man, Jesus, is known to us from the Pauline discussions of the second Adam. The author of Ephesians had already given the name *œconomia*[2] to God's plan of salvation, and this he discussed in a way which showed he was quite master of the Pauline scheme

[1] Ign., *Mag.*, 9, 2. *Philad.*, 5, 2; cf. 9, 1   [2] Paul's Eph. 1: 10; 3: 9

of thought. Thus even in this connection Ignatius was only a pupil of the great master.

It is clear that, with the conception of Christ as the incarnate God, His humanity was in danger of becoming a mere mask: we shall have plenty of opportunity to pursue this subject further in the life of early Christianity. Ignatius already knew of communities in which the idea was at home, and he strove energetically against it. What appeared particularly objectionable to the latter was the idea that the incarnate God could really suffer, for suffering was simply irreconcilable with the Greek conception of God. For this reason, Ignatius placed all the greater emphasis on the reality of the sufferings of a Christ who was truly incarnate; and this again led to the thesis, which would have been impossible for Paul, that the Lord was "in the flesh" even after the resurrection. He derived this deduction from John;[1] probably beyond John's intention, even if it corresponded to the naïve view of the Church: yet a deduction that Ignatius defends in this passage. For him, Jesus Christ was "perfect" man; the divine pneuma and the human flesh were united both in His life on earth and after His resurrection. Therefore Ignatius, obviously enamoured of the paradox they contained, formulated the pair of antitheses which, from this time onwards, resound through Christian dogma: One is our physician; He is of both the flesh and the spirit, begotten and unbegotten, God in the flesh, true life in death, from Mary and from God; first suffering, and then without suffering, Jesus Christ our Lord.[2] He does not give a theological proof for this statement of the case, the traditional faith of the Church being his guide. That faith postulated the resurrection of Christ in the flesh because of the hope, formed on Jewish models, of one's own resurrection. The Pauline doctrine of redemption[3] presupposed that, while on earth, Jesus was a genuine man of flesh and blood, and that, as such, He waged war to the knife against sin. When Ignatius twice asserts[4] that his own sufferings would only have meaning if Christ had really suffered in the flesh, we are brought near to this line of thought.

[1] John 20; 20, 27; 21: 5, 12, where we should note that it does not say that Jesus ate with them
[2] Ign., *Smyrn.*, 2–5. *Trall.*, 10 *Eph.*, 7, 2   [3] *Vide supra*, pp. 117 f.
[4] Ign., *Trall.*, 10. *Smyrn.*, 4, 2

Whether those whom he attacked can really be called gnostics, is a question which cannot be answered. In any case, Ignatius gives warnings against people who assert that they have more knowledge (gnosis) than the bishop, and he exhorts the Church to lay hold of "the knowledge (gnosis) of God, that is Jesus Christ".[1] On another occasion he describes the teachings which he attacks as false opinions and old myths of a Jewish kind, and adherence to them as "Judaizing". Perhaps the enemy celebrated the Sabbath instead of Sunday; they certainly made a great deal both of the Old Testament and its authority as against the gospel message, and also of the eminence of the O.T. priesthood. Thus Ignatius insisted on the decisive and independent significance of the gospel, and the superiority of the high-priesthood of Jesus[2]—we are reminded of the thesis of Hebrews. However, the opponents were not Jews but uncircumcised persons, and even though he says that they deny the soteriological significance of the death of Jesus, they are nevertheless the same persons as all the other passages repudiate. It is noteworthy that they do not call themselves "Christians",[3] but obviously had a name for their own sect. Not sufficient is known for a more exact description of these heretics.

Those who had been redeemed by Christ constituted a single great spiritual unity of saints: that was undoubtedly a doctrine obvious in itself and essential to Ignatius;[4] and all the letters which he wrote rest on this dogma.

Meantime, another unity has become of importance, a unity which covered not only his human and official, but also his theological interests: it is that of the individual church and, in particular, the church as an organism governed by a threefold order of clergy. At the head of the church stands *one* bishop, under him the college of presbyters; the deacons occupy the third rank. The unity of the church is personified in the bishop; he is in the place of God, and the presbyters are to be compared with the college of Apostles. He is the highest authority for doctrine, commissioned by Jesus Christ, just as Jesus was commissioned by the Father and was of one mind with Him; thus

[1] Ign., *ad Poly.*, 5, 2. *Eph.*, 17, 2
[2] Ign., *Magn.*, 8, 1, 9–10. *Philad.*, 6, 1; 9, 1; 8, 2
[3] Ign., *Magn.*, 10, 1   [4] Ign., *Philad.*, 5, 2; cf. catholic church, *Smyrn.*, 8, 2

the bishop must be looked up to as to the Lord himself.[1] All the functions of the church are subject to his oversight; nothing can take place apart from him, neither baptism nor agape nor celebration of the Lord's Supper.[2] The command of subjection to him applies without exception to every member of the church, including presbyters and deacons.[3] If the church keeps to that pattern, she will be protected in all the attacks of hostile heretics. It is to be hoped that these latter will one day repent, return to the unity of the church, and submit themselves to the bishop.[4] In Clement of Rome, we found the first beginnings of the doctrine of the divine appointment of the offices of bishops and deacons; but, in Ignatius, we find the completed monarchical episcopate, and the custom was regarded as authoritative in both Syria and Asia Minor. As distinct from Clement, Ignatius built up no theory in regard to the necessity of this institution, or its accordance with scripture; rather he started from it, and was simply concerned with continually pressing home the out and out divine authority of the bishop as the spiritual monarch of the individual church. This institution would be an impregnable bastion against all attacks from without and all dangers of schism within. In so doing he became the classical authority for the Roman Catholic doctrine of bishops.

[1] Ign., *Magn.*, 6, 1. *Trall.*, 3, 1
[2] Ign., *ad Pol.*, 5, 2. *Eph.*, 3, 2; 6, 1. *Magn.*, 3, 2. *Smyrn.*, 8, 1–2
[3] Ign., *Eph.*, 4, 1. *Magn.*, 3, 1. *Trall.*, 12, 2. *Magn.*, 2
[4] Ign., *Magn.*, 6, 1–7, 2; 13, 1–2. *Trall.*, 7. *Philad.*, 3, 2; 8, 1. *Smyrn.*, 5, 3; 9, 1; cf. *Eph.*, 10, 1–2

Chapter Fourteen

MARCION

WHEN THE CHRISTIAN CHURCH HAD GROWN CONSCIOUS OF possessing a life of its own, it began to interpret the Old Testament in the form of types and allegories. The result was to deny the book to the Jews and to claim it as the text-book of the Church. Christians, as the spiritual Israel, recognized only one method of interpretation, which they called spiritual, but which was, in fact, allegorical. This method of interpretation really transformed the sacred book. It began with the prophecies of Christ and the Church, and then tried to wring secrets from the text by the free play of ideas. The literal understanding of the Old Testament was set aside and branded as Jewish error. But if a teacher had come forward, and refused to let himself be blinded by the shimmering gleams of this "spiritual" ingenuity, and had looked the Old Testament plainly and simply in the face, in spite of all cries that he was Judaizing, a catastrophe would have happened. The book would have slipped out of the hands of the Christians again into those of the Jews. If such a teacher had read, and firmly grasped, Paul's doctrine of the abrogation of the Law through Christ, he would have seen how the problem of the Old Testament was to be solved. He would of necessity have come to an understanding of Christianity that would lead him far from the paths hitherto taken by theologians. This possibility became actuality in Marcion.

Marcion belonged to Sinope in Pontus, the present-day Sinope on the Black Sea, where his father was bishop.[1] His family was well-to-do, and he himself is frequently described[2] as a shipowner. This shows that he belonged to the highest social class of the important port and commercial city, but he did not remain in peace at his home; apparently his father excommunicated him from the church on theological grounds. Later, perhaps, he struggled for recognition in Smyrna on the west coast, and was cast out by Polycarp. It is certain that,

---

[1] *Epiph.*, xl, 1, 3–8 (2, 94 f., Holl), Harnack, *Marcion* (TU, 45), 24*, 24*–28*
[2] *Rhodon und Tertullian* in Harnack, 16* f.

in full manhood he came to Rome in the reign of Antoninus
Pius, sought and gained influence in the church there, until
bitter quarrels broke out once more. In July, A.D. 144, he
separated himself from the church catholic, founded his own
fraternity, which spread with astonishing rapidity "over the
whole of mankind", as Justin bears witness scarcely ten years
later. Marcion died possibly about A.D. 160.[1]

He wrote only a single work which he called *Antitheses* where
he brought his teaching together. It has not been preserved, as
can easily be understood in regard to a writing which was so
subversive to the Church. We have to content ourselves with
deducing the content from the notices contained in the writings
of opponents, particularly in Tertullian's five volumes against
Marcion.[2] Literal quotation only very rarely occurs, so that we
can form no idea of the literary quality of this extraordinary
man. But the notices about his teachings are so detailed, and
agree in so many essential points, that it is possible for us to
describe his doctrine with considerable confidence. What, however, we cannot do is to give, on the basis of written sources, a
sketch of the development of his religious ideas. What came
first and what came second, on what point definitive offence
was taken, we are nowhere told; we can only reconstruct sub-
jectively the course and the inner connection of his doctrines.
Nor can we give a clear answer to the question of his relation
to the Syrian gnostic Cerdon. Irenæus and, following him,
Hippolytus assert that Marcion was dependent on him, but, at
the bottom, this assertion is due to the prevailing tendency to
trace genealogical connections between different heresies. No
available material gives clear information about the work and
teaching of Cerdon, and the Marcionite tradition never mentions him.[3] This much is certain however: that the Syrian's
influence, if he be historical at all, can only have been oj
secondary importance; for Marcion's teaching is in every way
the expression of a self-consistent religious experience, and this
is rooted in the one person.

The basic thing that he rejected was allegory in all its forms.[4]
In so doing, he fell foul of the whole of theology hitherto, as we

[1] Harnack, 6*, 16*–20*   [2] Assembled by Harnack, 256*–313*
[3] Harnack, 31*–39*   [4] *Ibid.* 259* f.

have already said, and of its understanding of the Old Testament. He boldly and forthrightly attacked the learned intricacies of the exegetes, and read the straightforward and plain meaning of the Old Testament with a direct mind. This meaning was often only too clear, and what he found offended him in the highest degree. It is possible that, by his very nature, he was suspicious of all sham learning—he would not have anything to do even with philosophy;[1]—it is also possible that he was affected by anti-Semitic influences, possible also that the gospel had sharpened his understanding. In any case, he recognized with extraordinary clarity the incongruity between the spirit of these ancient Jewish books and the spirit of Christ. The moral elevation of the prophets, the religion of the Psalms, he never saw: but he was antagonized by the anthropomorphic traits of the God of the Old Testament. He saw a God who had created a world full of the most deplorable imperfections; a God who created men, and drove them to fall into sin; who frequently repented of what He had done, and who overlooked the most serious sins in His favourites, although He punished them cruelly in others.

With his views of the Bible, he intermingles his own experience of life: why did God create snakes, scorpions, crocodiles, and all the creeping things? Why must propagation and birth be accomplished in a way that is nothing else than a sum total of dirty and disgusting processes?[2] Here we find a natural and, in certain respects, even a pathological depreciation of the world at large such as had not grown out of Christianity, but must be regarded as due to Marcion's social background. With eyes darkened in this fashion, he read the Old Testament and its naturalism, and saw in the God of the sacred book the same God of imperfection, cruelty, and repulsiveness of whom life preached to him every day.

The proof was plain that the Old Testament was right in proclaiming its God as the creator of the world. It was true—but both were worthy of one another, this God and this world! Yet this God was not therefore absolutely evil. He was not a "wicked principle"; rather He was simply of inferior worth.[3]

---

[1] According to his emendation of the text: Col. 2: 8; cf. Harnack, 51, 122*
[2] Harnack, 268*–273*   [3] *Ibid.*, 269*–274*

What He was able to do fell short of His plan and intention; He strove for perfection with insufficient means and thereby wrought mischief upon mischief. He had pointed out to men the foundation of morality in His "law"; in this respect, the Law was rightly to be regarded as "holy, righteous, and good", indeed as "spiritual".[1] But He wished to enforce His commandments by a system of punishments which rested upon the idea of retaliation. Its principle was an eye for an eye, a tooth for a tooth, blood for blood, and this made Him an unmerciful judge who punished the sins of the fathers on the children down to the fourth generation.[2] His ideal was "righteousness", and therefore He might be called the "righteous God". His chosen people, the Jews, had acknowledged this righteousness and striven after it: but it was a righteousness which caused one to shudder on account of its fearful cruelty.

That was the first strand of Marcion's thought. The second began from the Christian point of view that this Jewish and Old Testament righteousness had been most definitely rejected by Christ, and replaced by something better. Jesus had replaced the Old Testament law of retaliation with the new commandment of patience and forgiveness, and instead of the bloody cruelty of the Jewish God, Christ showed gentleness and compassion: the Sermon on the Mount abrogated the Law.[3] The essence of Marcion's proof consists in working out the contrast between the Old Testament and the gospel's message, and it was buttressed both by him and his disciples who kept bringing forward new series of antitheses, for a final decision rested upon correct understanding in this issue. If he was right—and Marcion had no doubt about it—then Christ had nothing at all to do with the Creator of the world, His book, His people, or His religion; rather He proclaimed another God hitherto strange and unknown, the God of love, kindness, and compassion, who was to be understood as the genuine and true God, supreme above all else. Yet complete reality was to be ascribed even to the Creator of this world, the God of the Old Testament; this was proved by the Old Testament itself whose truthfulness Marcion never for a moment doubted, and the

[1] Harnack, 108*, 263*   [2] Ibid., 280* f., 271* f.
[3] Ibid., 280* f., 262*

sum total of the facts of experience of daily life and of history added further proofs.

Thus there were two gods—a lower and a higher, a "righteous" and a "good", one known and proclaimed by Moses and the Prophets, and the other an unknown, strange god. The latter had first been revealed in Christ, who delivered us from the power and the law of the other god, and raised us to a new sphere of life. Incisive logic had led Marcion to his doctrine of two gods, and neither the theological dogma of monotheism, nor dubious philosophical considerations, caused him to shrink back from the last consequences of his position. Whether he was acquainted with the dualistic conceptions of Persia, or gnostic modes of thought of a similar kind, and whether these had facilitated his system is an enigma. It is certain that they were not his starting point, nor in any way the inspiration of his thesis. His main contention is clear enough, and does not require the help of such assumptions. Men of that period were accustomed to find a multitude of intermediate beings between God and man, including both the devil and the divine logos.[1] Moreover Marcion's teaching was in reality neither dualistic in its starting point, nor in the way in which it was worked out.

Was it not clear to Marcion, however, that by this teaching he was contradicting the whole of primitive Christian tradition? No. Rather with the same thoroughgoing heedlessness of the consequences of this thought, he found in Paul the apostolic justification of his system: in him, and in him alone, the true teaching of Jesus had been grasped, unambiguously expressed, formulated in multitudinous ways, and made safe against false opinions. None of the other apostles had understood their Master: they had held Him to be the Messiah of the Jewish God, had understood and misinterpreted His words from that standpoint. The warnings and exhortations of Jesus had not borne fruit.

In spite of beginning sometimes to understand the gospel rightly, in the end they had gone aside into error, and become the protagonists of Old Testament legality. Therefore Christ had revealed the truth once again, and had called Paul as its herald; he alone had maintained it in its purity. It was for this

[1] Cf. Marcion on 1 Cor. 8: 5. Harnack, 307*

reason that he had opposed the original Apostles; he had rebuked Peter because he did not "walk uprightly according to the gospel of truth" (Gal. 2: 14); he had fought against the "false brethren privily brought in", against the "false apostles" (Gal. 2: 4; 2 Cor. 11: 13), and had accused the apostles of falsifying the word of God (2 Cor. 2: 17).[1]

For him, Galatians was the fundamental polemic against a Jewish form of Christianity: here at the very beginning every "other gospel" was explicitly rejected, the attitude of the first Apostles was censured, and then it was demonstrated that the Law was entirely set aside by Christ who taught the one fundamental truth as definitely as possible. Moreover the difference between the two gods had been clearly expounded in the Pauline epistles: it was only necessary to read them with unveiled eyes. In 2 Cor. (4: 4) the Apostle said: "The god of this world hath blinded the minds of the unbelieving, that the light of the gospel of the glory of Christ, who is the image of God, should not dawn upon them." Thus the God whose image and revelation was Christ was opposed to the god of this world who would protect his own, i.e. "the unbelieving" from knowledge of the true God, and had therefore blinded them—just as he had frequently done, according to the testimony of the Old Testament.[2] Moreover, he whose eyes had been opened by this passage of Paul's, would have no difficulty in finding the teaching about the two gods in numerous other passages in the Pauline letters, and therefore none in recognizing Paul as the apostle of truth and the servant of the good God. Regarded in this way, his epistles have complete authority, and become the fundamental sources of Christian knowledge. They give the criteria by which the gospel tradition of the Church was to be judged; for the first Apostles' lack of understanding, and the Judaizing zeal of the false brethren, had brought about a far-reaching displacement, indeed falsification, of the genuine evangelical tradition. Whereas Paul had expressly asserted (Gal. 2: 6; Rom. 1: 16) that there could, and must, only be one gospel,[3] viz. his own, the Church had made it into four gospels which always, but wrongly claimed apostolic origin for themselves, in spite of the fact that the Apostles never wrote any-

[1] Harnack, 257*–9*   [2] Ibid., 308*   [3] Ibid., 306*, 309*

thing. Rather, these gospels had been falsified throughout in a Judaizing sense, and were therefore, of course, fitted to recommend that the Church, which was walking in evil ways, should submit to the authority of the Old Testament and be deluded by the creator of the world.

Hence Marcion set himself boldly to the task of restoring what he held to be the genuine and true gospel, i.e. that preached by Paul. He began with one of the traditional gospels, viz. Luke. We cannot say with certainty why he made this choice. Perhaps the reason was that he regarded the author, Luke, as a disciple of Paul, and believed him to be more faithful to tradition than the other evangelists. For a remark of Tertullian can be understood to mean that, first, Paul, and through him, Luke, had been illumined by the original evangel; but to understand his remark in this way ignores the fact that, immediately beforehand, Tertullian had recorded Marcion's attack upon the traditional names of the evangelists.[1] We may also surmise that Luke's gospel had long been in use in Sinope, and had therefore been particularly well known to, and highly appreciated by, Marcion from his youth. At any rate he took it as his raw material, and began to carry out a critical sifting of Luke's text.[2] It was a purely "subjective" criticism that he exercised. The kernel and essence of the evangelical message remained fixed for him in the sense and scope already described, and Paul supplied him with further hints. He began boldly to remove the Judaizing interpolations from the gospel, and to restore the spoiled passages by altering the text. That his work could not be applied in every detail, nor brought to an end once for all, he never concealed from himself; both he and his school kept on wrestling with the problem, and the Marcionite text of the gospel went through many changes.[3]

The same problem faced him, as was unavoidable, in the Pauline letters. Many passages did not agree with the fundamental teaching of the Apostle as recognized by Marcion, and gave the impression that Paul had recognized the Old Testament as coming from the most-high God, and recording a

[1] Harnack, 358* [2] A reconstruction of the gospel in Harnack, 177*–255*
[3] Harnack, 43

revelation that pointed towards Christ. Such passages could only be Judaizing interpolations introduced by forgers belonging to the church; he who desired to read Paul in a pure form must first of all remove these foreign passages, and restore the text where it had been spoiled. Marcion attempted even this task and he carried it through with a high hand and much self-confidence.[1] He did this to a larger extent than, but always with the same good conscience as, that with which many a critic of the nineteenth century started from his own system of "Paulinism", excised anti-pathetic verses, and changed words which he disliked. Marcion let imagination run riot, but we still have every reason to remark the logic of his thought, and marvel at his self-confident, unwavering boldness; even in this respect he was an extraordinary person.

The result of his critical work was a canon of Scripture which united the genuine, and alone authoritative, gospel with the Pauline epistles. This combination was rooted in necessity, and was not the product of the accident of a particular tradition. Neither of the two parts was intelligible without the other; each guaranteed the sense and meaning of the other. Paul was the authority for the essential thought and the broad outline of the gospel. He taught its soteriological significance and the way in which it was to be accepted. He also showed that the Christian message had been misunderstood and falsified at an early date, and likewise what were the dangers of Judaistic side-tracks. Paul was thus the guardian and the expounder of the gospel. The gospel text itself gave the record about Jesus, His works and preaching, His death and resurrection; in short everything that Paul presupposed as known, and that he used as the basis of his instruction. Thus the two parts of the Marcionite canon constituted a genuine unity, whose significance was still further increased by the fact that the Old Testament was no longer regarded as sacred Scripture. That meant, however, that Marcion set on one side the Biblical canon which had hitherto been recognized by Christendom, and replaced it with a new one. He was the first really to proclaim, on a theological basis, the existence of a New Testament as a collection of writings, and to put it, not alongside, but in the place, of the

---

[1] Reconstruction of the Pauline text in Harnack, 40*–176*

Old Testament. Thereby, acting on his own initiative, and relying entirely on his own resources, he carried out an enterprise which was only in its beginnings in the church catholic, and was faced with all sorts of hindrances. The reactions of Marcion's achievement soon made themselves felt. We shall have to speak of them in another connection. What is important for us to notice, at the moment, is that Marcion had now an authoritative written source at hand, out of which he could draw further ideas for the building up and the extension of his teaching.

First of all, we note that Marcion himself exercised a noteworthy reticence, and everywhere avoided fantastic speculations; it was always more important for him to strengthen the foundations than to decorate the superimposed structure. Secondly, after his negative criticism directed against the creator of the world and his book, he taught the resplendent glory of the good God and His gospel. Marcion was no doctrinaire theorist but sought God with earnestness and a warm heart, and he seized on the profoundest meaning brought out by his researches. In particular he believed that he was really proclaiming a new understanding of God to Christian people who were in danger of backsliding into the commonplace thoughts of the past.

His *Antitheses* began with the words:[1] "Oh fullness of wealth, folly, might, and ecstasy, that no one can say or think anything beyond it [the gospel], or compare anything to it!" What Paul said in Rom. 11: 33 of the depth of the wealth, in 1 Cor. 1: 18–23, of the foolishness and power, of the preaching of the cross; and Luke, in 5: 26, of the wondering astonishment which fell upon all those who witnessed the miraculous power of Jesus—all this was comprehended in Marcion's exclamation. It is an attempt to describe the complete newness of the divine message, far beyond all human thought and power of conception. Marcion is never weary of teaching that, before the coming of Christ, mankind knew nothing of this God; that He was fully unknown and unknowable because no bonds of any kind united Him with the world and humanity; He dwelt as a "stranger" in His third heaven (2 Cor. 12: 2) far from the alien

---

[1] Harnack, 256*, corrected by Burkitt, *Journ. Th. Stud.*, 30, 279 f.

world: "No one knows the Father except the Son and he to whom the Son will reveal Him." It was the Jewish god who had created the world out of material substance; he had also created Adam, weak in body and soul, and then, assailed by the wiles of the devil through the Law, he had brought sin and death upon mankind.[1]

Then came to pass what is incomprehensible and overwhelming: the pity of the good God was excited by the lot of mankind, though they were strange and even hostile to Him; from pure compassion, He decided to redeem them from their distress.[2] He sent His Son into the world, the perfect revelation of the Father. He appeared as Jesus Christ in the fifteenth year of Tiberius (A.D. 28–29) and preached the gospel. He was neither "born of a woman", nor "subject to the Law"—these words, says Marcion, were interpolated in Gal. 4: 4 by Judaizers, as also was the story of the nativity in the gospel. How could the pure Son of the most-high God have defiled Himself with the filthiness of human birth! He clothed Himself with nothing earthly, originating from what was material; nor with flesh which had been formed by the Creator of the world: rather He appeared "in the likeness of man" (Phil. 2: 7) in an apparent body, a "phantasma", such as the angels wear.[3] He preached the gospel of the unknown God, taught gentleness and patience instead of cruelty and wrath, love of enemies and forgiveness instead of hate and retribution, compassionate kindness instead of a calculating righteousness. He taught these things as the will of God and showed them forth in both word and deed. He came to abrogate and not to fulfil the Law, and not the contrary, as the spurious verse, Matt. 5: 17, asserts.[4]

He had shown His divine kindness and patience even towards the creator and frequently had regard for his laws. Jesus had never attacked him directly or characterized him as a liar, but had so clearly expressed the pure divine teaching that the intelligent hearer could draw for himself the inevitable conclusion. In the parables, He had unmistakably described the essential content of that teaching. No man can serve two masters; an evil tree cannot bring forth good fruit nor a good

---

[1] Harnack, 264*-7*, 271*, 274*-7*　　[2] *Ibid.*, 122, 264*, 284*, 292*, 295*
[3] Harnack, 283*-7*, 74*　　[4] *Ibid.*, 252*, 262*

tree bring forth evil fruit; no one should put new wine into old
skins, nor new patches upon an old garment—was that not
clear enough? Moreover, wealth, happiness, and earthly show
had hitherto passed as signs of divine favour: and rightly so,
for this was in accordance with the law and regulation of the
creator. But Christ blessed the poor, the hungry, those that
wept, those who were abused and persecuted; and He pronounced woes upon the rich, the full, and those who laughed.
He turned away from the righteous and the Pharisees, and
visited publicans and sinners.[1] Thus the gospel re-assesses all
previous values. Jesus' gospel of salvation is for all who need
help in the whole of the wide world, and not only for the
subjects of a chosen people as the Messianic promises of the
Jewish god declares.[2]

That is how Jesus taught; then on the cross, He died the
death accursed by the creator god (Gal. 3: 13), but which Jesus
paid as ransom-money and thus redeemed us, "the strangers",
from our previous thralldom and gained us for the good God.[3]
He redeemed not only those who were then living or who
should live, but also the dead; for He descended into hell, and
liberated all the sinners: Cain, the company of Korah, Dathan
and Abiram, Esau and the whole multitude of heathen who
suffered in the fiery wrath of the revenging god. But the
righteous persons of the Old Testament: Abel and Enoch,
Noah and the Patriarchs, besides David and Solomon, remained below in the place of their promised reward, in a kind
of blessedness which their god had been able to provide for
them. They could not be redeemed, because they were be-
witched by communion with their own god, and lacked faith:[4]
thus they did not dare to *believe* the unheard of and the new,
and that was what mattered and would matter. Faith was complete and total self-surrender to the highest God. This meant
at the same time the denial of the creator-god and his earthly
plan of salvation as found in the Old Testament.[5] The first was
the Redeemer, the second was the Judge; love was due to the
first, fear to the second. The decision was exclusive, because—
you cannot serve two masters.

[1] Harnack, 127, 260* f., 265*, 292*–94*   [2] *Ibid.*, 289*
[3] *Ibid.*, 288*   [4] *Ibid.*, 294* f.   [5] *Ibid.*, 296*

Redemption won in this way worked itself out only in the future for it concerned only the soul; as long as a man was still in the flesh, he belonged bodily to this world and its Lord, and must bear its oppression and persecution: true Christians had also to bear the same distress and the same hatred.[1] They defended themselves as well as they could, not with force or by showing resentment, but by turning aside and withholding themselves from everything that would further the objects of the creator-god. The body as a material element was their enemy and thus they mortified it by fasting. Meat-eating was entirely forbidden, and wine belonged to the prohibited things: Paul had given directions by way of example in Rom. 4: 21 and 1 Cor. 8: 13. All sexual intercourse furthered the aims of the god of this world, and therefore was prohibited by Marcion to his disciples: the true disciples of Christ did not marry, and if they were already married when they came to know the truth they separated from their spouses.[2] This Christian church of Marcion's only propagated itself spiritually, and it spread far and wide in the world, and lasted for centuries. The Church Fathers tell us nothing further about his principles for the conduct of life, a fact which proves that at least they had nothing to find fault with there. Marcion's disciples obviously lived quietly and in retirement, and constituted churches with close inner bonds, churches which had much of the earnest strenuousness and decided other-worldliness of early Christianity; thereby they made a great impression on those belonging to the church catholic. A remarkable number of them died as martyrs: a fact which proved attractive to many.

The Marcionite movement flamed up rapidly and, after it separated from the church universal, became a powerful and successful antagonist of early Catholicism which was at that time first taking shape. The pagan philosopher, Celsus, dealt with the Marcionites in A.D. 180, in his polemic against the Christians; he regarded them as a second and equally important branch of the Christian movement.[3] That they permeated the whole world was the testimony of Tertullian of Carthage about A.D. 200, just as it was that of Justin of Rome about A.D. 150.[4]

[1] Harnack, 295* f.   [2] *Ibid.*, 149 f., 307*, 311*, 277* f.   [3] *Ibid.*, 325*
Tetr., *c. Marcion*, 5, 19. Justin, *apol.*, 26, 5. Harnack, 152, 6*

The large number of hostile writings belonging to the second century of which we hear, shows how acute was the danger for the church catholic, and in what regions it existed; for, in addition to western Asia Minor, we find mention of Corinth and Crete; the three world capitals, Antioch, Alexandria, and Rome; besides Carthage and Lyons.[1] In the east, the Marcionite church extended still further and was firmly rooted particularly in the region where Syriac was spoken. Here it was still a danger even in the fourth century, and the Fathers had to issue earnest warnings against it; whereas by that time its power in the west had been completely broken. The strict carrying out of the imperial laws against heretics at last drove the Marcionites out of the towns into the villages, where, in the fifth century, they were oppressed by active bishops, and compelled to receive conversion. Their last remains survived in remote corners of the orient for centuries, although many had been absorbed by Manichæism.[2]

We have no information about the inner life, the constitution, and the evolution of the church. Those who attacked the heresy never troubled themselves about anything except its doctrines. The Marcionites' constant criticism of church doctrine, and the polemic of the church Fathers, naturally brought about a large theological evolution of the former. We can observe manifold differences in the reports about Marcion's Bible and teaching, reports which can be explained as further developments carried out by pupils, as distinct from the earlier theses of the master; a few leaders of the Marcionite schools are known to us by name. Wherever they are dealing with additions of secondary importance or with corrections, we always find that they smooth down the crudities of the original teaching. Thus in addition to the body and animal soul which man owes to the creator-god and which is destined to perish, another "spirit" was also ascribed to him as an original gift of the most high God. This gift at last makes him man in the full sense, and it is this spirit which the God-sent Jesus saves, because it belonged to God even although it had fallen into enemy hands. This was of course a very illuminating thought of a genuine gnostic character, but it destroyed Marcion's fundamental idea of God's

[1] Harnack, 152, 314*–327* [2] *Ibid.*, 156–160

absolute remoteness from the world and from mankind, and of
how He saved man out of purest love, although he was a complete stranger to Him.[1] Others made the devil into the evil
principle and a third god; thus the god of the Old Testament
became "the mediator" and so was conceived on a considerably
higher plane. On the other hand, the regions which had come
under Manichæan influence held firmly to the two gods, and
they set the creator-god, as the evil god of darkness, in contrast
to the good god of light: and this resulted in a modified kind
of Manichæan theology.

Only one of all these disciples, Apelles, attained any large
and independent significance. He had heard Marcion in Rome,
had afterwards gone to Alexandria, and then returned to Rome
as an enemy of Mani and his dualism. In Rome he exhibited
much literary and propagandist activity. He worked with
Marcion's system of ideas and even with his New Testament,
but he introduced an element of enthusiasm which was entirely
remote from Marcion, in that he gave credit to the visions of a
prophetess, Philumene by name, and regarded them as sources
of revelation.[2] But he then separated the creator of the world
from the Old Testament, and denied Marcion's radical pessi-
mism. This world, he said, was created by an angel of the most
high God, indeed to His honour, and after the model of His
own higher world: but it remained incomplete and bore "the
sting of repentance" until, at the request of the sorrowful
creator, Jesus Christ the Son of God was sent down at the end
of the æon to heal the world. The Old Testament was a lying
book of the god of the Jews, i.e. one of the angels of fire who
had fallen away from God, and become evil. He was the same
as had decoyed human souls to come down from the heavenly
heights, and had clothed them with the sinful flesh of an earthly
body.[3] Origen has preserved a number of passages from a work
of Apelles, entitled the *Syllogisms*, which is devoted to proving
the inferior value of the Old Testament.[4]

An orthodox writer towards the end of the second century,
Rhodon by name, had a discussion with Apelles then growing
old. Fragments of his report of this discussion have been pre-

---

[1] Harnack, 165   [2] *Ibid.*, 404*-412*
[3] *Ibid.*, 406*–409*, 417*   [4] *Ibid.*, 413*–16*

served.[1] We are told strange things. Apelles was of the opinion that doctrine ought not to be criticized, but that everyone should retain the one in which he believed. Then those would be saved who set their hope upon the crucified Lord, but they must of course be "full of good works". The Pauline theology of the cross, and his exhortation to have a faith active through love, are expressed with an uncouthness which must have appeared unheard-of. But worse things were to come. In praiseworthy contrast to Marcion, Apelles recognized only *one* principle, but he immediately added that the question of the Godhead was the darkest of all problems. Although there was only one principle, he grasped it, "not by way of knowledge, but by an inner feeling". And when conjured by his opponent, he again answered and swore: "In very truth he did not *know* how there could be an uncreated God, but he *believed* it." Rhodon then laughed outright and scoffed at a teacher who could not prove his teaching; but, at the same time, and with genuine astonishment, we recognize a spirit in Apelles which was independent of the outlook of his period, which had grasped a great truth, and which had even expressed it almost in modern terms, viz. that the religious idea of God does not belong to the sphere of logic, but to that of "emotional" thought.

Marcion had not actually said that, but it was of the essence of his spirit; for his great aim was to liberate theology from all forms of logical systematization; the intuitive knowledge of God as "entirely other" and quite unattainable from the standpoint of the world; the denial of everything creaturely, and thereby also of every form of natural and historical knowledge of God; the estimate of redemption as a miracle of love which could not be thought out. Here Jesus' genuine message of God, and Paul's real experience, were put into vivid words, even if one-sidedly, boisterously, and with such reckless passion that all the other, and frequently not less significant, values of the Christian religion went to pieces. But is not a prophet always one-sided when seized by the spirit?

[1] Harnack, 404*

Chapter Fifteen

GNOSTICISM

SHORTLY AFTER THE TURN OF THE FIRST CENTURY AND IN the time of Trajan, Dion of Brussa delivered an address to his fellow-citizens which has since become famous.[1] Being proscribed, he moved to and fro in the world as a wandering philosopher in voluntary poverty, but later on he became again a highly respected and wealthy patron of his home town. He says that in Olbia, near to the mouth of the River Dnieper, he had once delivered an address in Greek to the inhabitants, and had dealt with the conception of a well-ordered *polis*, i.e. a state; he reproduces the sequence of thought in detail. From the state and its constitution by man, he proceeds to treat of the divine cosmos and, after he has spoken first of all as a philosopher about gods and men and their fellowship, he gives a myth[2] which "is sung in a marvellous way at the secret ceremonies of initiation of the Magi"; and the myth had been communicated to them as the teaching of the wise and upright Zoroaster.

Like a divinely guided span of four noble horses, the world revolves ceaselessly in a gigantic orbit in an endless succession of periods of time. The outermost horse is the strongest and the most beautiful of all, and runs in the longest path: it is of a light colour shining with pure brilliance and with the glowing splendour of sun, moon, and stars—the heavenly æther, worshipped as Zeus. The second horse bears the name of Hera, and is black in colour: but where illuminated by the sun it is light coloured—the air. The third is sacred to Poseidon and is known to the Greeks as Pegasus—the sea. The fourth, called after Hestia, stands fixed and immovable, bound by steel reins, and constitutes the centre of the whole movement—the earth. Thus the glorious span of horses run amicably together until, after a long time, the fiery snorting of the outside horse ignites the others, sets the mane of the innermost in flames, and so burns up the entire cosmos. The Greeks call it the burning of Phæton. On a second occasion, and after many years, the horse of Poseidon shied and flooded its neighbour with sweat; and that

[1] Dio Chrys., *Or.*, 36, v. Arnim   [2] *Or.*, 36, 39–61

was the universal flood of Deucalion. To men, these appear to
be meaningless catastrophes, whereas they are controlled by
the firm reins of the chief governor, and brought to a good end.

Now, however, the metaphor changes: the leading horse
overpowers the others, and takes them upon itself, just as one
wax figure is made out of four. After a short time, which, only
according to human ideas appears infinitely long, it stands in
glorious beauty as the victor. The world that had been destroyed in the flaming æther, has become a new and higher
existence. Then the Lord God perceived a void and was seized
by desire of driving the chariot and, yearning for the various
kinds of natures, began to create the present world. A flash of
lightning shone out and changed the bright flame to a gentle
fire. Then the moist element penetrated the whole, as the seed
which had been given life by the divine spirit, and created all
things: this is what the sages of the mysteries laud as the
"holy marriage" of Zeus and Hera. Thus comes into being a
new world, young, and of shining beauty, just as it proceeds
from the hands of the Creator, more glorious than any human
mind can conceive and any tongue can worthily describe: only
the Muses and Apollo themselves would be able to do it in the
divine rhythm of purest harmonies.

For a long time, this myth of Dion's was regarded as the airy
imagery of a speculative theology, that was intended to put
his Stoic theories into a many-coloured garment. But the happy
discovery of a monument to Mithra and its skilful elucidation,
have recently shown that Dion was really speaking the truth:[1]
he was giving the contents of a hymn of the "Magi", i.e. those
Persian missionaries who laboured in Asia Minor, who mingled
the ancient Persian theology of Mithra with astral elements of
Babylonian origin, and who Hellenized the whole by assimila-
ting it to Stoic doctrines. Dion's oration was delivered at the
time of a flourishing syncretism which mingled the religious
ideas of all peoples and put their gods on an equal footing with
each other. In Dion only the names of Greek gods appear, but,
under this disguise, Persian gods are concealed according to
that broadminded way of conceiving things[2] which had formally

[1] F. Cumont in the *Revue de l'histoire des religions*, vol. 103 (1931), pp. 33–44
[2] H. Usener, *Götternamen*, 341

identified the Roman Jupiter with Zeus, Hera with Juno, and which allowed Tacitus[1] to discover Mars, Mercury, and Isis among the Germans.

This syncretism of the gods is one of the most significant phenomena which accompanied the growth of Græco-Roman world civilization. It levelled the way for monotheistic currents of thought, and, in both a negative and a positive sense, constituted a precondition for the rise of world-religions. Dion's oration shows us how an oriental, esoteric doctrine compounded of various elements—in regard to the nature of the world, its end in fire, and the new creation of a more beautiful heaven and a better earth, i.e. a typical eschatology—when clothed in Stoic ideas became a cosmogonic myth unveiling the purpose, and the divine constitution of this world. It was Trajan's time, and Dion, for all his training in logic, and his Greek cast of mind, felt that philosophy alone no longer satisfied. In the present oration, however, he was trying to meet the needs of a new time, and he spices his oration with the mysterious echoes of oriental religion in order to satisfy the yearnings of a large circle of educated people.

It was no accident that Plutarch about the same time wrote a monograph on Isis and Osiris[2] in which Egyptian myths, helped by allegorical interpretation, are made to chime with Greek thought, orientated philosophically. In so doing, Plutarch was not merely a confessed Platonist, but one by conviction. Yet he was also a worshipper and a priest of the Delphic Apollo. He dedicated the monograph to the Delphic priestess Clea, who had been consecrated by her parents to the mysteries of Osiris. Egyptian elements had long been accepted in Hellenism. Persian and Babylonian elements were now added. All these gods began, as it were, to speak Greek and to philosophize, and so became acceptable in every sense. The orient began to conquer the Hellenic world, and even to vanquish the occident. For a while the reawakened Greek consciousness, in its best representatives of the Antonine period, offered resistance; but afterwards the oriental tide flowed irresistibly over the whole empire.

We shall now turn our attention to another stratum of society.

---

[1] Tac., *Germ.*, 9   [2] Plutarch, *de Iside et Osir.*, p. 364 e., 369 e., 370 c

In the museum at Leyden there is a magical papyrus written about A.D. 350 which proudly bears the title of the *Eighth Book of Moses* or the *Book of Unity*. Among a multitude of most trivial recipes designed to meet the superstitious needs of the lowest class of people, it has preserved an old and valuable gem of the history of religion.[1] This consists of a prayer, in two different recensions, which beseeches the most-high God to come down from heaven; it is really the cult-prayer of some early gnostic church, and it contains a myth of the creation of the world.

God must be praised in every language and every tongue, just as the first and highest beings had once praised Him: first Helios, who had been installed and entrusted with all power by Him, and who had put the stars in their place and founded the world by means of a beam of light that was filled with God. He praised the most-high God in the language of the hiero-glyphics, after having mounted up to heaven in the ship of the sun, which is like a round shield. With him went the dog-headed ape, which pronounced the secret numeral for the year, *abrasax*,[2] and the sparrow hawk which croaked with its greedy beak. God was also praised by the first angel who is responsible for punishments, i.e. the judge of the dead, Osiris, and by the "Nine-fold", the sacred nonad of the gods of Heliopolis.[3] This last clapped three times with his hands, and God laughed; seven times His "Ha ha" resounded, and seven gods arose from His laughter.

On the first occasion, light appeared and shone through the universe, and became the god of the cosmos and of fire. Everything was still water; but when God laughed the second time, earth heard the echo, cried aloud, rose up, and separated the water into three parts—the ocean above, upon, and under the earth. A god appeared and was set over the deep; the rise and fall of the tides was due to him. On the third occasion, God laughed grimly, and Nous, understanding, appeared with a heart in his hand, and received the name Hermes. At the fourth laugh, Genna appeared, the goddess of propagation. At the fifth laugh, God's face darkened, and then Moira, the goddess

---

[1] A. Dieterich, *Abraxas*, 16–20, now with a translation in K. Preisendanz, *Papyri Graecæ magicæ*, ii, 93–7 and 109–114

[2] *Vide infra*, p. 284   [3] A. Erman, *Aegypt. Religion*, 30

of fate appeared with a balance, the symbol of Justice. Hermes quarrelled with her because he claimed justice for himself. The most-high God decided that justice should proceed from both, but he gave Moira the sceptre of world dominion. Then he laughed for the sixth time and was glad; Kairos appeared, the god of the fortunate moment, carrying the royal sceptre which he handed to the most-high God. The glancing crown of the god of light was put upon his head, and he was granted the power to rule over everything; a queen wearing a crown of light was placed by his side. Its light, however, was borrowed, it waxed and waned; she was the moon-goddess and the mistress of growth and decay.

God now laughed for the seventh time and groaned deeply; Psyche appeared and everything began to move. God said to her: "Thou shalt move everything, and everything shall be joyful, if Hermes leads thee." Then everything was set in motion and at once filled with the breath of life. God saw it and clicked with His tongue; then Phobos, armed terror, appeared. When God bent towards the earth and whistled aloud, the earth re-echoed, and bore the Pythian dragon which knew everything in advance, because it originated from sounds made by God. The earth reared itself up and threatened to break into heaven, but God said: "Iao" and all stood still.[1] The greatest god then appeared, he who had ordered the past and future of the world, and no longer was anything out of order in the kingdom of the heights. Even Phobos, who, as the elder, wished to resist him, must give place to him at the command of the most-high God. As compensation, he was granted permission to precede the divine Ninehood and have equal power and honour with it.

The writing breaks off at this point for no discernible purpose or reason. It had satisfied the magician so far: but he now conjures up the god, addresses him, chatters, clicks his tongue, whistles, and continues with his hocus-pocus. It is clear enough that some genuine, ancient tradition has preserved here a popular, gnostic cosmology, and one which gives, at the same time, a graphic illustration of the structure of all these systems. There is a most-high God without name and without properties;

[1] *Vide infra*, pp. 269, 290

the only thing said about Him is that He "comprises the whole", and that He is the last source of all power, and of all that comes into being. From Him all the gods originate whom men know and distinguish: they arise from the laughter, the tongue-clickings, and the whistlings of the most-high God. In other systems, it is the laughter and weeping and fear, the outcries and glances, which give life to creatures;[1] but the fundamental idea is the same. A group of gods appears, but the particular order of succession is meaningless to us. At best we should be justified in regarding Helios as the first. Then others appear, they strive among themselves, and are clothed with power—but it remains a question how the different "world rulers" are related to each other. It is as if the mystagogue's glance could only take in a small bit at once.

At first, we have Egyptian images: the barge of the sun with the shield of the sun, the praying dog-headed apes, the sparrow-hawk, are all universally-known images of the Egyptian cult; and Osiris, the judge of the dead, as well as the divine Ninehood are unmistakable even if they are only shadowy forms. At this point, however, the Egyptian source seems to have ceased. Only at the end do we find the Ninehood again unmistakably. What now follows comes from a Jewish source: first of all light is created, then the wastes of water; then dry land rises and separates the waters. And the last god who originates from the whistling is no other than Yahweh, and thus as in the Old Testament, he is described as the organizer of the whole world, and as "the greatest of great gods". The other gods appear to be Greek, even if more than once a doubt arises whether their Greek character would stand close examination. It has even been suggested that they were modelled upon Iranian deities.[2] In any case they have been affected by Greek philosophy: Hermes is the nous or logos; his struggle with Moira reflects the problem, which was frequently discussed by Stoics, whether reason or blind necessity determined the course of the world.[3] The Pythian dragon which knew everything in advance is still the ancient dæmonic oracle. An arbitrary mixture of most

[1] Dieterich, 24–8
[2] R. Reitzenstein, *Die Göttin Psyche*, 33–44. *Hellen. Mysterienrelig.*, 3rd edition, 359 f.
[3] Dieterich, 75

various elements, syncretism in its purest expression, characterizes the fragment. This medley of religion is modified by
ideas drawn from contemporary philosophy, and its purpose is
to introduce a higher wisdom; and it presents a genuine
cosmogony, like the myth of Dion. In addition there is here a
large and varied number of divine figures, behind which, in the
last analysis, is the great One from whom everything arises
that possesses power and life. Even this strange doctrine is a
form of gnosticism, but the thought is that of untrained minds.

It is not easy to come to close terms with the systems of
gnosticism which the church writers, from the second to the
fourth century, are never tired of recording. These writers are
never objective, and never try to be so. Rather, they pick out
and emphasize anything strange or repellent, and coarsen it,
if they get the chance. We never get a real glimpse into the
teaching and life of a gnostic church; and, in view of the in-
credibly large number of systems, and the ceaseless flow of the
movement, every description must be regarded only as a snap-
shot of one particular form. Hence we must attempt to get as
close as possible to the original sources, i.e. to the writings
which belonged to the sects themselves; and this can be done
in a few cases.

Hippolytus of Rome, in his *Book of Heretics*, gives records
about the "Naassenes", who used to call themselves after the
Hebrew name for snake (*naash*). At a later date, they described
themselves as gnostics who alone plumbed the deeps of the
godhead. A tractate belonging to this sect had come into the
hands of Hippolytus[1] and he gives his readers a very ample
selection from it—it is possible that only this selection had
come into his hands, and not the complete original. This was
a learned theological monograph based upon a short hymn
addressed to Attis. The hymn was regarded as scripture, and
now explained in a gnostic fashion. It was sometimes sung as a
solo in the theatre. It hails Attis, whom the Assyrians call
Adonis; the Egyptians, Osiris; the Greeks, the Horn of the
Moon; among the Samothracians he is called Adamnas; among
the Thessalians, Karybas; among the Phrygians, Papas; and he

---

[1] Hippol., *Refut.*, v, 6, 3; 7, 3–9, 9; reconstructed by Reitzenstein, *Poimandres*,
83–98 and reviewed in Reitzenstein und Schaeder, *Studien zum antiken Synkretismus*
(1926), pp. 161–173

is called by still other names. Thus the hymn, which may have originated in Hadrian's time, is a witness to syncretistic "pantheism"; it honours Attis as the god worshipped by every race.

The gnostic preacher found in this hymn the teaching of "important mysteries", and he now proceeded to give wordy and pedantically overloaded descriptions of the myth of the first man, as the solution of the riddle of the universe. As in the legends of all races, man, as we know him, arose out of the ground, but was modelled on the form of the heavenly, original man. At first, he lay motionless and without breath, until a soul was given to him; and this it was that brought suffering and servitude for both the original man and his replica. What is the soul and whence does it come? Passing along roundabout ways which twist and turn in every direction through a multitude of mythologies, we are at last given to understand that the soul which dwells not only in man, but in the entire world of life, is the original man himself and is both male and female. Being a fertilizing germ, he brings everything into being; he is the motionless pole in the flux of cosmic appearances, the logos and the pneuma through which those who are born again are made like him in essence. But the whole account is so sketchy that it is not possible to work it out definitely and clearly. The myth of the original man occurs in innumerable gnostic systems in very varied contexts,[1] and the sermon of the Naassenes gives us a reflection of this variety. It is very ancient teaching, perhaps of Iranian origin, which had regained vitality in this restless period. It attained to some significance within Judaism, and it gave an impulse to the idea of the Messianic Son of Man as found in Daniel. We can trace it also in Philo, and behind the Pauline theory of the first and second man,[2] but only in gnosticism did it attain its full development and effectiveness; and here it remained active for several centuries.

The Naassene sermon is instructive also on other grounds. Similarly to the Leyden cosmogony, in its oldest recension it mingles Jewish elements with a multitude of pagan ideas—this epithet is the simplest. So doing, it betrays a tendency, which

[1] W. Bousset, *Hauptprobleme der Gnosis*, 160–233
[2] Reitzenstein, *Poimandres*, 109 ff.

we have already discussed in another connection,[1] to adopt
Jewish ideas and deal with them syncretistically, whereas the
sacred text of the hymn to Attis has no trace of this sort of thing.
The reason is that this form of gnosticism had come into contact
with Christianity, had frequently introduced New Testament
quotations into its text-book, and had interpolated Christian
phrases, but, fortunately, so superficially, and sometimes so
clumsily, that these interpolations can be sorted out again
without difficulty. This work, however, reflects, on the literary
plain, the concrete religious evolution of many of these sects
and, taken on the whole, that of gnosticism as such.

Hippolytus, however, supplies us with still further and, in
this case, more fruitful material. The gnostic Justin wrote a
book called Baruch as the "Scripture" of his church, and this he
surrounded with great secrecy; no one was to talk about it
outside. Hippolytus gained acquaintance with this writing and
he reproduces *verbatim* a chapter from it.[2]

Herodotus tells us that when Heracles was searching for the
cattle of Geryones he met a girl who was half human and half
snake: he united with her in love and she bore three sons. The
girl is a symbol of the origin of the world. At the beginning of
all things were three "unbegotten" principles: two male and
one female: the good God who possesses no other name and
who is omniscient; the father of all creation, who is invisible
but not omniscient and whose name is Elohim; and the woman
Eden who possesses two forms and is moved by passions, and
who is also known as Israel. Elohim unites with her, and in
mutual love, they beget twenty-four angels: twelve take after
the father and are called Michael, Amen, Baruch, Gabriel,
Esaddaios, and so on; twelve take after the mother: Babel,
Achamoth, Naash, Bel, Belias, Satan, and so on. The whole
multitude of angels is Paradise, the single angels are named
allegorically the trees of Paradise; "the tree of life" is the third
father-angel, Baruch; "the tree of knowledge" the third
Eden-angel, Naash. But Mother-Eden is nothing else than the
earth itself: the twelve angels of Elohim take material from her
upper, human part and create the man, Adam, with his earthly
soul; Elohim breathes into him the spirit, pneuma. Thus Adam

[1] *Vide supra*, p. 161   [2] Hipp., *Ref.*, v, 24–7

is the product of an agreement of Eden and Elohim to work in partnership, and is the seal of their marriage; and in the same way, Eve is created after him. The animals arise from the animal part of Eden.

The picture now changes, and Eden becomes the enemy of the human race. She gives her twelve angels power to bring evil into the world. They divide into four groups—typified in the Bible by the four streams of Paradise—and, in allotted periods and distances, they wander in circular paths: the place where they are at any particular time, determines the strength of their influence upon the earth. Why should Eden be so wrathful? Because at one time Elohim wished to mount into the higher regions of heaven in order to see if he could still improve the world. He took his angels with him, but left Eden behind; she could not follow her husband because she was burdened with the earth. From above, he saw the supramundane light, the doors of heaven opened, and he stood before the "Good", who invited him to sit at his right hand. Then he cried in fear: "Lord let me destroy the world that I have created: for my spirit is in prison in man, and I wish to receive it back again." The Good prevented him from doing evil, and advised him to remain above, and to leave the world to Eden; and this is what he did.

Then Eden grieved because her husband had abandoned her, and she decided to avenge herself on Elohim's spirit that dwelt in man. Her angels become the agents of her hostility. Babel, i.e. Aphrodite, brought immorality and divorce among men, and Naash tormented them in other ways.

Now, however, Elohim sends his third angel, Baruch, to give help. He warns men not to eat of the tree of knowledge, i.e. to learn from Naash. They may eat from any other trees (Gen. 2: 16), for the eleven other angels have passions, but are not hostile to the law, Naash alone being an exception. He seduces Eve to adultery, and Adam to perverse immorality. Then Evil and Good work upon mankind, both coming ultimately from the father, Elohim: his ascent to the "Good" shows the way to man when he is endeavouring to rise, but the betrayal of Eden causes all evils to break in upon the spirit which dwells in man. Baruch came again to Moses and summoned the children of Israel to turn to the "Good", but once again Naash excited the passions of the soul, which was born in Eden, against the spirit, and he successfully contested Baruch's warnings, although they had been preached by the prophets.

At last Elohim turned to the heathen and chose Heracles as a prophet. He fought and vanquished the twelve angels, a deed which the myth honours as the twelve labours of Heracles, but finally succumbed to the power of Omphale's love, who was no other than Babel or Aphrodite. She took his strength from him, i.e. she made him forget Baruch's commandments and covered him with her clothes, viz. the powers of Eden. His mission was in vain.

At last in the days of Herod, Baruch was sent to Nazareth, to Jesus the son of Joseph and Mary when he was minding the sheep as a twelve year old boy. "Preach the word to men—thus he was commanded—and proclaim to them the father, Elohim, and the 'Good', and then mount up to the 'Good' and there take your seat by Elohim, the father of us all." Jesus fulfilled the commandment, and Naash was not able to deceive Him: so he brought Him to the cross. But Jesus abandoned His body to mother Eden: "Woman, behold, thy son." (John 19: 26), He cried to her, and handed over to her His psychic, earthly part, but committed His spirit to the hands of the Father, and departed to the "Good". That is how this myth ends. Hippolytus says that it explained other Greek myths and words from the Bible, and he does not hesitate either to tell us the oath of the sect, or to record how they drank from the water of life and were baptized in this heavenly spring. Even Elohim did this, and the rite blotted out all repentance, whereas earthly men and psychics are baptized in earthly water.

This artificial myth contains a number of conceptions characteristic of gnostic thought, which considerably extend our previous horizon. First of all we observe the preference for a base in Holy Scripture. The actual words are treated allegorically, and so give shape to the dogmas in many respects. Besides Greek myths, Old Testament passages are used in the main, and the Mosaic story of creation supplies the data for depicting the beginnings of things and the tragedy of human corruption. The names of the persons who take active part are

borrowed from the Old Testament. Echoes from the New
Testament are very rare, and are marked only when Jesus
appears in the concluding act: it is not by chance that John is
the gospel cited.

As far as the contents are concerned we see that the theology
of redemption is the basis of the whole.[1] Man consists of a lower
and a higher element; his spirit is of divine origin, but he is
exiled in a body endowed with a "psychic" soul and he suffers
in this world. A divine messenger comes to redeem him, points
him the way to God, and precedes him. We have already discussed the same things in different forms in the Naassene
doctrine of the first man. Although it must certainly have been
in the other parts of Baruch's book, no extant reference explains
how to obtain the redemption which had been brought about
by Baruch and Jesus. According to all analogies, it is not likely
to have been effected by a simple intellectual acceptance of the
theories. Rather, redemption must have been effected by a
mystic and sacramental communion with the spirit of the
redeemer, and by a way of life intended to liberate the soul that
dwelt in man from the earthly passions which were active in
his body and soul, i.e. from the falsehood and deceit of Eden.

We have shown that this system of redemption lay behind the
Pauline theology. There is a crucial difference, however, in that
for Paul, redemption is a pure and incomprehensible act of
God's love on behalf of guilty and hostile mankind. Marcion
grasped that fact in a certain sense, and carried it to extremes.
Moreover, in Paul, the spirit of Christ is not a natural element
of man given in creation, but a heavenly gift which brings
redemption. In the book of Baruch, on the other hand, the
human spirit is itself of divine origin. What it suffers is not connected, in the Pauline sense, with its own sin and guilt, but is
the effect of a divine tragedy: and even then the concept of
guilt is artificially balanced between the two protagonists. Thus
redemption is a necessity for the father, Elohim, a matter which
he must bring about for his own sake. Indeed, it is a liberation
of himself, for it is his own spirit which he rescues from the
fetters of the earthly. Redemption takes place in the form of
an ascent to God, and this sect must have been told of the

[1] *Vide supra*, pp. 120 f.

"heavenly journey of the soul", or, rather, "of the spirit", as they express it. The idea of God is the same as we have already discussed.[1] The One, Great, Good, Almighty, remains in the background as the final source. The active gods are of lower rank, and are both male and female: the higher qualities are ascribed to the male gods. Their mutual antipathies give rise to the drama of the mystery of redemption. Astral theology plays a certain part: the twelve angels of Eden run their course and, in turn, rule over events on the earth because they are the signs of the zodiac. It is expressly said that the third angel acts as the herald of both Elohim and Eden, and conveys their will. Whether this idea is linked with the "third messenger" of Mani,[2] and whether it comes directly from Baruch or in a roundabout way through Iranic ideas, must remain an open question.

If we test the relationship between this gnostic system and Christianity, the case will be somewhat different from that of the Naassenes. First of all, we note that the Jewish elements are more marked everywhere. It is not without purpose that the redeeming messenger of God is called Baruch, and we can confidently describe this gnosis as Jewish at bottom, i.e. we can assume that the Old Testament elements were from the beginning the components out of which the system was built up. The case is different with the Christian passages. Jesus appears only at the end, unexpectedly, and when the act of redemption is taking place; and it is rather strange to hear of Him after we were expressly assured that Baruch had gone from the Jews, and had "finally" chosen Heracles. It is striking that he should then come back regretfully to the Jews, and turn—once more "finally"—to Jesus of Nazareth. Obviously Jesus was lacking in the original, and Heracles was himself the Redeemer after he had freed himself from Omphale's toils, thereby giving mankind a saviour. The Heracles of Greek mythology does not remain in the woman's bonds, but goes to heaven and is accepted among the gods. In this case, there is a formal and final rounding off, in so far as the figure of Heracles constitutes both the

[1] *Vide supra*, p. 268
[2] Bousset, *Hauptprob. der Gnosis*, 74 f. H. H. Schaeder, *Urform. u. Fortbildung d. manichäischen Systems* (1927), p. 102

starting point and the final aim of the myth. The figure of Jesus is brought in only at a later date. His death on the cross is explained in the usual way from the hostility of the lords of this world, in this case of Eden, and His death is understood as a separating of His divine and mundane components; this view, together with the perverting of the last words on the cross, corresponds to the gnostic conception elsewhere. What we have here was borrowed from some other system that had already been Christianized.

The examples that we have cited so far show that gnosis arose apart from any Christian influence. Indeed, it is older than Christianity, and is a phenomenon of pagan syncretism, which mingled Greek and oriental religion in the greatest variety of forms, filled them out with mystical traits, and, at the same time, combined them with philosophical ideas and modes of thought. Thanks to its aggressive propaganda, Judaism shared to a considerable extent in the development of gnosticism. But in its critical early period, Christianity was practically untouched by gnosticism which, at that time, was itself obviously only just showing signs of beginning. First in Colossians, do we find Paul called on to repel an influence which had arisen in the Lycus valley. This influence had gnostic elements and, as a consequence, Paul himself made some positive use of his opponents' forms of thought and expression. After this, similar, mutual reactions are continually occurring: we have discussed them more fully in the case of the Johannine writings. But only in the period that we have now reached, and after we have examined a few typical examples of gnosticism in its simplest form, are we able to deal intelligently with the question as to the effects of such teachings on the Christian church.

What could these systems contribute to the Christian standpoint, when they were so remote from Christianity itself? So long as they were purely pagan and syncretistic, nothing of importance. The matter of greatest moment, the theology of redemption, Paul had already put into a classical form which, at best, could only have been worked out a little further. Enthusiasm, prophecy, and sacramental mysticism might have been able to gain stimuli from gnostic fraternities. Astrology was almost ineradicable at that period, and could have been developed further, along with such observances of certain days as are dependent on it; ascetic tendencies, which were already present and in a certain sense sanctioned by Paul, found new occasions and forms. In other words, gnostics of the earlier type were in a position to send isolated impulses into the Christian church. They made themselves felt in peculiarities of cult, of ethics, or of speculation, some being tolerated and others attacked. Most of the influences up to the end of the first century were of this character.

The situation was different as soon as ever a strongly Judaized gnosis appeared on the horizon of the Christian churches, and opened their eyes to a new way of regarding the Old Testament. Allegorization of the Scriptures had been adopted as a matter of course amongst the Christians, and now the same method was applied with greater boldness and with astonishing new results. The consequence was that the gulf separating Christians from orthodox Judaism widened, and this was felt as pure gain. At the same time numerous questions and doubts were settled, if only the creation and the defects of this world; the Fall and all the evil impulses of the body, as well as all the dubious stories of men of God in the Old Testament, were no longer brought into connection with God, the Father of the Lord Jesus Christ, but were ascribed to an intermediate divine being. If Jesus was regarded as some such revelation of a divine being, i.e. as the logos or the spirit, why should one not find another godhead of more or less secondary character in the God of the Old Testament, and thereby gain a clear understanding of God, and not one oppressed by ethical doubt? Moreover, did not the glimpse of the secrets of supra-mundane happenings attract the unhealthy curiosity even of the simple Christian? To the present day, he is ever and again eager to fathom what Paul condemned no less sharply than Jesus, as belonging not to the sphere of religion, but to that of "carnal wisdom" and unseemly curiosity?

However, if one had gone so far, the next step was almost inevitable. One must be on the look-out to give the person to Christ a place in the system of new knowledge. In this respect there were not a few points of contact for speculative construction. We have made the acquaintance of one of the simplest and therefore one of the most instructive forms, in the book of Baruch. This gnostic myth, in its Christianized form, could have been given out as a legitimate further development of early Christian teachings, and have gathered a church round about itself. These people would believe themselves on a higher level than the masses who moved on the lower grounds of the tradition of the church catholic; and so would regard themselves as the genuine Christians endowed with full insight. So long as such new systems put forward pagan elements strongly and in crude form, and regarded Christ only as one messenger of God among others, they had little power of attraction for normal Christians. Gnosis only became dangerous when it developed systems which placed Christ in the centre of world events and which paid court to any disaffections on the part of the orthodox. A struggle with such gnostics flamed up in the middle of the second century and the church bears the marks of it to the present day.

It is not part of our task to trace the evolution of gnosticism in greater detail, or to describe the exceedingly numerous systems. As a significant phenomenon belonging to the beginning of the declining period of the ancient world, gnosticism is a movement in itself. It must be discussed within the framework of the general history of religion belonging to that period, and its branches stretch out in both space and time, beyond the borders of our account of church history. For our purpose it only comes under observation as far as Christianity was attacked by it, and as the development of the church was influenced by controversy with it. Hence we are not only permitted but required to limit ourselves to the characteristic types: and we ought to deal only with the two most mature gnostic systems out of the overwhelming mass. This means that we must deal with those which come nearest to traditional Christianity, which most strongly influenced the churches, and which, correspondingly, had to withstand the sharpest opposition on the part of the Church: the doctrines of Basilides and Valentine. At the same time, however, we are dealing with those which alone can claim higher significance in the spiritual warfare of ancient times. Apart from the advent of Christianity the whole of gnosticism would have been just as unobserved and obscure as all the other mystical and magical phantoms of the period. Moreover, the gnostics never became of literary significance in the field of spiritual life in general. Literary men occasionally accepted samples of the fare it offered, as we have seen in the case of Dion, but never thought of regarding it as literature proper. Nevertheless influences proceeded from gnosticism, which enabled churchmen to put forth works of higher literary value although that happened only generations later.

As soon as we come to the task of giving an account of the teachings of Basilides, a difficulty arises that is characteristic of the entire movement, a difficulty at which we have already hinted. All these systems were in a state of continual and rapid evolution, and the polemic writers of the church naturally had no interest in antiquarian researches, but attacked the teaching in the form in which it influenced the church of their time. This is particularly striking in the case of Basilides. Clement of Alexandria took the trouble to look up the original writings of Basilides, which he cited, as also what was said by his disciples.[1] Irenæus of Lyons[2] about A.D. 180 described the system, which apparently showed several further developments; the same holds true of the various notices in Hippolytus.[3] But the points with which we are concerned are clear enough.

Basilides lived in the time of Hadrian and Antoninus Pius (A.D. 117–161) in Egypt, particularly in Alexandria, although he made missionary journeys through the nomes of the delta.[4] He wrote a considerable work under the title of *Exegetica*, which, in practice, amounted to a commentary on the gospel. A few fragments have been preserved. The thirteenth book[5] dealt with the parable of the rich man and Lazarus, and found therein hints of the doctrine that the origin of nature was without root in time or space—if we rightly understand his enigmatic words. Our authority, Hegemonius, quotes from this book a report about the dualism of the "barbarians", i.e. the Persians. The passages describe the war of light with darkness

---

[1] Harnack, *Altchristl. Literatur*, i, 157–161; Hilgenfeld, *Ketzergesch. d. Urchristentums*, 207–217, cf. E. de Faye, *Gnostique et Gnosticisme* (2nd edition), 39–56

[2] Iren., i, 24, 3–6 (i, 198–203, ed. Harvey)

[3] Hippol., *Ref.*, vii, 14–27, and in the *Syntagma* ap. Epiph., 24 (i, 256–267), Holl

[4] Clem., *Strom.*, vii, 17, 106, 4; Epiph., xxiv, 1, 1

[5] Hegemonius, *Acta Archelai.*, 67, 4–11, ed. Beeson

and the resulting peculiar character of what was created. But
we are not told what attitude Basilides himself took to this
theory. Clement of Alexandria,[1] too, quotes several passages
from the twenty-third book. Basilides is there dealing with the
problem how God could permit the innocent sufferings of the
martyrs. His answer is that there are no such things as innocent
sufferings, because that would contradict the righteousness of
God. The martyrs suffer in punishment of their sins, otherwise
secret. And if they really had none—a rare case—their sufferings
were to be set on a level with those of infant children. Even
these had a predisposition for sin, and it was not their merit
that this impulse had not come to effect in practice. The will
for evil was present in any case; this, and not merely the accomplished act was wicked and deserved punishment: there is an
unmistakable reference to the Sermon on the Mount, with its
attitude to adultery and murder.

Thus the formal, philosophically conceived, righteousness of
God is for Basilides a fundamental postulate of his system, and
this he carries through logically regardless of the contradictions
in practical experience. His idea of sin is, in a sense, earnest and
profound, corresponding to Paul's doctrines and the Sermon
on the Mount. Thus, all suffering is, for him, a just punishment
for sin; to that extent, it is good. It may be punishment for sin
committed in an earlier life. For he takes the Old Testament
principle of punishment to the third and fourth generation, and
explains it from the standpoint of metempsychosis; and, only on
this assumption, can he understand the Pauline saying: "I was
alive apart from the Law once" (Rom. 7: 9). That could not
apply to human existence, for this was always subject to some
law; it must have been said about a life in another, perhaps an
animal body.[2]

The soul which has been destined and chosen for redemption,
is of a supra-mundane nature, foreign to the earth. Its knowledge of God proceeds from this nature, and faith is not one of
its functions, but self-subsistent; it is the most glorious orna-
ment of the soul. Thus the redeemed have received three things

[1] Clem., *Strom.*, iv, 12, 81, 1–88, 5

[2] *Ibid.*, iv, 12, 83, 2; *Exc. ex. Theod.*, 28. Origen in *Epist. ad Rom.*, v; Vol. 6,
p. 336. Lommatzsch

by the will of God: (a) the power to find everything acceptable in order that the logos of each may be saved for the All. (b) To have no desires, and (c) to have no hatred. Thus, even in the most inward part, they remain untouched by the attacks of this world: "Suffering and fear belong to material things, like rust to iron." Thus also sins committed in ignorance or involuntarily are forgiven, i.e. simply washed away. We may add: only when sins are born of the will and thereby have contact with substance must they be atoned by suffering. If we say, in addition, that Basilides personifies righteousness and, together with its daughter Irene, i.e. peace, numbered it with the highest ogdoad, we shall have dealt with the authentic passages from his writings.[1] They do not give a complete picture, but a few points which other passages help to connect up, and fill out. Thus they make it possible for us to get an idea of Basilides's way of thought.

Besides these literal extracts from the writings of the master himself, our best sources afford not a few notices in regard to the opinions of the "Basilidians", particularly in the writings of his son, Isidoros. He also had written a book called *Exegetica* in which he expounded the words of a prophet, Parchor by name. Moreover, Basilides himself had his own apocryphal authorities: a certain Glaucias, a person described as a translator of Peter; and Matthias, of whose tradition we hear elsewhere; further names of prophets are mentioned,[2] Barkoph and Barkabbas "and other imaginary figures". For Isidor, and obviously also for Basilides, prophetic talent was a special gift of God to the elect; and if the Athenians had ascribed a clarvoyant dæmon to Socrates, and similarly Aristotle to all men, this was done only in recognition of a theological truth preached by the prophets. The philosophers just mentioned had not themselves discovered, but only accepted, it. Thus Isidor in his commentary on Parchor.[3]

On another occasion, we hear[4] that the Basilidians described the passions as "addenda", as spirits which had laid hold of the rational soul only on the occasion of some primeval rebellion;

---

[1] Clement, *Strom.*, iv, 12, 88, 5 (unlike ii, 3, 10, 1–3). v, 1, 3, 2. iv, 12, 86, 1; 88, 5; 24, 153, 3; 25, 162, 1
[2] *Ibid.*, vii, 17, 106, 4; 108, 1. Agrippa Castor in Euseb., *H.E.*, iv, 7, 7
[3] Clem., *Strom.*, vi, 6, 53, 2–5   [4] *Ibid.*, ii, 20, 112, 1–114, 1

at a later date these spirits had been joined by all sorts of animal and plant spirits which induced the soul to imitate their own "properties" with the help of imagination. Isidor clearly recognized the danger of this conception for moral conduct, and in writing *Of the Twofold Soul*, would not permit reference to the power of these "appended" forces to be regarded as excuses for sin. "The rational part of us must remain master and overcome our lower nature." We have just seen how Basilides himself, by using the metaphor of rust on iron, explains the relationship of the passions to the soul: here we have a further development of the theory.

A fragment, preserved by Clement, gives us the attitude of the school to marriage.[1] The word of Jesus about the three kinds of eunuchs (Matt. 19: 12) is expounded quite correctly, and the "eunuchs for the sake of the kingdom of Heaven" is explained as referring to those who avoid marriage on account of its being bound up with earthly cares—which agrees fairly well with Paul's personal opinion. But "to marry is better than to burn" says the apostle: he who must be always on his guard in order to keep himself pure, lives in a divided hope: he would do better to marry. But he who for any reason does not wish to marry, and yet is afraid of sin, should not separate himself from the brethren. In the holy fellowship nothing could attack him, and their laying on of hands would bring him help. He need only desire to do the good, and he would then be successful. In human life there are things which were natural and necessary, and others which were only natural. To dress oneself was natural and necessary; sexual intercourse was natural but not necessary. It is more than doubtful whether the sexual practices of a gnostic sect which were apparently observed by Epiphanius some two hundred years later[2] reflect any of the theories of Basilides. There is one important notice[3] to the effect that the Basilidians observed a feast of the baptism of Christ by a nocturnal ceremony which preceded the day itself. It was observed on either the 10th or the 6th of January, i.e. in connection with an ancient Egyptian feast of Osiris at which holy water was drawn by all from the Nile during the night.

[1] Clem., *Strom.*, iii, 1, 1–3   2 (=Epiph., *haer.*, xxxii, 4, 4–9)
[2] Epiph., *haer.*, xxvi, 4–5; cf. xxvi, 17, 4–9
[3] Clem., *Strom.*, i, 21, 146, 1–2; cf. K. Holl, *Ges. Aufsätze*, ii, pp. 143, 152–4

To these details which have come down to us by the accident
of tradition, we now add the sketch of the system of Basilides
with which Irenæus presents us.[1] The "unborn and nameless
Father" is exalted and alone. He first begot Nous, the understanding; the logos was begotten by Nous and then a series of
emanations from Phronesis, Sophia, Dynamis—reason, wisdom,
power—to the great powers and archangels who dwell in the
first heaven, which they themselves had created. A new
emanation of spiritual powers then took place. They created
for themselves a second heaven, and so on, until the holy
number of three hundred and sixty-five heavens was reached.
That this was a holy number was proved by the magic word
abrasax, 365 being the sum of the numerical values of its Greek
letters. The lowest of these heavens was the one which we see,
and its inhabitants were those which had created our earth
and which shared its rule among themselves. The highest of
these was the god of the Jews who wished to subject all other
people to his elect, but thereby set the other angels and their
nations against himself and his people.

When the anonymous Father saw the distress of mankind, He
sent His first-born, Nous, as Christ, in order to redeem those
who should believe on Him, from the rule of the creator of the
world. He therefore appeared upon earth as man, revealed
Himself to the nations, and worked miracles. But He bore
human form only in appearance, because, really, He was an
incorporeal being. Thus He did not really suffer on the cross.
On the *Via Dolorosa*, He handed the cross over to Simon of
Cyrene, to whom He lent His own figure, and who was killed
as if he were Jesus, while the true Jesus Christ in the figure
of Simon stood near by, and laughed at His enemies.
Then, invisible to all hostile powers, He ascended to the
Father.

He who knows this secret is liberated from the power of the
creator of the world: he must confess Him who came in human
form, who is regarded as crucified, whose name is Jesus, and
who was sent from the Father in order to destroy the works of
the creator of the world according to the Father's plan of
salvation (*œconomia*). But he who confesses Jesus the crucified

[1] Iren., i, 24

is still a slave, and under the authority of the angels which created our bodies.

Salvation has to do only with the soul, for the body is by nature corruptible. Prophesyings originate from the creators of the world and, in particular, the Law comes from their overlord who had fetched from Egypt his own people, the Jews. Among the Basilidians no one troubled about the prohibition of sacrificial flesh and other matters, and there were no problems in the sexual sphere. They used magic, images, exorcisms, and other forms of witchcraft. They named the angels, and distributed them among their three hundred and sixty-five heavens. In the same way, the Saviour, when descending and ascending through the empires of the spirits, was called Qawlaqaw—a pedantic Hebrew reminiscence coming from Isa. 28: 10, and occurring among the Naassenes as the name of the original man.[1] He who knows all these matters in their proper connections, and the names of the angels, will be invisible to all the angels and spiritual powers, and incomprehensible to them, like Qawlaqaw; he will pass unrecognized through all the heavenly regions. Naturally these are secrets which are only possible for the few and which must be guarded by initiates in the strictest confidence. Thus Irenæus.

His account does not mention the basic doctrine, although it is proved by the separate passages already discussed, viz. that the human soul is of heavenly origin and is related to the son of the most-high God, the redeemer Nous. That is why Nous descends to the earth—also taught in the book of Baruch—and raises to life again the divine power of the human soul. Everyone reached and convinced by this message is transformed to a copy of the original model. He receives the powers and the capacities of the redeemer, so that he himself can now find his way back unrecognized and unhindered to his heavenly home, where the God, who is perfectly good and absolutely righteous, sits on His throne unapproachably distant and majestic.

Here we have the gnostic idea of God, gnostic doctrine of redemption, gnostic cosmogony with the incorporation of the God of the Jews as a spirit of lower rank, gnostic anthropology—including a marked leaning to magic and all sorts of esoteric

[1] Hippol., *Ref.*, v, 7, 41, 4

teachings—and yet one thing is certain: Basilides maintained he was a Christian. In his system, Christ is not one dæmon among many, but the only begotten Son of the most-high God, His only and perfect revelation; through Him everything else had been created. He is the redeemer of mankind and brings the elect of all nations back to God.

We have seen that gnostic literature usually took the form of expositions of sacred books. Basilides was the first to expound a Christian book, and indeed nothing less than "the gospel". We cannot say whether one of our four gospels, or a selection, prepared by Basilides himself, of a gospel-harmony, constituted the text. That it was not apocryphal is shown by all the extant citations of the gospel which the Basilidians quoted. The most significant fact is that this book, written to expound gnostic doctrine, is the very first commentary on a gospel. No Christian, who was a member of the church catholic, had, up to that time, made a gospel the subject of a continuous exegesis; and it was still to be a long time before Papias wrote his expositions of the sayings of the Lord, and Theophilus of Antioch (about A.D. 180) his commentary on the gospels. Further, Basilides dealt with the gospel as sacred scripture, and therefore explained it allegorically, in exactly the same way as the Church was accustomed to explain the Old Testament. On this point, the Church had not yet gone so far as to put the gospels on a similar level to the traditional book, i.e. the Old Testament, and so treat it as itself Holy Scripture; the New Testament canon was still at the prenatal stage. In this respect, again, gnosticism stimulated the Church and called forth new activity just because it had gone on ahead.

If we consider the teachings of Basilides, we have no difficulty in understanding how seductive they must have seemed to many orthodox Christians. There was no trace of that syncretistic paganism which had always been felt objectionable; instead of that, Christ stood clearly and gloriously in the foreground as the Son of God, in a vigorous monotheism. That there was an endless number of angels was also the opinion in the Church. Basilides taught their names and their mutual relationships, and much about the origin of heaven and earth; that was surely not forbidden? And when he spoke of the divine origin of the soul, and founded his doctrine of redemption upon it, what was he doing differently from the author of Acts, who, indeed (17: 23, 28) tells that the Apostle Paul preached about the "unknown God" and quoted Aratos: "For we are His off-spring." This is but what Basilides said, and indeed more exactly and clearly. The only objectionable thing was that he did not accept the Old Testament in its entirety. He thought little of the prophecies, and nothing of the Law; nor did he recognize the children of Israel as the elect of God. It is true that the orthodox teachers preached otherwise, but was it so very certain that they were right? Paul himself had said (Gal. 3: 19) that the Law was given by the angels, and such an authority as the author of Hebrews (2: 2) had expressly re-peated it. Basilides made exactly the same assertions, but pro-ceeded logically to liberate Christian thought from all the troublesome problems which the old book of the Jews offered to the moral sensibility of a Christian, and indeed, to his idea of God. He replaced the Old Testament, and gave the gospel, as scripture, all the greater reverence in the central position of Christian teaching.

All this and much more was true, and was often said; and he who was completely convinced went over, together with others of like mind, to a schismatic church of the new teachers, and became a sectarian. But much greater was the number of those who remained faithful to the church and who regarded such opinions as quite in keeping with the old doctrine: they opened the doors of the church to gnosticism and unwittingly brought the church into a danger which would soon require all her powers to ward off: the danger of being overrun by the power of gnosis and being drawn into mortal combat with ancient religion.

The most comprehensive and effective system of Christian gnosis goes back to Valentine. He came from Egypt to Rome where he laboured for a lengthy period, about A.D. 160–170, and indeed hoped to become bishop. Later he appears to have left Rome and gone to Cyprus.[1] The various branches of his teaching and school of thought struggled most vigorously with the Church and were most definitely repudiated. Loud

[1] Epiph., *haer.*, xxxi, 7, 1–2; *Iren.*, iii, 4, 3 (2, 17 H.); Tert., *adv. Valent.*, 4

complaints have come down to us from the orthodox,[1] that the
Valentinians preached in the churches, making full use of the
customary phrases and deceiving the simple. Then the seducers
took offence because they were repudiated as heretics, although
they were saying and teaching exactly the same thing as the
orthodox. But that was precisely why they were regarded as the
most dangerous opponents of the Church; and such they were
in fact. They were honourably concerned to do her justice, and
to recognize her as the first stage to perfect knowledge.

Thus the sources are particularly rich in regard to Valentine's
form of gnosticism. Besides reliable reports we possess a not in-
considerable number of quotations from Valentine himself and
his school, even if no complete documents.[2] Of course the
methodological limitations which we had to assume in the study
of Basilides hold good in this case also, but by comparing
various sources, it is possible to begin with the notices of
Irenæus in regard to the Ptolemaic School, and work out details
of an older form,[3] which we may possibly ascribe to Valentine: it
can scarcely have undergone serious changes by the editing of
his disciples.

Above the universe, on invisible and ineffable heights, dwells
the prime Father who is also called Bythos and Chaos. He is
invisible, incomprehensible, superior to time, unbegotten, and
dwells in eternal peace. At His side is His Ennœa also called
Sigē, or Charis, i.e. God's thought, silence, and grace. Personification of divine properties is by now quite familiar to us: it
is a new thing, however, that the prime God should have a
consort. That belongs to the nature of the system, for according
to Valentine all the divine emanations proceed forth in duality;
the mystery of marriage (Eph. 5: 32) is predominant even in
the world of the gods. The first two gods give birth to Nous or
Monogenes, the only-begotten, together with Aletheia, truth,
the latter two produce Logos and Zoē, word and life; and from
these proceed as the final pair of the higher ogdoad, Anthropos

[1] *Iren.*, iii, 15, 2 (2, 79 H.); de Faye *Gnostiques*, 57–141, pp. 251–67
[2] Harnack, *Ges. d. Altchr. Lit.*, i, 174–184; Hilgenfeld, *Ketzerges.*, pp. 293–308,
Ptolemaeus, pp. 345–368, Marcus, pp. 369–383, Herakleon, pp. 472–505, Eastern
School, pp. 505–22
[3] *Iren.*, i, 1–8; cf. Hippol., *Ref.*, vi, 21–55 and Ps-Tertullian, *adv. omn. haer.*, 4.
Exc. ex. Theod., 43–65. Cf. K. Müller, *Götting. Nachr.*, 1920, pp. 205–241. Ed.
Schwartz, *ibid.*, 1908, p. 128, pp. 134–9

and Ecclesia, man and church. Almost all these names are chosen with good conscience from the Biblical sources, including the "chaos" of Genesis and the silence from which according to the Wisdom of Solomon the word of God arises.[1] The germs of hypostatization, recognizable[2] even in John, now attain to full development.

From Logos and Zoē proceed a further decad of five pairs of gods, from Anthropos and Ecclesia a series of six pairs, so that the "pleroma", i.e. the "fullness of the Godhead",[3] consists of thirty "æons", which are conceived, in reality, only as rays of the one ineffable Godhead, but the differences between them express the descent from the highest to the lowest divinity. Among all these beings, the only-begotten Nous alone possesses the possibility of perfect knowledge of the highest God, and gives information to the others about Him. He alone is the divine principle of revelation. His preaching awakens in all a yearning for God, which yearning, however, is a silent desire.

Only the last of the thirty æons, Sophia, lets her desires grow into an unbridled passion, and tries to grasp the nature of the Father. But she would have been overcome by the sweet rapture of her feelings, and have dissolved into the All, had not Horos, the guardian of the borders of the pleroma, held her back, supported her, and brought her back to her senses. Now she understood that the Father was incomprehensible, and so she cast away her former desires and passions;[4] thus she was able to remain in the pleroma. But now at the command of the prime Father, Monogenes brings forth a new pair, Christ and the Holy Spirit, in order that the latter might restore order to the pleroma which had been disturbed by Sophia's action. Christ teaches the æons that they owe their origin to the Father, but their form to Nous, whereas the spirit teaches them how to agree with one another, how to thank God, and thus how to attain genuine peace. This they now do, and all become similar to one another in form and sense. They sing, in chorus, the praises of the prime Father, and then produce Jesus the Saviour as the perfect fruit of the pleroma. He is also

[1] *Vide supra*, pp. 242 f.   [2] *Vide supra*, p. 230   [3] *Vide supra*, p. 214
[4] *Iren.*, i, 1, 1-2, 3 (vol. i, pp. 8–16, ed. Harvey)

called Christ or Logos, after the one who begot Him, and He is surrounded by a host of angels as His satellites.[1]

The yearning cast out from Sophia and the pleroma is known as "Enthymesis", and it becomes the first being in the hitherto lifeless void. It is a pneumatic substance still without form, until it is shaped by Christ, and receives a personal nature: it is the lower Sophia, or, using the Hebrew name, Achamoth. Like her mother, she possesses heavenly yearning, and experiences similar suffering. The guardian of the border opposes her urge for the pleroma, and frightens her back by using the name, Iao, which has magic power. She now suffers in the highest degree the pains of all the passions, whence there arises the original model of the world: from her love for the Giver of life, everything that possesses a soul; from her passion, everything that is material; in particular, moisture comes from her tears, out of her laughter comes light, out of her sorrow and anguish, the elements.[2]

At the supplication of the higher Sophia, Christ takes pity upon her and sends to her aid the Saviour or Paraclete, who heals her and "gives form to her knowledge". As a result she rejoices in the sight of the angels which acccompany Him, and so gives birth to a pneumatic substance. The world is now formed of these three elements, matter, psyche, pneuma. In particular, it is created by the demi-urge, the creator of the world with his six angels, and he himself is created by Achamoth out of psychic substance. Thus there arises a new and lower "ogdoad" of Achamoth with seven angelic figures. The demi-urge creates the seven heavens for himself and his angels, and out of the world of dæmons and earthly elements creatures are called into being on the model previously set by Achamoth. His own form and likeness are used when he creates man out of matter and psyche, body and soul. But without his suspecting it, Achamoth sows the pneumatic substance, born of herself, into the human soul, and therefore prepares it for the reception of the perfect logos in the future. The redemption of mankind means, therefore the liberation of his pneuma, which longs for God, from union with lower substances.[3] Thus there is repeated

[1] *Iren.*, i, 2, 4*b*–6 (pp. 18–23 H.)   [2] *Ibid.*, i, 4, 1–2 (pp. 31–36 H.)
[3] Valentine in Clem., *Strom.*, ii, 20, 114, 4

once more the drama which has already been played twice in this world—by the higher Sophia and by Achamoth.

The Saviour descends to the yearning spirit of man. As the firstborn of those whom He is to redeem, He has already accepted from Achamoth the pneumatic element, and from the demi-urge, the "psychic Christ". Matter is not capable of redemption, and thus the Saviour has no earthly, material body. The way of redemption is the same for mankind as it had been for Sophia, the "shaping of gnosis": i.e. the full knowledge of God and of Achamoth, by initiation into the mysteries. This perfection is, however, only granted to the "pneumatics", who carry within themselves the divine seed, which is sown ever afresh by Achamoth. When all the pneuma scattered in the world is perfected in gnosis, then redemption is completed, then Sophia-Achamoth enters into the highest pleroma, and becomes the bride of the Saviour; the pneumatics lay aside their souls, and, unhindered and unseen by all the heavenly powers, they ascend to the pleroma in order to be married as pure spirits with the Saviour's angels.

But also the "psychics", who have not been reached by pneuma, are promised a redemption. The demi-urge, who is entirely without inkling until the arrival of the Saviour, had not shut himself up from the teaching of the redeemer; and so even he labours, according to his power in perfecting the world, and shows particular care for the prosperity of the Church.[1] The latter preserves the divine revelation in its holy scriptures, although most of its members are not able to understand them completely in their spiritual sense, because they themselves lack the pneuma, and are bound to this world. Thus they strive valiantly, in faith and by good works, to reach the goal prepared for them: in the end, the souls of the righteous, together with the demi-urges, will enter into the middle space, between heaven and pleroma, where Achamoth still dwells, and where they will find rest. The earthly world will be destroyed with fire, and will exist no longer.[2]

The whole, exceedingly complicated system is transformed

---

[1] *Iren.*, i, 7, 4–5 (pp. 63–4 H.)

[2] *Ibid.*, i, 4, 4–6, 2;6, 4–7, 2 (pp. 38–55; 57–60 H.), also *Exc. ex. Theod.*, pp. 43–65

further and rebuilt in the various schools; it is also buttressed by a detailed scriptural proof,[1] which relies almost entirely on the Gospels and the Pauline epistles, and only uses the Old Testament in a few quotations from Genesis and Psalms. The method of interpretation is of course allegorical; accordingly, the wandering sheep is Sophia; Simon, who sings the hymn of greeting to the child Jesus, is the demi-urge who rejoices in the Saviour; the prophetess Hannah, who awaits the redemption in the temple (Luke 2: 36), is Achamoth awaiting the re-ascent of the Saviour. The parable of the tares amongst the wheat shows the existence of the spiritual seed side by side with psychic elements in a pneumatic man. The daughter of Jairus is the symbol of Achamoth, who is awakened to knowledge by the Saviour, and the words of Jesus, when suffering on the cross, express the pains of Achamoth.[2]

Valentine's disciple, Heracleon, wrote, probably after the middle of the second century, a detailed commentary on John, of which Origen has preserved many excerpts.[3] Here allegorization is complete; e.g. the demi-urge speaks through the Baptist, and the woman of Samaria is a type of the pneumatic woman who is dissatisfied with the Jacob's Well of the Old Testament, who therefore turns to the living water of gnosis, and who longs for her future spouse in the pleroma.[4] This method was exactly the same as that customary in the Church, and neither its application nor the tendency of its exegesis was out of harmony with the spirit of the Fourth Gospel. In the end, it was the re-examination of the whole presuppositions of gnosticism and its denial of validity to the Old Testament, which created a feeling of doubt among readers within the Church.

A thorough discussion of the Old Testament by another of Valentine's disciples, Ptolemy, has been preserved.[5] Writing an

---

[1] *Iren.*, i, 3, 1–6; 8, 2–5 (pp. 24–31; 68–80 H.), *Exc. ex. Theod. passim*; Hipp., *Ref.*, vi, 34–5, etc. Cf. Carola Barth., *Interp. d. N.T. in der Valent. Gnosis*, 1911 (*T.U.*, 37, 3)

[2] *Iren.*, i, 8, 2–4 (pp. 68–73 H.), *Exc. ex. Theod.*, 53

[3] Origen's, *Commentary of John*, ed. by E. Preuschen, p. cii. Brooke, *The Fragments of Heracleon* (Texts and Studies, i, 4). Hilgenfeld, *Ketzergeschichte*, 472–498

[4] On John 1: 26 (Orig., vi, 200) and on 4, 12 ff. (Orig., xiii, 57; lxiii, 68); W. v. Löwenich, *Johannesverständnis im 2. Jh.*, pp. 82 ff.

[5] Epiph., *haer.*, xxxiii, 3–7; cf. Harnack, *Berl Sitzungsberichte*, 1902, pp. 507–545; Edition in *Kleine Texte*, No. 9

open letter to an eminent lady, Flora by name, he subjects the
five books of Moses to religious criticism, and displays keen
understanding. First of all he distinguishes the three parts of the
Law: the first is from God, the second is from Moses—as Jesus
explicitly declares, e.g. in regard to permission for divorce
(Matt. 19: 8)—the third from the Jewish "elders", to whose
tradition Jesus ascribes a commandment such as the privilege
of what is given to God (Matt. 15: 5–6). Even the part which
goes back to God is not a unity, but itself falls into three stages.
The first stage is the pure commandment of God, in which no
foreign element is mixed, and which Jesus did not wish to
abrogate, but to fulfil: the Ten Commandments. The second
consists of the commandments which have been adulterated
with injustice, such as that of retaliation where one wrong act
is repaid by a second. The third are the ceremonial laws, which
possess only symbolic and typological meaning.

This raises the question: Who was the divine originator of
this Law? It is not perfect, and therefore does not come from
the perfect God, the unbegotten One; still less does it come
from the devil since it contains what is truly good. Thus the Law
is the work of an intermediate god, who proclaims righteousness
as he understands it. The lady now asks how the lower beings,
belonging to this middle position, and especially how the
nothingness of the devil, could arise from the "One original
principle recognized and confessed by us"—for the goodness of
nature only begets things similar and equal to itself. In answer,
she is directed toward future teaching, which will tell her of
"the apostolic tradition which we have accepted from hand to
hand, together with the proof of all the sayings from the teaching of the Saviour". Thus she was to be initiated into the
system, and introduced to its scriptural proof; and she would be
convinced that this gnosis was truly Christian.

At this point we pause. Much more could be said about
Valentine and his school, about gnosis and the other systems.
Later on, we shall have the opportunity of filling out the
picture which we have just sketched, but these few examples
must suffice for us to understand the evolution of the Church
in the second century. In particular, the last examples clearly
express, by their explicitly Christian character, the decided

antithesis, indeed the strangeness and danger of gnosis to which the Church was fully alive. The danger was not to be found in the subjective character of the Biblical exegesis; nor in the unlimited freedom in transforming, or in fabricating gospels; nor in the docetic Christology which makes a mask in one way or another out of the humanity of Jesus; nor in the number of dæmonic or divine figures. More dubious and, when carried through logically, quite intolerable is the denial of the Old Testament: but the *Epistle of Ptolemy* contains so many concessions that, in this case, there seems a possibility of coming to a mutual understanding.

The decisive thing always is the conception of God, with all its consequences. For Christianity, the fundamental principle is the supra-rational fact that the same God, who commands and judges, also redeems the helpless sinner by pure compassion: that is what Jesus put into simple words, and Paul, into the forms of a searching dialectic. Gnosis solves the problem by dividing the Godhead into two, and placing the two halves on different levels; but in so doing it surrenders the profoundest depths of ethical urgency in our experience of God. The miraculous now becomes comprehensible and the unthinkable can be understood: God becomes a philosophic abstraction of the kind beloved by mystics.

The drama which takes place in Valentine's pleroma shows most clearly the sense of this "Divine Comedy" of redemption. It is the self-unfolding and self-understanding of the Godhead. Everything that is begotten flows from the natural necessity of the divine nature, and, in its progress from the one to the many, leads to a differentiation and a continually increasing manifoldness, to an ever more strongly marked diminution of the divine nature. But, with the same inevitability, what is divine, having found one of its forms even in man, turns back to its original source, overcomes the differences step by step, and finally disappears in the One-Whole, the formless and indefinable "fullness of the Godhead", which no longer possesses individuality or personality.

That might have been said also by a philosopher; and pantheism from the days of the Stoa to those of Hegel has really given a series of new forms to this idea of God. But in gnosticism, the mysticism of the orient is added to philosophical pantheism. The path of the individual, in its ascent to the divine Nirvana, is not only to be found by pure thought, but also by magical formulas and actions, and by the control of superhuman powers. This feature is to be found in all gnostic circles and is unmistakable in Valentine,[1] in spite of the high level of his thinking.

Gnosis has been described as the "acute Hellenization of Christianity":[2] we must recognize in addition an equally acute "re-orientalization". But it was not the many colourful figures of the Greek and oriental heaven which threatened Christianity. These were easily overcome. But among the gnostics, the god of oriental mysticism rose up in power and might to contend with the Father in Heaven to whom Jesus had taught His disciples to pray.

[1] Cf. K. Müller, *Gött. Nachr.*, 1920, pp. 188–200
[2] Harnack, *Lehrb. d. Dogmenges.*, 4th edition, i, 250; cf. also F. C. Burkitt, *Church and Gnosis*, 1932

LITERATURE

The footnotes refer to the sources, or as occasion requires and in much abbreviated form, to collections of material or researches of fundamental importance. The following works are cited in a still more abbreviated form:

Arch. Rel. Wiss=*Archiv. für Religionswissenschaft.*

Billerbeck = Strack und Billerbeck, *Kommentar zum Neuentestament aus Talmud u. Midrasch.* 4 vols. 1922–28.

Bousset, W., *Die Religion d. Judentums im späthellenischen Zeitalter.* 3rd edition, ed. Gressmann (=Handb. z. N.T., vol. 21), 1926.

Bousset, W., *Jüdisch-christlicher Schulbetrieb in Alexandria und Rom.* (=Forschungen z. Religion u. Literatur des A. u. N.T. vol. 23), 1915.

Beucheler, Franz, *Carmina latina epigraphica*, 1895.

Chrysippus, cited according to *Stoicorum Veterum Fragmenta*, collegit Jo. ab. Arnim. Vols. 2 and 3 (1923).

C.I.G.=Corpus Inscriptionum Graecarum.

C.I.L.=Corpus Inscriptionum Latinarum.

Damascus Document=W. Staerk, *Die jüdische Gemeinde d. neuen Bundes in Damaskus.* 1922. (Beiträge z. Förderung christl. Theologie, 27, 3.) The original has recently been published in a new edition by L. Rost in the *Kl. Texte.*

Deissmann, Ad., *Licht vom Osten*, 4th edition, 1923.

Dibelius, Martin, *Jungfrauensohn u. Krippenkind*; Sitzungsberichte d. Heidelberger Akademie (philos.–hist. Klasse). 1931–32, No. 4.

Diehl, Ernst, *Inscriptiones latinae christianae veteres.* 3 vols. 1925–31.

Dittenberger, Wilh., *Sylloge Inscriptionum Graecarum*, 3rd edition. By Hiller v. Gaertringen, 4 vols. 1915–24.

Dittenberger, Wilh., *Orientis Graeci Inscriptiones Selectae.* 2 vols. 1903–05.

Ephesuswerk=*Forschungen in Ephesos*, by Heberdey, Keil, and others, 4 vols. 1906–31.

Eusebius, H. E.=Eusebius, *Kirchengeschichte*, ed. by E. Schwartz, small edition, 1908.

Friedländer, Ludwig, *Darstellungen aus der Sittengeschichte Roms*, 10th edition edited Wissowa, 4 vols. 1921–22.

Gött. Nachr.=*Nachrichten der Göttinger Gesellschaft der Wissenschaften, philosophisch-historische Klasse.*

Handbuch zum Neuen Testament, in Verbindung mit W. Bauer u. a., edited by Hans Lietzmann: here further material and support for the New Testament citations is frequently to be found.

Harnack, Adolf, *Geschichte der alt-christlichen Literatur bis Eusebius*, 4 vols. 1893–1904.

Harnack, Adolf, *Die Mission und Ausbreitung des Christentums i. d. ersten drei Jahrhunderten.* 4th edition, 2 vols. 1924. English Translation: *The Mission and Expansion of Christianity.*

LITERATURE

Harnack, Adolf, *Studien zur Geschichte d. Neuen Testaments u. d. Alten Kirche*, vol. 1, 1931 (=Arbeiten z. Kirchengeschichte, vol. 19).

Head, Catal. *Ionia=British Museum, Catalogue of Greek Coins of Ionia*, by B. V. Head, 1892.

Hicks, *Inscr.*=E. Hicks, *Greek Inscriptions in the British Museum*, vol. 3, 1890.

Hilgenfeld, Ad., *Ketzergeschichte des Urchristentums*. 1884.

Inschr. *Magnesia=Die Inschriften von Magnesia u. Mäander*, edited by Otto Kern, 1900.

Inschr. *Pergamon=Die Inschriften von Pergamon*, edited by M. Fränkel, 2 vols. 1890-95.

Irenæus is cited according to Massuet's sections but in Harvey's edition.

Josephus is cited according to the edition of B. Niese (1887-95).

Juster=Jean Juster, *Les Juifs dans l'empire Romain*, 2 vols. 1914.

Kl. *Texte=Kleine Texte für Vorlesungen und Uebungen*, edited by Hans Lietzmann.

Meyer, Eduard, *Ursprung und Anfänge des Christentums*, 3 vols., 1921-23.

Miletwerk=Milet. Ergebnisse d. Ausgrabungen u. Untersuchungen, edited by Wilski, Knackfuss, Wiegand, and others. 1906 ff.

Müller, F. H. G.=*Fragmenta Historicorum Graecorum*, ed. Car. Müller. 5 vols. 1841-70.

Österr. Jahreshefte = Jahreshefte des Österreichischen Archäologischen Institutes.

Pauly-Wissowa = *Pauly's Realencyclopädie der classischen Altertumswissenschaft*, neue Bearbeitung von Wissowa, Kroll, Witte, Mittelhaus. 1894 ff.

Philo is cited according to the edition of Cohn and Wendland; abbreviated titles are used for the different writings. The volume and page numbers of the large edition are given in brackets.

Reitzenstein, R., *Die Hellenistischen Mysterienreligionen*, 3rd edition, 1927.

Roscher, *Lex.* = *Ausführliches Lexikon der griechischen und römischen Mythologie*, edited by W. H. Roscher. 1884 ff.

Schürer, Emil, *Geschichte des jüdischen Volkes im Zeitalter Jesu Christi*. 3 vols., 4th edition, 1901-11.

T.U.=*Texte und Untersuchungen zur Geschichte der altchristlichen Literatur*, edited by Gebhardt and Harnack.

Wendland, Paul, *Die Hellenistisch-Römische Kultur*. 2nd edition (1912) (=Handbuch zum N.T. Vol. 2).

Wilcken, Ulrich, *Chrest.*=Mitteis und Wilcken, *Grundzüge und Chrestomathie der Papyruskunde*. 4 vols. 1912.

ZNW.=Zeitschrift für neutestamentliche Wissenschaft und die Kunde des Urchristentums.

A SHORT BIBLIOGRAPHY FOR ENGLISH READERS

ANGUS, S.
The Environment of Early Christianity, Duckworth (1931)
BINNS, L. E. E.
The Beginnings of Western Christendom, Lutterworth (1948)
BLACK, MATTHEW
An Aramaic Approach to the Gospels, Oxford (1946)
BURNS, C. DELISLE
The First Europe, Allen & Unwin (1948)
CADOUX, C. J.
The Life of Jesus, Penguin (1948)
CHAPOT, V.
The Roman World, Kegan Paul (1928)
DAVIES, W. D.
Paul and Rabbinic Judaism, S.P.C.K. (1948)
DODD, C. H.
The Apostolic Preaching and its Developments, Hodder & Stoughton (1938)
DUNCAN, G. S.
Jesus: Son of Man, Nisbet (1948)
FAIRWEATHER, WM.
The Background of the Gospels, T. & T. Clark (1921)
FAIRWEATHER, WM.
The Background of the Epistles, T. &. T. Clark (1935)
GLOVER, T. R.
The World of the New Testament, Cambridge (1931)
GOGUEL, M.
La Naissance du Christianisme (1946)
GOODSPEED, E. J.
A History of Early Christian Literature, Chicago (1942)
HARNACK, A.
The Mission and Expansion of Christianity (2 vols.), Williams & Norgate (1908)
JACKSON, F. J. FOAKES and LAKE, K.
The Beginnings of Christianity, Vols. I–V, Macmillan (1920 etc.)
JAMES, E. O.
In the Fulness of Time, S.P.C.K. (1935)
JAMES, M. R.
The Apocryphal New Testament, Oxford (1924)

KNOX, W. L.
The Acts of the Apostles, Cambridge (1948)
KLAUSNER, J.
Jesus of Nazareth, Allen & Unwin (1925)
LIGHTFOOT, J. B.
The Apostolic Fathers, Macmillan (1891)
LOISY, A.
The Birth of the Christian Religion, Allen & Unwin (1948)
MACGREGOR, G. H. C., and PURDY, A. C.
Jew and Greek: Tutors unto Christ, Nicholson & Watson (1936)
MANSON, T. W. (ed.).
A Companion to the Bible, T. & T. Clark (1939)
NIEBUHR, R.
An Interpretation of Christian Ethics, S.C.M. (1936)
THE OXFORD CLASSICAL DICTIONARY (1949)
RICHARDSON, ALAN
The Miracle Stories in the Gospels, S.C.M. (1941)
ROSTOVZEFF, M.
The Social and Economic History of the Hellenistic World, 3 vols.
    Oxford (1941)
SCOTT, E. F.
The First Age of Christianity, Allen & Unwin (1926)
STREETER, B. H.
The Four Gospels, Macmillan (1924)
STREETER, B. H.
The Primitive Church, Macmillan (1929)
TARN, W. W.
Hellenistic Civilization, Arnold (1930)

SELECT INDEX